To Gautam
Best wishes
Phillip

Belgium Dec. 2012

Cyber Risk & Resilience for (non-I.T.) Managers

Understanding and managing internet connectivity risks

Phillip King-Wilson

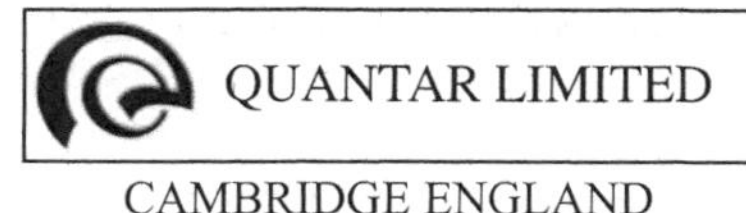

CAMBRIDGE ENGLAND

Cyber Risk & Resilience for (non-I.T.) Managers. Understanding and managing internet connectivity risks

First hardback edition printed 2012 in the United Kingdom.

A catalogue record for this book is available from the British Library.

ISBN 978-0-9574091-0-1

Published by Quantar Limited, St. John's Innovation Centre, Cowley Road, Cambridge, CB4 0WS United Kingdom.

www.quantarsolutions.com

For more copies of this book,
please email: info@quantarsolutions.co.uk

Tel: +44 1223 420 252

Designed and Set by Troubador Publishing Ltd
9 Priory Business Park, Wistow Road, Kibworth Beauchamp, Leicester, LE8 0RX, United Kingdom.

www.troubador.co.uk

Printed and bound in the UK by Biddles, part of the MPG Books Group, Bodmin and King's Lynn, United Kingdom.

www.biddles.co.uk

Contents

	Foreword	v
	Acknowledgements	vii
1:	Introduction	1
2:	The Internet and Security Threats Posed	8
3:	International Standards and Best Practice Adoption and Use	36
4:	Psychological Effects Upon Judgment and Decision Making	70
5:	Managing Uncertain Information	93
6:	Strategy: Definitions, Models, Theories and Perspectives	111
7:	Risk Management, Operational Risk and Enterprise Resilience	139
8:	Business Process Mapping, Analysis and Their Problems	173
9:	Managing Cyber Threats	192
	Bibliography	271
	Index	287

Foreword

This book is about "rethinking" the nature of risk management, I.T. risks and business continuity planning in general. Whilst managing I.T. risks has always been an integral part of business operations, the current environment of increasing integration of technology within our daily lives has established a new paradigm. There is now a greater emphasis on ensuring financial and data losses are not permitted through a lack of awareness, inappropriate controls, systems or people. Cyber threat management and resilience has become a discipline it its' own right.

The management of business process interdependency with I.T. systems and networks is now a paramount factor in maintaining enterprise resilience. The 1980's and 1990's managerial focus of functional silos is no longer appropriate for managing internet risks. Recurring successful breaches of I.T. systems and security that are revealed publicly are drivers for increasing legislation and a subsequent shift of responsibility from the I.T. director/CIO towards general Board level accountability.

Previous divestment of responsibility to those operating at the I.T. department "coal-face" has been removed by those organizations seeking to signal their quality of risk management. Without the blanket of trust to cover operational integration between suppliers and their customers, businesses stand to lose their competitive standing.

The impact of successful attacks is a presumption of a lack of procedures, systems or managerial control from external observers can range from loss of customers to breaches of increasingly onerous laws, and even impact negatively upon stock price.

An effective strategy for managing cyber risks requires the organization to adopt a holistic, enterprise-wide approach. Systems, processes, organizational culture, management structure, skill sets comprise the basic building blocks in building network risk resilience.

As the number and types of attacks experienced continues to accelerate and evolve, allied to increasing process and systems interdependency, many organizations are concluding that they can no longer operate with technological responsibility to vest solely in the I.T. director or CIO.

With disparate types of attackers, both real and potential, posing a threat to ongoing normal operational efficiencies and longevity, a historical viewpoint of I.T. risk management can no longer keep up with day-to-day threats. This post-mortem style of I.T. risk management has to now be supplemented with real-time and strategic forecasting risk management frameworks, policies and procedures.

Operational risk management, in general terms, has the objective of enabling an organization to attain its' strategic goals. The pervasiveness of such a program has, by definition, to be melded into the overall business processes and operations of an organization.

The aim of this book is to broaden the scope of thinking of managers in respect of the number and type of components that a cyber threat management program should include. In addition, it seeks to assist in the design and implementation frameworks that will enable an organization to achieve its strategic cyber threat management goals and maintain them on an ongoing basis.

Whilst there is no one size fits all cyber risk management and resilience program that is applicable for all sectors, sizes and types of organization, it is hoped that this publication can, at the very least, create a starting point for assessing the content and structure required of such a program.

Acknowledgements

This book is based upon a combination of several pieces of research, extensive practical experience allied to the views and commentaries of experts in the academic and business fields.

Special thanks go to the many academic professionals within the U.K. universities who have assisted in both the provision of data and details of their experiences of internet attacks on corporate networks. I am particularly grateful to individuals who have added to my knowledge on an ongoing basis over the years, sharing their thoughts, providing insight on a broad spectrum of sectors and from their peers; Dr. Iain Phillips, Dr. Pawel Piotrowicz, Dr. Andrew Gray, Dr. John Welch, and Chris Williams. Further thanks go to Peter Hamlyn and Chris McLean, without whose assistance this book would ever have been possible.

The author must also thank editor in chief, Minh Tran-Duy, for her patience and for her help in bringing this book to its conclusion.

Chapter One

INTRODUCTION

THE CONTEXT OF THE BOOK AND ITS CONTENT

> "Trading hurt by failing servers"
>
> "…technology was put to the test earlier on Tuesday when record trading volumes put the US system under severe strain…at about 3.40pm, automated trading orders began to get 'hung up' with many trades left unexecuted…The heavy volumes also caused a sudden mid-afternoon plunge in the Dow Jones Industrial Average…as with the problems at the NYSE, a failure of the company's servers was behind the glitch"
> Thursday March 1st 2007.

Over the past decade, the focus of organizations on risk management has increased, being increasingly regarded as a means of appropriating rents (profits) from leveraging existing knowledge of how different types of risk may be eliminated, reduced, ignored, or managed more effectively.

Allied to this trend has been an increasingly regulated business environment, developed as a result of major corporate failures and consequent global capital market impacts, such as Lehman Brothers, WorldCom, Enron and Pacific Gas and Electric Co. Various regulatory bodies reviewed the means by which corporations were being managed, reported and audited. New regulatory practices were imposed, for example by the Securities and Exchange Commission (SEC) in the USA, the European Commission in Europe, the OECD for the international financial community and, at country level, the Public Company Accounting Reform and Investor Protection Act 2002, commonly known as the Sarbanes Oxley Act 2002, which is a US federal law, amongst others.

Alongside these shifts have been increasingly complex risk management developments, whereby the goal of all organizations is a re-stating of their long-term viability, including the ability to withstand exogenous shocks resulting from risks which impact on organizations. This has been coined 'enterprise resilience', that is, the capacity for complex systems to survive, adapt and grow despite surrounding turbulent changes. Such resilience to risk goes beyond protection, business continuity and profitability. Enterprise resilience includes various elements, many different from the other. Whilst a commonly accepted definition is difficult to arrive at, the methodology of attaining enterprise resilience is surprisingly common within academic literature and mainstream writing.

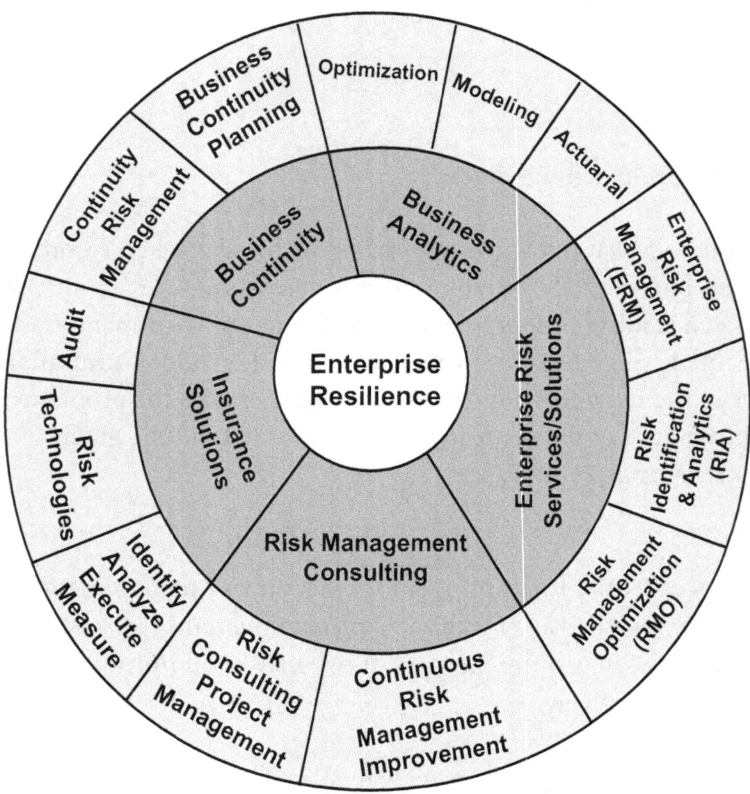

Fig. 1.1 Enterprise Resilience Positioning

The origins of resilience are derived from the concept of sustainability, but in many cases the concept was based upon reducing un-sustainability rather than strengthening sustainability's systemic underpinnings. Many accept that complexity, dynamics, and the non-linear nature of interdependent systems imply that the notion of sustainability as a steady-state equilibrium is not realistic. Further, certain academics posit that the concept of resilience emerged as a critical characteristic of complex, dynamic systems in a range of disciplines, including economic, ecology, psychology, sociology, risk management, and network theory.

Further, management theorists have identified the need for resilience in managing within dynamic and unpredictable environments. A logical extension of the notions of sustainability and resilience is that of enterprise resilience, which is a concept predicated upon an expanded view of risk as one containing a broader spectrum than previously having been the case. Traditional items within the risk management function, such as financial, natural hazards, physical security, legal and compliance, are allied to non-traditional items such as innovation, intellectual property, corporate culture, and client relationships.

In attaining enterprise resilience, organizations have a large body of knowledge to draw upon. Regulations may mandate specific behavior, but national and international risk management standards, industry associations, and other regulatory bodies, all offer best practice guidelines which, whilst not being mandatory, provide sufficient frameworks for organizations to achieve their goal.

To what extent, then, do organizations truly seek to establish enterprise resilience as opposed to meeting and complying with the increasing number of regulations which reduce their scope for operational innovation and increased profits? Why, if there is a strategic advantage to be derived from establishing a resilience program, would organizations not embark upon one? With such a large body of knowledge to draw upon, why would organizations not use best practice guidelines to enhance their business operations?

According to the perspective of appropriating rents (profits) from existing knowledge external to the organization, barriers to the adoption of an enterprise resilience program within organizations are seen as barriers to the appropriation of rents from existing external but accessible knowledge. Where adherence to regulatory requirements takes precedence over attainment of enterprise resilience, organizations may be said to be regulation dominant.

Contrary to the common belief that organizations seek to achieve a high level of enterprise risk management sophistication, there are many who claim that, in the real world business environment, two risk management types exist; those of seeking to deliver the optimal results for company owners through regulatory compliance rather than utilizing optimal risk management practices, and that of strategic enterprise risk management, which drives towards achieving enterprise resilience.

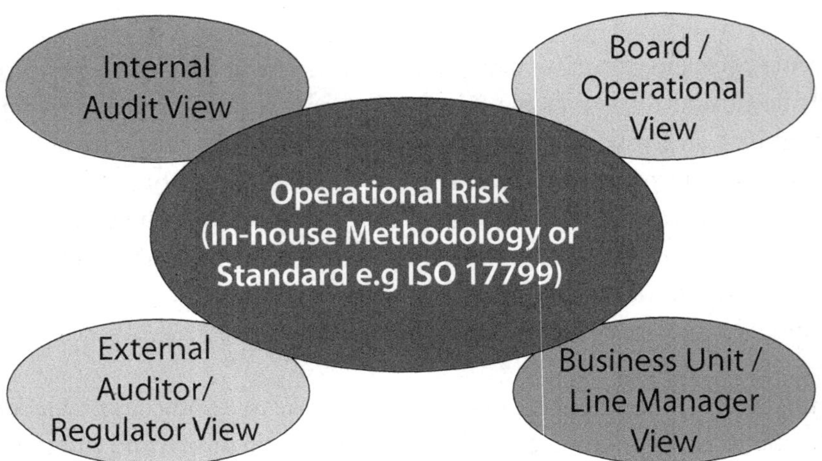

Fig. 1.2 Risk Management Objectives

This book seeks to assess the various issues relating to how to benefit from both pre-existing knowledge within organizations as well as external and widely available knowledge. Additionally, the various regulations and standards that currently impact upon the business environment are reviewed as to whether they can make a positive contribution to the development of cyber threat resilience.

Chapter 2 introduces the context of this book and the rationale for the need to manage cyber threats by looking back at the evolution of the internet and understanding the foundation of a technology that has become so pervasive in all aspects of personal and commercial life.

A review of the threats posed and by whom may require a reassessment of the "who and why" common perspectives of so called hackers. Attack methodologies are touched upon in order to more fully understand the context and environment in which risk managers and I.T. professionals operate, as well as provide a greater knowledge of the complexity of the task of securing our data posed.

Chapter 3 provides an overview of various standards and best practices that can be utilized in enhancing operation risks. The main obstruction to organizations adopting standards and other relevant frameworks, however, is the "not invented here" syndrome, precluding what would appear on the face of it, to be a logical transition to increase competitiveness and maintain the life of a business.

The various standards and regulations that may apply in the case of creating cyber risk management programs are reviewed and the current thinking on why/which organizations do indeed adopt and use external information is included within the chapter.

Clearly, the affects of psychology upon judgment and decision making play an important role in managing risks, adopting external information and other areas. In Chapter 4, the various components, factors and influences are reviewed in order to more fully understand why organizational blockages can occur in rolling out programs that may affect personnel and create a negative view internally. In the context of cyber threat management, the components of a resilience program affects a vast array of personnel, in both numbers and functions and as such it stands to reason that such intrusiveness may meet with resistance or worse, political maneuverings to counteract the scope, effectiveness or perhaps budgeting for a cyber threat resilience program.

Information volumes are already vast within most organizations and continue to grow at an exponential rate and are expected to remain so. Chapter 5 looks at the implications for assessing and utilizing the various flows of information within an enterprise and the difficulties presented in cases of inconsistency, uncertainty, incompleteness or absence.

In the case of risk management in general and more specifically for cyber threat management, data, its provision, analysis, assessment and quantification are key. It is therefore important to understand why and when some information may need handling in different ways and which may need to be disregarded if negative influence and impact is to be avoided.

In Chapter 6, strategy is reviewed in terms of the definitions, models, theories and perspectives that are attached to the term in its' broadest sense. One famous quotation states that the question of which strategy a company is following should not be asked. Rather, the observer simply has to view the actions of management in order to answer the question.

However, the many views and models impact on how an organization operates, undertakes its day-to-day activities, and gives direction and a mission for those employed. In terms of risk management and resilience, strategy impacts upon major components such as in setting the risk appetite for the enterprise. Understanding the strategic landscape and why one model/perspective/etc is better suited to risk and cyber threat management enables senior managers to propose changes to align corporate strategy with the degree of acceptable risk facing the organization.

The chapters then begin a more detailed focus upon the task of risk management, cyber threat management and the creation of enhanced enterprise resilience. Chapter 7 commences the process by providing the basis of risk management and its composition, factors affecting its scope and success.

The specificity of network operational risk is addressed, highlighting the differences between more traditional risks, such as market or credit risks, versus network (and thence cyber) threats. Understanding why these risks are different and require different management techniques is critical to relating to how and why they have the potential to impact an organization in a multitude of ways, with consequences that may be beyond the scope of assessments undertaken to date. It can be argued that the risk models that have been used for other forms of risk faced by the enterprise are inappropriate for network/cyber threat modeling. Knowledge of the underlying reasoning and what models are available for risk management of these risks will assist in determining how, why and when components of a cyber threat management program are utilized and are the most appropriate for a particular enterprise.

Chapter 8 stands apart from the previous two chapters in that it addresses a particular problem peculiar to cyber threat management, that is, in mapping business processes and technology/data interdependency. Most organizations have undertaken some form of business continuity planning program, which ordinarily will have included technology risks. However, the specificity and ever-increasing integration of technologies/data within processes, allied to comparable rates of automation, requires understanding. The shift towards cloud computing, for example, will create a totally new risk environment and the mapping of systems, processes and data will change fundamentally once again.

The final chapter provides the outline basis and options available for managing cyber threats over a sustained period. The mitigation options available vary in type and cost considerably, with both technological and non-technological being available to most enterprises. Providing an overview of cyber threat management components, the risks, mitigation options, the reader should, at the very least, have a broader perspective of the cyber threat management environment, the context in which I.T. professionals operate, the complexity and scale of the task and the absolute need to manage such threats.

The figure opposite is designed to provide a basic overview of the items within the book and guide the reader along a logical path to the conclusion of this book and is meant for illustration purposes, rather than making any statement as to the efficacy of utilizing the content for a cyber threat management program.

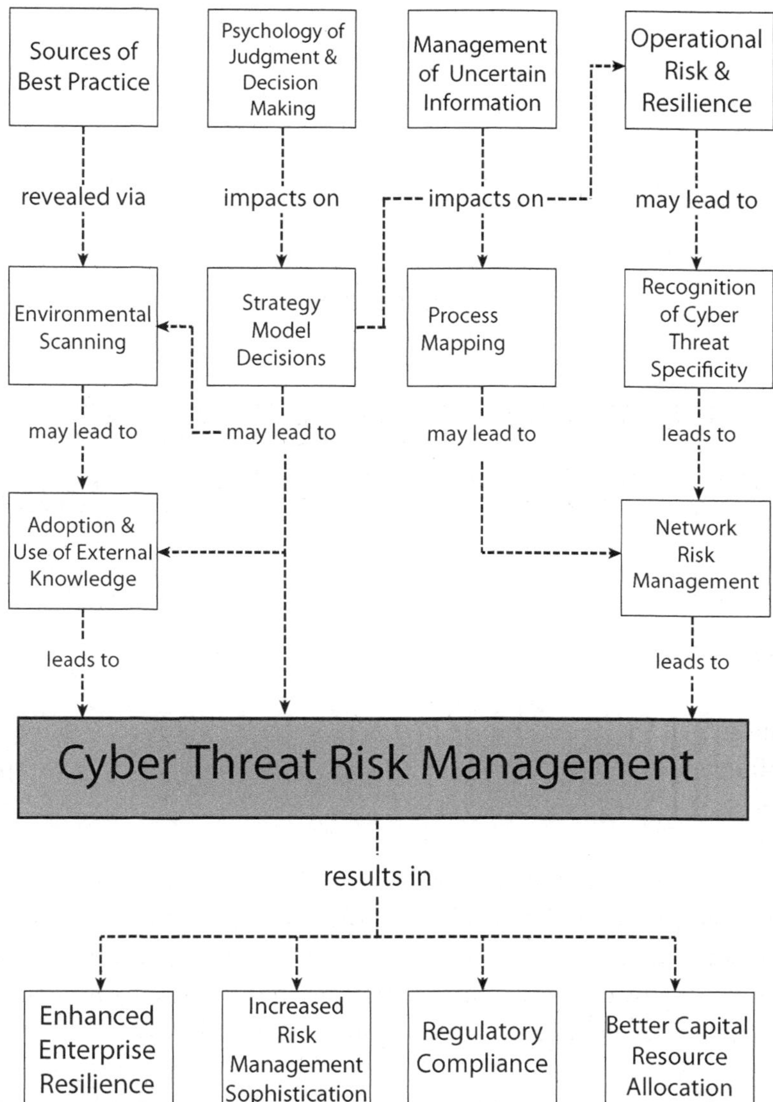

Fig. 1.3 Cyber Risk Management Model

Chapter Two

THE INTERNET AND SECURITY THREATS POSED

How the Web Was Born

In understanding the power and the threats posed by the internet when a corporate network is linked to a public network, it is necessary to understand how it developed and grew beyond the initial expectations of use.

The internet is best described by analogy that that of being a postal system where each host computer has a unique address. The information is passed from one computer to the next, over a network, until the proper addressee is found, in much the same way that mail is routed between post offices until it reaches the one from which the mail carrier can deliver it to the specific home or office of the addressee.

The internet was borne out of ARPAnet, the US government's Advanced Research Projects Agency Network, as a defense and research network. The US Department of Defense decided to build ARPAnet as an alternate means of communications to back up the telephone system in case of nuclear war. The internet was designed to move information via packets from one computer to the next through these interconnected networks.

This meant that if one part of the network was destroyed, an alternate route for the packets could be found and the information would still get through to the addressee. The standard communication language for this packet transport is Transmission Control Protocol/Internet Protocol (TCP/IP) – a unique method governing the movement of Internet and World Wide Web information. An important point is that any computer or network that utilizes TCP/IP can be part of the Internet.

The National Science Foundation (NSF) built upon the ARPAnet foundation by creating NSFNET, which was intended to connect universities and research centers. Governments and university agencies, as well as some corporations paid for the infrastructure and computer platforms, but no single company or institution controlled the entire network. The side benefit of this effort was the creation of a virtually free network. Academic researchers, engineers and other technologists quickly made this network their own.

In 1989, Tim Berners-Lee, a British researcher working in Geneva, Switzerland, at CERN (Conseil European pour la Recherche Nucleaire, now known as the European Laboratory for Particle Physics), was frustrated by the lack of portability and compatibility in the vast quantities of research materials stored at the centre. Additionally, many of the projects undertaken at the facility were enormous in scope and inevitably brought about the need to be able to manage all the information generated by the research.

The team faced compatibility of document types, file systems and other issues, but also that of organizing and linking the entire catalogue of materials available at the facility. None of the existing formats provided a mechanism to do that.

Berners-Lee envisioned a world in which access to data would be simple task, accomplished in a consistent manner regardless of which terminal or systems were being used. The concept of universal readership was formed, embracing the idea that any individual on any type of computer in any location should be able to access data using only one simple and common program.

As he began to expand on the initial concept of universal readership, Berners-Lee realized that the traditional ways of thinking about information in linear or sequential order was not necessarily the best way to present that information across disparate systems. This realization eventually led to the use of the now-familiar concept of links on the web.

Additionally, there was no limitation or restriction against anyone adding sub networks and computer systems to the internet, so the growth of the system was, and largely still is, uninhabited by regulations, budget constraints, political boundaries or controlling agencies.

Thus, originally, the internet was designed for military and academic purposes for research, providing access to data over long distances and as a communications infrastructure for a relatively small number of institutions and persons that knew and trusted each other. This is the origin of the internet's network structure, with many of today's protocol standards for data transmission and packet switching have been designed in an environment in which, essentially, everyone was considered trustworthy.

The Problem Description: A Security Threats Summary

Since the internet has evolved from an academic and military resource to a public world-wide computer network utilized by numerous commercial and non-commercial organizations and individuals, and on which modern society has become ever increasingly more dependent, there have been many security issues, some of them exposing weaknesses in the security model of the internet itself.

While the importance of computing has advanced in our society, one of the first and biggest problems concerning the evolution of computing has been the improvement of applied internet security technology. With increasing speed and complexity of technology and software development, the number of security issues as well as their severity and impact on businesses and governmental organizations has tended to grow drastically. Similarly, the number and public profile of security incidents caused by the growing number of intruders that are actively exploiting weaknesses in current security models and by intrusion software becoming more sophisticated have also experienced rapid growth.

While defense against specific intrusion software is often futile, because private attacking software and techniques can be developed that either can hardly be identified or possess no methodological weaknesses which could be used to stop them, security issues have to be overcome by using coherent, logically applied, systematic security improvement and protection efforts.

In order to develop a defense strategy against future threats, it is necessary to take into account that proposed solutions require the inclusion of effective countermeasures against an unknown threat potential.

An approach to this solution therefore has to be formed upon a differentiated set of measures based and assessed against current weaknesses and threats, and against upcoming security issues, extrapolated by analyzing existent weaknesses and core problems in the security infrastructure of corporate users. It is generally accepted that current threats such as distributed attack tools do not represent security vulnerabilities themselves, but rather they multiply and visualize the potential of existent problems present in current security architecture models. This aspect will increase with the rise in prominence of hosted applications and cloud computing leverage by corporate users.

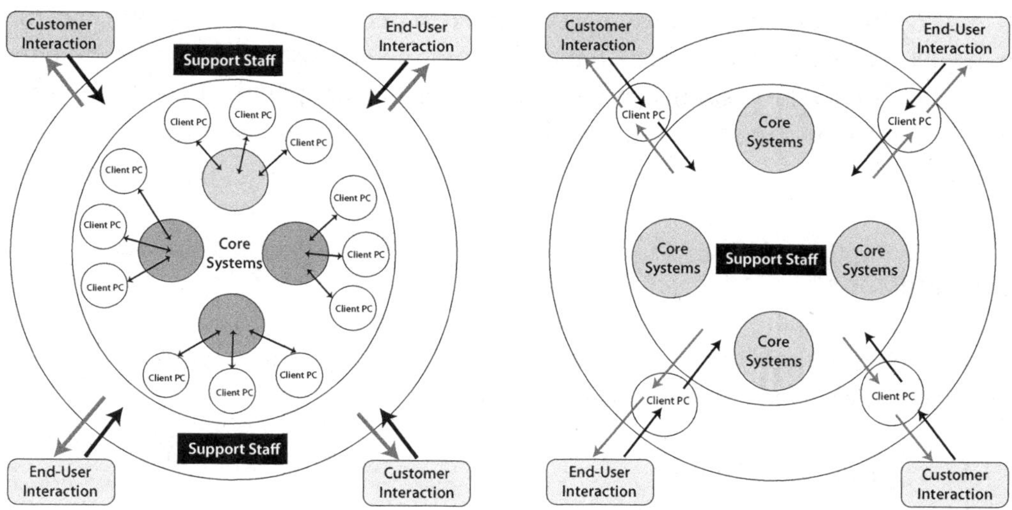

Fig. 2.1 Traditional Versus Internet/Network Client: Core Systems Interaction

In reviewing the above diagrams, it is possible to understand the fundamental difference between historical end-user to core systems interactions and those facilitated via the internet/networks. Previously, core systems were security hardened and the touch-points for the end-user were via client PC's at, for example, shop/bank branches, with support staff manning these.

Now, the layers comprising the I.T. infrastructure are reduced and the customer interacts, via their own PC/internet enabled device with the core systems. The fundamental difference lies in the fact that previously, the core systems' security was reliant upon the organizations' I.T./network security teams, whereas now the security is reliant upon the security at the end-user touch-point. Taking internet banking as a prime example of this, until very recently, end-user security was regarded as the responsibility of the customer and was reflected within the terms of agreements of banking institutions.

Nowadays however, on the back of various security failures, both from a legal obligation perspective and from an operational loss viewpoint, the banking sector has realized that they stand to lose in the face of a successful mass attack on their customer base. This has resulted in smart card; token; biometric type security devices being issued as a de facto operational requisite and comes in part from reputational damage occasioned by data breaches/losses. This subsequent visible publicity has in turn been fuelled by the pervasiveness of new communications technologies such as social networking, which was not accounted for during risk management strategy at the outset of launching internet banking.

Cloud computing will remove another layer of security effectively, through the transmission and holding of data remotely from the end-user and the core systems, but controlled by the customer and again being dependent upon their ability to protect access from that data, but without the complexity of smartcard/token/biometric authentication.

The landscape

In describing the relative levels of security a computer system purports to have, it is first necessary to understand the two key issues of:

- Secure against what?
- Secure against whom?

Without being able to answer to both of these questions, an accurate assessment of security cannot be made. For example, a GSM telephone conversation can be encrypted for security, however, without recognizing that there may be a security failure through the simple means of recording at the sender or recipient's ends, the potential points of failure in security are ignored. In this way, network computer security is more than the individual technological aspects allied to the technology, but rather it is context sensitive, more than being technology sensitive.

The networked environment is similar in many respects to the physical one in respect of the threats that exist within each. Embezzlement, bank robbery, extortion, vandalism all exists in both domains. Physical threats in the physical world can also be achieved through the internet medium, through threats to railway controls, process control units (SCADA systems) and other sensitive networks such as those for air traffic control.

If it is accepted that analogue threats are the same as digital ones, then it is possible to review past events in the analogue world in order to understand those threats which may exist in the digital networked one. Although the appearance of the attacks may be different, the psychology and motivation behind such attacks frequently remains the same, as do the types of attacker. Criminals tend to attack with the same levels of intent, motivation and resources. Organized crime has increasingly used its major resources to attack supposedly more secure enterprises, with the intent of acquiring data to sell on or for financial gain. Smaller sized crime gangs or individuals attempt to gain money via scams and phishing on various websites.

Equally, privacy violations have had the same, historic motivations, i.e. obtaining data relating to individuals for legal or illegal activities. In the past this data would have been acquired from legal data sources, such as public records, tax records, and credit scoring agencies. In the modern era however, there is now an ability to collect and aggregate data about individuals that would otherwise be, at best difficult and at worst impossible. Examples of this are commercial databases that have accumulated data on individuals who have credit facilities, but have not opted out of marketing campaigns and other types of communication.

Increasingly, the use of social networking sites has also enabled profiles to be created about users and combining this data with low-cost computing power creates the ability to crack passwords through names, places, interests, family members listed publicly on such social networking sites. Although there have been recent moves towards providing different default settings to prevent general publication of personal information, the fact remains that many users remain exposed to information gathering that may be used in the future against them.

Taxation agencies, private investigators, law enforcement agencies have all traditionally used data correlations to seek out such things as illegal activities and potentially corrupt people in sensitive positions. Similarly, marketing organizations have increasingly gathered data within sectoral databases.

Utilities organizations have in the past developed telephony-based monitoring systems that sought to reduce the cost of inspections and meter readers. These systems were then hacked by the criminal fraternity to monitor patterns in a different way – observing when people left for their annual holidays, in order to gain time to execute their burglaries.

There are however, certain ways in which computer crime differs from physical world crime due to the characteristics and capabilities that are unique to the internet and corporate networks; automation, attacks at distance, and technique propagation.

The strengths of computers lie in their basic abilities to undertake mundane tasks repetitively, without error. Historically, companies have experienced theft that was common, but was of so little consequence that it did not bother to defend effectively against it. However, in the case of computer salami attacks, for example, (slicing very small financial values from a transaction) the computer is able to acquire large volumes of very low values at high speed. This obviously has a potentially high financial loss scenario for companies that would otherwise be unconcerned by such attacks. In addition, the cost of acquiring sufficient computing power to perform these types of attack is very low, making it worthwhile for even amateur criminals to attempt the technique.

Equally, as described above, the number of commercial and government databases that have public data available has grown exponentially and software is widely available that provides the ability to correlate data according to the end user's requirements. The automation of data collection for specific, illegal purposes is therefore easily attainable. The manner in which networks operate means that due to the internet, a computer in the US is just as easy to log onto as one in Australia, the lack of physical proximity is of no consequence.

There is therefore a capability to attack at distance, without risk of exposure, with a low probability of capture if the right steps are taken, and even if apprehension is possible, perhaps the legislative system where the attacker resides is less than thorough.[1]

Since attackers do not have to have the same physical proximity to the target as in the physical world, the implications are that every computer attached to the internet is equidistant to the next and therefore equidistant from every attacker on the internet. The end result is that any attacker, in any location, has the same possibility to attack and probability to succeed as the next.

Given the borderless nature of the internet, some operators of illegal online activities have sought to ensure that they will evade the legal jurisdictions of many countries by ensuring all hosting and transmission of data is made from a "user-friendly" domain and is a form of jurisdiction shopping unavailable to their physical world counterparts.

A further difference lies in the ease with which successful techniques can propagate through the digital environment. Rather than there being a single attacker who finds a simple means to attack a corporation, with only a small impact, the ability to disseminate the information on how to attack, on a widespread basis means that previously regarded low level attacks have to be reassessed as to their true potential impact upon the corporation.

Computer based attacks have therefore grown exponentially. The manner by which computer viruses/worms have spread has not been through generally high levels of ability held by the perpetrators, but rather the ability to download viruses, virus toolkits and other attack tools and use them to attack on a global scale. In the case of computer attacks such as virus creation and propagation, only the first attacker need possess a relatively high skill level, the rest are able to simply emulate and distribute the attack tools.

---

[1] A good example of this phenomenon has been written in *The Cuckoo's Egg: Tracking a Spy Through the Maze of Computer Espionage*. This is a 1989 book written by Clifford Stoll and is his first-person account of the hunt for a computer cracker who broke into a computer at the Lawrence Berkeley National Laboratory (LBL).

Attack Types

Internet attacks may be generally categorized as being one or more of the following type; criminal; publicity; or legal attacks. In the case of criminal attacks, the motivation is simple to understand i.e. obtain the maximum financial return from an attack; however, the latter two have the capability of being the more damaging.

Internet scams now have a long track record, with the most common being sales of internet services, general merchandise, auctions, pyramid and multi-level marketing schemes, and business opportunities and therefore mirrors the most common offline scams.

In cases of destructive attacks, causing damage to another person/corporations/property, these are frequently the work of terrorist groups, insiders (including employees who may be disgruntled for whatever reason) or black hat hackers, whose motives may be to cause maximum damage but without the objective of obtaining profit from their actions.

These types of attack are often targeted at a single entity/person, without regard for any subsequent collateral damage caused to other people/organizations. In cases of intellectual property theft, there is a need to distribute the means by intellectual property may be exploited illegally in order to gain financial revenues, whilst simultaneously protecting those rights from illegal copying and redistribution without financial recompense. This would include proprietary information within organizations, as well as the systems themselves (for example commercial databases cost large amounts to develop and propagate with data, so the software itself is sometime more valuable than the data residing within it). Common theft includes software piracy and movie and music piracy. The internet allows widespread distribution at speed and the ability to replicate and pass on the material. Although, unauthorized copying has long existed, technology and the internet combined have the capability to impact across multiple sectors in a manner that previously did not exist in the case of the individual copier.

Brand theft has found new meaning through the internet and the potential for damage to a brand is much higher. Early examples were domain names that logically would be owned by real-world brand owners, subject to "cyber squatters" holding brand owners to ransom in exchange for the sale of "their" brand domain names. Attempted theft still occurs online, with activities such as page-jacking and typo piracy, where a domain name is acquired that is very close to the real brand owner's name.

Whilst privacy violations are not necessarily criminal, they are often a prelude to identity theft, which in turn is used for covering the true identity of a perpetrator or in the facilitation of illegal activities.

There are two principle types of privacy attacks, those that are targeted and those that are primarily data harvesting, with fundamental differences between them. In a targeted attack, an attacker is seeking as much information as possible about one person or organization. Data harvesting is where correlations are used to identify targets that have particular characteristics that are attractive to the attacker.

Surveillance has always been possible, such as with eavesdropping conversations. However, the internet and corporate networks in general have made this a simple task via pattern matching and scanning networks. Packets of data sent around the world are usually unencrypted; therefore they have attributes that can be read by mail scanners, sniffers and other tools.

Mail scanners, work by identifying key words in an electronic conversation and this methodology is used by law enforcement agencies and other governmental organizations to attempt to identify terrorist and drug activities. They are also used by enterprises to monitor employee behavior to identify a CV for example, which may result in the company longer trusting them or changing data access levels for a particular individual.

Obviously, such methods can also be used for illegal activities, using the same widely available tools. Typical targets are credit card data, bank account information, passwords and other useful information. Where security is sought by using data encryption for packets, this in itself attracts unwanted attention by assailants. The cracking of algorithms that form the basis of many commercially available encryption programmers has become feasible through the availability of high-end processing power at low cost.

Pattern matching can be used alongside traffic analysis, which focuses not on the content of the communication, but rather the characteristics of the communication. Examples are who communicates with whom; when, how long for; how quickly are replies sent; what communications occur after an initial one. Each characteristic gives information about the sender and recipient.

Publicity Attacks

The concept of a publicity attack is to simply act in a manner that will result in the media carrying coverage of the attack on the system. Since most systems are hardened against such types of attack, those undertaking them successfully tend to be those with a high degree of skill. The objective of such attacks is usually simply to attract media attention rather than having any financial objective underlying the attack. The most frequent of such types are those seeking to expose security flaws in software and hardware solutions or the lack of ability of computer security personnel to secure a corporations' security perimeter.

The impact of a publicity attack can be severe as a result of a loss of trust by consumers, with the consequent loss of earnings damaging share price. In extreme instances, they have led to a failure of shareholder confidence, withdrawal leading to hostile takeover bids.

It is therefore the financial consequences of bad publicity, rather than the cost resulting directly from the attack that is important. In threat modeling, this must be taken into account of by security systems developers, since the motivation and consequent possible attack types is fundamentally different from an attacker whose motivation is solely financial reward.

Legal attacks are those that result in the legal system acting against the interests of the general public. This can occur when there is a belief or such a belief may be created by the defence team that a computer system and network is infallible and therefore any incidents are the result of actions and/or omissions by those seeking legal redress. Further, the disparate manner by which the internet and computer security failures are handled by various legal systems around the world creates greater complexity in this regard.

Attacks against the legal system are difficult to guard against too, since one expert witness testimony can be negated by another and evidence. Hackers, for example, have been used frequently by defense lawyers, to rebut the suggestion that a plaintiff was responsible for transferring funds from accounts.

Patterns and Motives & Adversaries

Real world adversaries are in general the same as in the digital world. As such, the categories are also much the same, these being criminals seeking financial advantage, industrial spies searching for a competitive advantage, hackers looking for secret information, and military intelligence and their agencies.

The differences between each category are their objectives, access, resources, expertise and risk.

Such differences are important, since they determine the types of countermeasures that may be successfully deployed against particular adversary types. A countermeasure successful at repelling a solitary attacker of one type would not necessarily be successful at preventing an organized terrorist group.

Further, access levels vary too, for example where a malicious insider has easier access to systems and networks belonging to the target than would be the case for an external hacker. Financial and other resources vary too, with terrorist groups and organized crime obviously having greater resources than individuals. However, more recent developments illustrate that governmental organizations and the media have used their extensive resources to obtain non-public data. Risk tolerance varies too, with some terrorists willing to lose their lives in the pursuit of their objectives, whilst for a lone criminal or publicity seeker, apprehension is to be avoided at all costs.

Hackers

The word hacker has had a number of definitions and connotations attached to it. These range from a corporate systems administrator who has high skill and knowledge levels relating to computing, to teenagers who have low skill levels and download attack tools and run them without having any real strategic intent aside from causing damage to anyone they can. It is primarily the media that has co-opted the word to describe a number of different types of computer user and whereas it was once used as a complementary term for somebody with extensive computing skill sets it is now used in a negative manner.

Today, hackers exist in a subculture, with hacker handles, vocabulary and rules, tend to be younger than twenty-five years old and are predominantly male. A small percentage have high skill levels, with the remainder using knowledge developed by the skilled to carry out often illegal and certainly unethical activities and are labeled by the skilled as being “script kiddies” or “lamers”.

Of importance to note, many highly skilled hackers have expertise that frequently exceeds that of systems designers. Software compilation tools have led to the simplification of creation of software, with the deletion of the requirement to have an in-depth knowledge of the underlying computer science. Further, the ways in which the two groups view a system are fundamentally different too, with hackers viewing a system from the outside as an attacker, rather than from the inside as designers view them. They also view a system more holistically than the designers, and may, for this reason understand attacks better than designers, who frequently develop piecemeal as individuals, with the assimilation of the work of different developers being the end product.

…e hackers' culture is one of individuals who feel a belonging to a … who cannot be coerced into making attacks against particular targets … rewards and there is no hierarchy.

…tool propagation (exploits) and their widespread distribution is by far the main …e relating to hackers. Initially, hackers researched the vulnerabilities of systems arising from internet attacks, wrote papers and published the findings, together with the means of preventing such attacks. However, the tendency now is for vulnerabilities to be published on the internet, together with links to available exploits to use against such vulnerabilities. As such, the ethical basis of how and why hackers operate has changed fundamentally over the past decade. Governments have changed legislation on a broad basis to eliminate the previous hacker defense of intrusion of networks solely to explore systems, rather than with malicious intent.

Malicious Insiders

By the very definition, insiders are already within the security perimeter of an organization and therefore pose a serious threat. They frequently have high levels of access within the organization and therefore the systems access and associated trust in their use is often also present. The worst case scenario for an organization is where the malicious insider is in fact part of the organization responsible for securing the perimeter, since their very presence prevents them from being denied access. The systems and processes of an organization may be exploited by an insider for means other than the direct use of the systems and networks for financial gain. They may, for example use the capabilities for a use unrelated to the activities of the employing organization.

Due to scarce availability of high level computing skills generally, many organizations employ sub-contractors, with each of these posing potential threats as malicious insiders. Detecting malicious insiders is usually achieved by using traffic pattern analysis, e-mail scanning and observation of the use of individual computers within an organization. There has been a rise in the types of products that have such capabilities and are offered by most of the large software houses for their corporate clients.

The advantages that accrue to such attackers is their knowledge of the organization, the systems and operations of the organization, as well as knowledge of what possible reactions that would result from an attack, thereby ensuring the means to conceal certain aspects of the attack whilst remaining within the employment of the target organization.

The motivations of this type of adversary are dependent upon the s
of them, since they may be motivated be revenge, financial gain, institu
or possibly publicity. They can fall within the sub-categories of being lone
hackers, or even national intelligence agents. In the case of the latter, the obje
to identify vulnerabilities within an enemy State's computer defense systems. T
methodology has been employed successfully by a number of Governments over time
and has played its' role in some of the largest national security failures.

Industrial Espionage

Historically there has been a grey line between what may be viewed as ethically executed competitive intelligence and industrial espionage. This line has become blurred in recent times, with examples of bribery in exchange for passwords, eavesdropping via telephone and computer networks, and recruiting hackers to break into competitors systems to obtain information.

Industrial espionage if increasingly well funded since it presents itself as a sound business case when the cost-benefit is assessed. Further, it may provide a crucial advantage over another enterprise or create competitive advantage. An example here is a major European car manufacturer who had digital plans for a new engine design stolen from its' corporate headquarters, costing the corporation an estimated nine hundred million euros. The limiting factors are those of the risk appetite of an organization, the legal implications within various jurisdictions (in terms of the actual acts and the consequences if caught) and the governance within an organization.

The Press

This group could be regarded as a sub-category of industrial espionage, albeit with the objective of seeking out a newsworthy story that often requires the acquisition of private or proprietary information. National security information and its' dissemination has caused problems for the press, since its' publication could cause fundamental problems over a considerable period of time. As such, some countries have a record of being able to ensure no publication, even where there have been security breaches, whilst in others; the press has used the defense of the public's right to know successfully and published. More recently, the defense has been used in the English courts but overturned as a defense by the US courts. The example of News International and mobile telephone hacking and the extent to which it was known and at which level of the managerial hierarchy is a case in point.

Organized Crime

This category comprises a number of profiles ranging from small groups with limited competencies, to major crime syndicates, in Russia, Poland, Asia and West Africa, who possess vast resources and an ability to acquire highly skilled workers.

Their motivations have remained as being financial advantage, with the means of acquiring finance being the variable. Computer crime is seen as a new avenue for exploitation and the ability to break into banks electronically poses far less risk of apprehension than physical attacks. One of the most common undertaken by organized crime is identity theft for the illegal use of credit cards. There has been a steady growth in this type of activity and has spread throughout the world generally as online retailing popularity has increased vastly.

Police Forces

The police tend to have more limited resources and skills than national intelligence agencies for example and their activities relating to computer crime is dependent upon the regime in which they operate. In some countries, the police have used their access to data capabilities for illegal means, such as vote rigging, as has been claimed in Russian and other former Soviet countries elections for example. They use their systems either directly by the use of identity theft for voting in the name of another person, or by bring pressure to bear on voters through the use of threats of violence or imprisonment.

The primary goal for police forces is to gather information relating to activities, people, organizations and their powers vary according to country, but can result in large volumes of data being acquired without permission being required from a regulator. It is generally assumed that police forces operate such systems and methods in the best interests of the people they serve, however, there have been numerous examples to the contrary and questions as to the recording and storage of acquired data continues to be a major issue.

Terrorists

These tend to have ideological objectives and it may be a group, an individual, international, or national and the label attached to such attackers is context and perspective dependent. They may be viewed as fighting for press freedom or fighting against oppressive regulations preventing governmental transparency, or they may be labeled as a threat to national security. Wikileaks is a prime example of this, with the issue of morality mixed with a real or perceived need to maintain national security at the cost of limiting freedom of access to information.

The objective tends to be the opposite of police forces, in that the aim is to cause damage and gathering information is of little or no importance. As such, attacks tend to be of the denial-of-service or destruction type. The psychology behind the actions is frequently an objective that is rational or logical even, if viewed as a long-term objective. However, the result is a frequently a series of short-term attacks that may appear simply to be acts of revenge, chaos creation or creating the maximum publicity possible.

National Intelligence Organizations

Most developed countries have some form of national intelligence agency, and most are well resourced, with high levels of access to technology generally unavailable to the general public. Their very nature makes such adversaries extremely risk averse and the use of in-depth research, equipment and expertise is utilized in avoiding detection.

National intelligence is based upon the gathering of information that the country should not know. Historically, the key principles have been eavesdropping and learning without the opposition learning that information of interest and use has been acquired. Discovery of this last can render the very information acquired worthless or pose a danger if it were depended upon to act or decide.

Intelligence objectives include military information, weapons designs, diplomatic information, and also includes industrial espionage in some cases, where the agencies are used to acquire commercial information on competitors in other countries for the benefit of the domestic organizations.

Traditionally, telephone communications have been the focus for eavesdropping, but with the advent of the Internet and e-mail, the opportunities for acquiring information have increased. Regulatory changes that would require all ISPs to maintain records for a considerable period and provide crucial information to national security units is currently under discussion and will have wide-reaching implications if implemented.

National security forces are able attract highly skilled computer experts and provide them with the resources they require to develop the means to monitor and acquire information on a level that has not been possible by commercial organizations. They have also recruited hackers and paid them by other means than simply cash and have founded various bodies and competitions in order to seek out the next generation of highly skilled computer/network personnel as well as the long-term objective of encouraging such individuals to join them.

Infowarriors

An infowarrior is a military adversary who seeks to undermine their target's ability to undertake a war by attacking the information or network infrastructure. Attacks range from preventing systems from operating as they should, to destroying networks/systems completely. Attacks may be covert in nature and the internet facilitates this frequently, leading to a misidentification of such an attack as being of terrorist origin.

Resources are similar to national intelligence organizations and their objectives tend to be short-term, preventing an opponent from waging war. For this reason, their acceptable level of risk is substantially higher than for national security organizations. Their targets have a tendency towards critical infrastructure, such as telecoms networks, command locations, logistics and in this manner are very similar to those targets exploited by armies.

Table 2.1 Categories of Attacker

Type	Objective/Target	Result/Effect
Hacker	Gain Access – various motives	Defaced sites to loss of access to computers
Lone Criminal	Transaction Systems	Financial losses / compromised system integrity
Malicious Insider	Financial gain or retribution	Loss of proprietary data, compromised organizational security
Industrial Espionage	Theft of competitors' proprietary data	Trade secret loss, R&D compromised, potential loss of pipeline developments and strategic advantage
Terrorists	Image damage to Governments and others, data access from security services	Damage to reputation, organization security compromised, high levels of publicity
Info Warriors	Cause damage to military and government targets and others perceived as being the enemy	Security compromises of critical infrastructure of military and other bodies and organizations
National Intelligence Agencies	Watching the watchers	Gain critical data on activities of the opposition and future potential opponents

Vulnerabilities

There is a difference between theories of attacks and types versus the real world actuality, in that a vulnerability does not correspond to a successful attack being mounted. There are a number of stages that need to be fulfilled in order for an attack to be executed successfully, including correct identification of a target, effective planning of the attack, successful exit post-attack. Where encryption algorithms have been deployed for such actions as secure e-mail that have subsequently been found to have a vulnerability within them, it has not automatically resulted in mails being decrypted and used by attackers.

A degree of technical knowledge and skill is required of attackers, such as knowledge of the communications protocols used, accessing the target network in order to make what, prima facie appear to be legitimate requests (for funds transfers for example), acquire funds in a secure account and exit without being apprehended. The absence of knowledge of the other variables or the ability to acquire the relevant information results in an inability to successfully execute an attack from beginning to end and the theoretical vulnerability and subsequent attack remains hypothetical.

Attacks have been categorized by various authors and bodies as generally having five stages:

1. Identify the attack target and gather as much information about it as possible;

2. Analyze the information and identify any vulnerabilities in the target that should enable the attack objectives to be successfully accomplished;

3. Gain the appropriate level of access to the target;

4. Perform the targeted attack;

5. Complete the attack (including erasure of evidence of the attack and avoid retaliation or capture).

The ease of attack is generally correlated to the availability of information and such information may be widely available from a number of sources, easing the degree of difficulty and/or removing some of the above stages of attack. A good example of such information are databases held by domain registrars that are available for public view, giving key information regarding domain names, domain name servers etc. When combined with freely available attack tools such as packet sniffers, there is a potential attack type to gather passwords, user names and so forth that can then be further used.

Information gathered is then analyzed offline in order to then identify vulnerabilities. It is widely assumed that perimeter defenses such as firewalls can prevent intrusion; however, probing a firewall and acquiring information as to type, for example, can lead to offline assessment of potential access points and weaknesses. Once identified, the attacker may then execute the attack and exit. The five steps are not meant to be a single action per step, since each step may require a number of attempts and iterations before moving to the next step. However, the ability to automate attacks makes this an easier task than in the past.

Once access to a computer has been attained and the relevant root privileges acquired, the following steps have been generally accepted as being undertaken as part of an attack:

- Discretely remove traces of the root compromise
- Gather some general information about the system
- Make sure re-entry to the system is possible
- Disable or patch the vulnerable daemon(s)

Countermeasures

These are methods with the objective of reducing vulnerabilities and may be simple or complex, and seek to deny an adversary from undertaking any of the steps of an attack. Since the security of a system is determined by its weakest link, security is often deployed in multiple layers and an effective set of countermeasures comprises:

- Protection
- Detection
- Reaction

Each of the three works in tandem with the others, in that a weakness in one requires the others to be stronger. An example of this is where a computer system has a number of security features, such as firewalls, intrusion detection, password protection for login, and so forth. If there is an intrusion detected but the system administrator fails to act upon such a warning, then there is still a vulnerability, despite there being layers of security in place.

It is this reliance upon protection mechanisms for security that causes the most issues from the network security team to the board room, since there are usually disparate views. For the security practitioners within organizations, security systems and procedures are vital for maintaining the ability to conduct business. From a financial perspective at CFO level, security is seen as a cost without a revenue offset. This view is slowly changing as cost-benefit analysis of capital allocation to security now includes off balance sheet items such as brand damage.

The Vulnerability Landscape

The vulnerability landscape represents the various types of attacks, with each system having proprietary landscapes, although frequently featuring certain common features. A visualization of the landscape is that of a series of peaks and troughs, where the peaks represent a higher degree of difficulty for an attacker and vice-versa.

Vulnerabilities are different from, but utilized in, achieving goals. The vulnerability landscape comprises four broad categories:

- The physical world
- The digital world
- The trust model
- The system's life cycle

They are often inter-related, in particular where a digital attack impacts on the physical world. Physical security is a problem that has been ongoing for centuries. Digital systems designers often miss the physical aspects of security. Good examples of such failures are where laptops are lost (and increasingly the case with smartphones) containing critical data such as product launch information, autofilled login fields giving access to corporate networks, or even military intelligence.

The objective of having a number of different physical security measures together is in attaining the point at which the sum of the whole is greater than the sum of the individual parts of the security system.

Digital/Virtual Security

A firewall may be viewed as serving the same function as a physical wall that secures something, similarly, a wall with a door with locks is analogous to the firewall, with access rights being given to particular people and checked each time they request entry and subsequently permitted through the secure doorway. Encryption is analogous to the creation of a separate room where nobody can overhear or see anything without being given access to the room by the person within. Secure logon through token based systems such as smartcards, random code generators have begun to be the norm for certain systems such as internet banking. However, with apps shifting transactional capabilities to smartphones, other forms of security systems focusing upon wireless technologies will emerge.

The Trust Model

Organizations have different trust models according to how each perceives threats to their operations. The access capabilities for an enterprise's assets all impact upon the vulnerability assessment and the protection required and encompasses all assets, including physical, financial, and intangible (such as patents and designs).

There is however a major difference between the physical and digital worlds in respect of trust, in that in the physical world it is possible to identify who holds a position of trust. In the digital world, remote access enables information gathering without risk of exposure and has the potential to enable access within the security perimeter. In the physical world, such breaches are clearer to identify with co-workers, CCTV and so forth. In the digital environment, potential and actual attackers are able to masquerade as somebody who possesses particular access rights and all without the risk of physical capture by security.

Life Cycle of a System

One of the least recognized aspects of vulnerabilities of systems lies in the ability to attack at particular phases of the lifecycle. An example of this is where a system is in the development phase that has a weakness built into it that later may be exploited by an attacker. Military intelligence agencies have worked with product developers in the past, creating products to be sold into questionable markets with engineered-in backdoors enabling agencies to then gather information that would otherwise have been impossible to acquire.

In the internet environment, the above scenario has been created and continues to expand due to various freeware movements that have products freely available for download and in particular apps at present. Many users have unsuspectingly installed software that may have had either a backdoor engineered in or has a point of weakness within it. There have been many recorded incidents, but it is not just the freeware sector that has had major security failures. The rate at which security updates and patches have been issued by the major software houses has increased rapidly as the threat environment evolves and becomes more insidious, with dedicated attacks increasingly executed against applications that have mainstream personal and business use. The current trend towards cloud computing will create further risks allied to uncertainty as to the security integrity of hosted applications.

Although the above might indicate a widespread security issue in the internet environment, the actuality is that a high percentage of networked systems are secure and many have been maintained and well audited over a considerable period. The real vulnerability enabling attackers to access and infect on a wide-scale basis is therefore created through the weak configuration of programs and the lack of experience of many end-users or in the absence of timely security updates provided by the manufacturers that are intended to strengthen vulnerabilities in software.

Current software and systems are easy to install and configure in their basic form. However, ensuring the overall configuration of systems and applications is secure are often the most difficult part, with default settings often used by users who are either unwilling to learn more about the impact such settings may have on their security, or a fear through lack of knowledge to select alternatives.

A further impact is the relatively low level of variation of software used by the majority. This impacts in that a security failure in a single software product has the potential to have the greatest impact on the total population of users of that software.

One final factor creating security weakness is the overall concept of security software development and deployment. The markets in both the personal and business sectors for security solutions are vast and offer an attractive market for software houses. However, the broad array of offerings creates the overall environment of piecemeal application purchase and deployment, as opposed to a conceptual environment of applications, hardware and security followed by product selection and deployment.

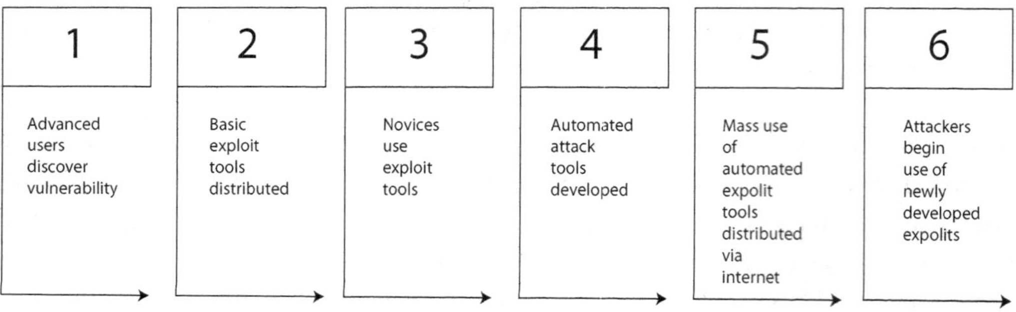

Fig. 2.2 Vulnerability Path

Basic Concepts of Security

Before coming to applied security measures, a description of some of the basic concepts that can be used to assess a solution and which can be applied to design a systematic approach are given. At commencement, it is advisable to find the lowest layer of information processing to which security measures can be applied to.

Excluding physical security and hardware design, the lowest layer of security has to be established at the operating system level since this will create the access control to any resource and system capability. It is necessary that this control can then be securely enforced by the operating system on which it is implemented.

The next layer is the secure transmission and storage of data in general, both locally and remotely. Of note is that access control has to be in place for this layer to effectively work and cryptography may be utilized to harden this security layer. Further security layers are problem specific, and in the case of the internet environment, network specific. The third layer of network security is the stability and security of any points of access to a network, single machine or to higher privileges.

It is only through consecutive rows of security layers that there may be protection against a problem. This methodology enables the construction of a scalable solution, with the capability to improve protection where necessary of the weak point in a specific layer if necessary.

Conceptual security measures: The systematic approach

A single goal of optimizing network security to mitigate the vulnerability potential over a maximum period of time should be set at the outset, with a second rule being to use common sense and apply logical concepts.

An un-trusted system, that is, a system that could already potentially have been compromised, must be deemed impossible to secure and should therefore never be connected to a network without security measures having been already implemented.

Some form of backup/recovery system should similarly be within a security system design from the outset, at the very least for unique data. Checksums and/or change logs, preferably cryptographic, should be included since these facilitate an ongoing comparison to compare the systems current states with their original states reliably and are fairly simple to implement and operate in much the same way as personal internet security products looking for changes to a home PC.

In order to eliminate vulnerabilities efficiently, a vulnerability checklist should be complied, ordered by priority. Security threats considered as critical to a systems' survival must be eliminated at all costs, whilst easily preventable risks should be avoided, such as not/late updating of software versions, or ensuring configuration is to the latest standards.

The role of the security administrator is to model worst-case scenarios in order to threat model and assess the potential for attacks. Some measures may not eliminate threats, but rather they raise the level of difficulty in executing an attack and this limitation as to effectiveness must be reviewed on an ongoing basis as attack tools evolve.

Designing a security model

In the same manner that a single host must be protected prior to linking it to a network, so the internal structural design of a network must be completed before exposing it to the internet. The generally accepted rule is to use a decentralized task security model, avoiding single, large resources that share many points of access. A single host that runs a concentrated number of services may be compromised more easily due to the wider availability of services for an attacker to exploit.

Problems in a Corporate Environment

Security policies dictate how an organization is to operate in relation to the required levels of security within it. It is analogous to the mission statement of an organization in that without it, the various sections that comprise an organization would remain unaware of the overall strategy and would not therefore be capable of tailoring its behaviors and attitudes to it.

The three pillars of a security policy comprise:

- **Responsibility**: clear and accurately defined roles and responsibilities within the organization for security.
- **Definition:** the security policy should be clearly defined, including details of its creation and development and identification and explanation of the criticalities of the system.
- **Consistency:** the policy should be defined and upheld at every level of the organization, with a clear description of whom, how and under which circumstances a change to that policy may be authorized.

It is generally accepted that corporations establish a security policies and a team that is solely responsible for protecting corporate resources by policy enforcement is assigned. However, this is problematic in that a small number of personnel controlling security measures cannot guarantee this protection, while the rest of the employees possibly lack sufficient computer/network knowledge to care enough about security.

Further, although it is possible to demonstrate lack of security, it is far harder to demonstrate its' guaranteed existence. A security policy may be enforced in respect of all technical measures, but it cannot be fully guaranteed that employees, lacking awareness, find ways to circumvent it (or that the policy is insufficient/staff are unaware of its' existence).

The accepted improved approach to corporate security is to define a minimum of security and of technical education for all personnel, and educate every individual in an adaptive manner, suiting their present state of knowledge. Taking this approach, however, makes it necessary to observe how well it is individually adapted, rewarding knowledgeable employees with respect, and helping those who face problems gaining the sufficient knowledge, possibly by assigning them to teams with more knowledgeable individuals. In recent times, video game styled online training has been utilized by many of the Fortune 500 companies in various areas, such as compulsory 30 minute online courses on how to use social networking and this could be adapted to security issues.

Classes of Attack

Buffer Overflows: are one of the most exploited vulnerabilities within the computing architecture. Most often an attack attempts to overrun a buffer in order to install malicious code that then operates with system privilege on the machine.

Distributed Port Scans: low-level port scans are used by hackers to systematically scan single ports on single agents in an alternating manner, mapping services and applications within a network.

Trojan Horses: can take several different forms:

- Trapping of keystrokes by network applications.
- Accessing memory owned by other applications (applications that attempt to interfere with the memory space of other applications.)
- Stealing local passwords.
- Downloading and invoking an executable file.
- Downloading and invoking ActiveX controls.

SYN Floods: attacks result in half open connections on the server when an abundance of half open states on a server can then prevent legitimate connections from being established.

Ping of Death and Malformed Packets: an attack involving IP packets that exceed the maximum allowed length resulting in software failure and physical machines being unable to operate.

Email Worms: one of the most common means by which enterprises have their security breached through end users, without technical knowledge, and often in breach in organizational security policies opening mails from unknown recipients and expose the organization to the attack hidden within it.

An increasing level of skill is required for the common attacks listed as the following list descends:

Denial of Service

1. Flooding – sending rubbish data or reply requests to a host to block its services.
2. Smurfing – using the IP broadcast system and IP spoofing to multiply floods.
3. OutOfBand/Fragment Attacks – exploiting vulnerabilities in TCP/IP stack kernel implementations.
4. SYN/RST Flooding – exploiting a vulnerability in TCP implementations (limited cache) to block incoming connections.
5. "Nuking" – using forged ICMP and TCP messages to reset active connections.
6. Specific DoS – generating requests that block one specific vulnerable service.

Malicious Software

1. Logic Bomb – program that causes damage under certain conditions (although this is also often just due to software or system bugs).
2. Backdoor – program feature enabling remote execution of arbitrary commands.
3. Worm – Program or trojan that spawns and spreads copies of itself.
4. Virus – programs or code that self-reproduces in existing applications.
5. Trojan – hidden program-in-a-program that executes arbitrary commands.

Exploiting Vulnerabilities

1. Access Permissions – exploiting read/write access to system files.
2. Brute Force – trying default or weak login/password combinations for telnet/pop3 etc. authentication.
3. Overflow – writing arbitrary code behind the end of a buffer and executing it.
4. Race Condition – exploiting a temporary insecure condition created by the execution of a program to gain access to sensitive data.

IP Packet manipulation

1. Port Spoofing – using 20/53/80/1024 etc. as source ports to avoid packet filtering rules.
2. Tiny Fragments – using 8 byte packets to bypass firewalls protocol-flag/port/size checks.
3. Blind IP Spoofing – changing the source IP address e.g. to access password-less UDP services that rely on IP checking.
4. Nameserver ID "Snoofing" – blind spoofing with calculated ID numbers to put false data into NS-caches.
5. Sequence Number Guessing – calculating TCP SEQ/ACK numbers for hosts with insecure random sequence numbers to establish a spoofed TCP connection from a trusted host.
6. Remote Session Hijacking – using packet spoofing to intercept and redirect running TCP/UDP sessions.

The Attack Lifecycle

All attacks follow the same logical progression, as shown:

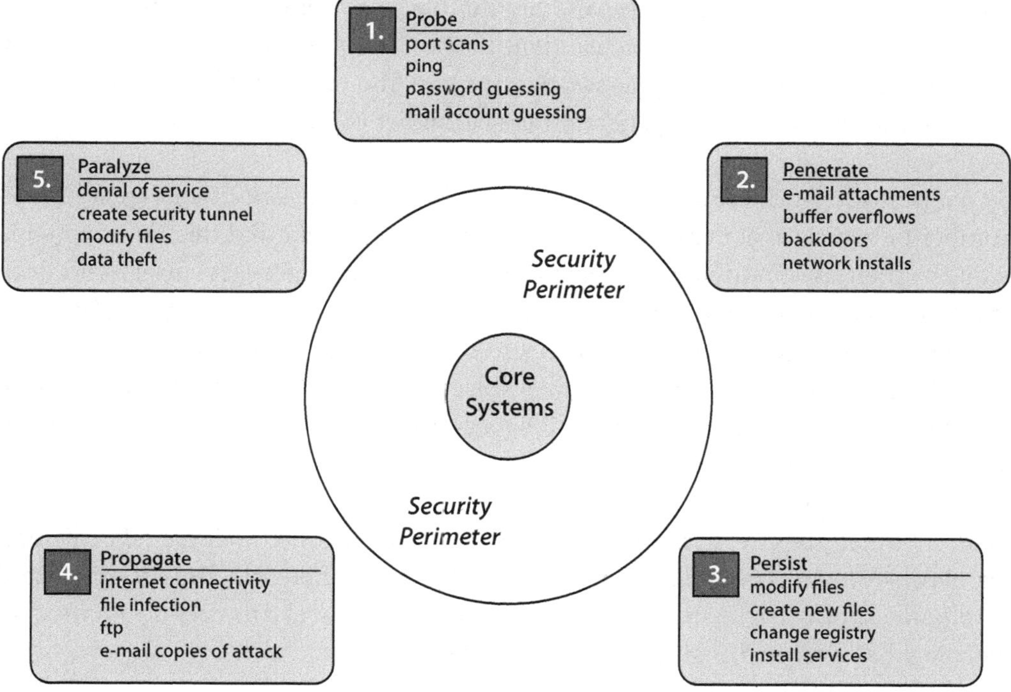

Fig. 2.3 Attack Lifecycle

1. Vulnerable targets are identified in the Probe phase with the goal being to find computers that can be subverted.

2. Exploit code is transferred to the vulnerable target in the Penetrate phase with the goal being to make the target execute the exploit code using some form of attack vector such as a buffer overflow.

3. Once an exploit has been successful, the exploit code attempts to create persistence for itself on the target system. The goal of the Persist phase is to ensure that the attack code will run and be available to an attacker even if the target system reboots.

4. Once an attacker has a beachhead in the organization, it is able to extend this to other targets. The Propagate phase seeks out vulnerable neighboring machines so that the exploit code can spread.

5. Of note is that it is only during the Paralyze phase does actual damage occur. Files may be erased, systems crashed and/or Distributed Denial of Service (DDoS) attacks launched.

There is a major dividing line between the Penetrate and the Persist stages, with the first two stages being highly subject to mutation i.e. the footprint of the attack constantly changes. The stages are also highly subject to being hidden from defenses using various methods. Since attack identification at the Penetrate stage frequently requires a certain amount of guesswork as to how the target system will handle the network packet, this tends to generate a large number of false positives.

By contrast the last three stages are highly stable over time, since there are a limited number of malicious activities that an attacker may undertake and this list of possible actions (such as modifying the operating system, adding a new user with root privileges, deleting files) has remained remarkably unchanged over the years. With the above in mind, organizations should seek to secure during the last three phases of an attack lifecycle rather than the first three, since in the latter case the attacks may take on different appearances and there will be a constant battle to keep pace in terms of security updates and patching.

In recent times, the effectiveness of signature based security methods has fallen behind the expansion and complexity levels of attack types. There has thus been a rapid development of behavior-based security systems, which seeks to decline attempts to execute what is viewed as suspicious activity within a host.

This approach is based upon the following categories of behavior:

- *Malicious activity:* where attempts are made to modify files, programs etc by an attacker.

- *Policy-relevant activity:* where a user might seek to operate outside of the bounds of what has been defined as undesirable within an organization, such as attempting to download some form of instant messaging software at work.

- *Application wrapping:* where an application has rules attached that effectively state that everything not expressly permitted is prohibited. This imposes severe restrictions upon the ability of the application to operate and can therefore be viewed as an extremely secure mode of operation.

All of the above is meant to illustrate how problematic network and computer security is. Generally, there is no consensus of opinion as to what the architecture requirements, limitations, implementations and operations should be. Rather, the context is different across various sectors and countries, and is also dependent upon vendor presence and distribution chains. It is highly unlikely that this situation will improve in the near future, since there are too many vested interests at stake and too large a market with a specific need for there to be a convergence of views.

Chapter Three

INTERNATIONAL STANDARDS AND BEST PRACTICE ADOPTION AND USE

Risk Standards Around the World

This chapter provides an overview of standards and best practices appertaining to operational risk. Comparing various risk management standards around the world in terms of their scope, process steps, and specific emphasis illustrates that there is a fundamental difference between the management of business risks, a sub-specialty area in the fields of finance and insurance, and operational risks, these being concerned with uncertainty in the execution of the activities of an organization.

Further, the extent and potential reasons for use or lack of use of information widely available is discussed, together with the constructs that determine usage within organizations, such as environmental scanning and judgment as to the degree to which the environment and/or information may be analyzable.

The origins of risk management are said to be in the field of Safety Engineering. As a result of the evolution of operational risk, a number of standards that prescribe and advise organizations on the best way to manage their risks have arisen. There are two levels of standard scope: Project and Organization. The distinction is based upon whether the standard states that the processes, steps and procedures it contains, are meant to be implemented at the project level, or are meant to be implemented by the entire organization. The standards all provide guidance and advice, and encourage organizations to adapt them to their own needs.

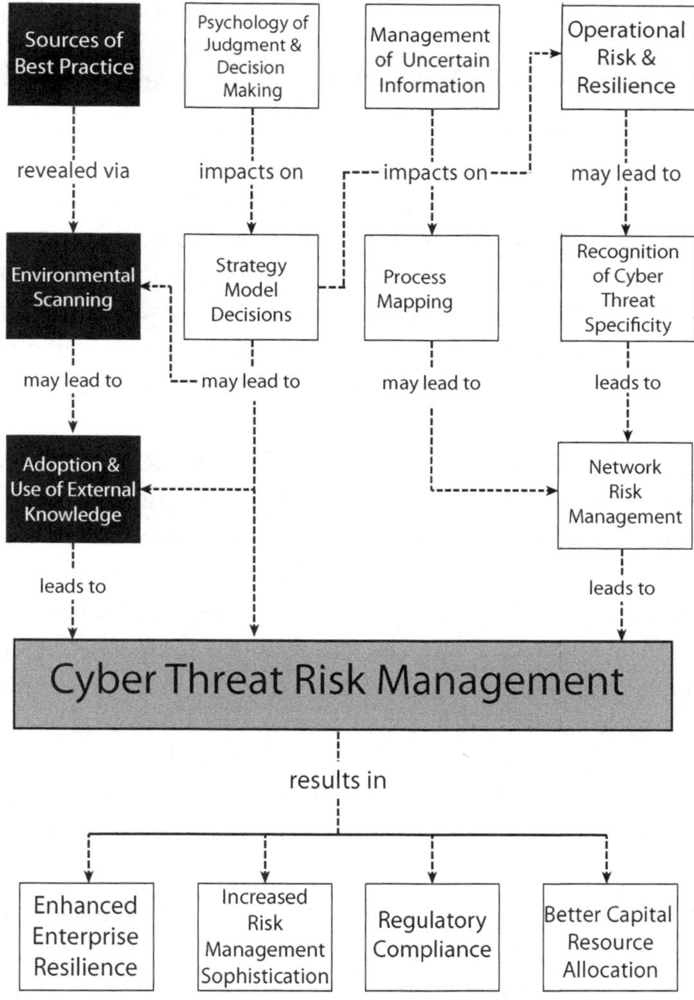

Fig. 3.1 Chapter 2 Focus

There is a high degree of similarity and consistency across standards, which may in fact indicate an emergence of a worldwide consensus regarding the way risk management, ought to be conducted. The main steps that can be identified are planning, identification, analysis, treatment and control. In some standards, the analysis step is labeled as 'assessment' and both the terms 'analysis' and 'assessment' frequently contain a process of estimation (of probability and consequences of the risk events) and evaluation (determining the overall magnitude of the risk event from which its priority is derived).

With is worth noting that the majority of tools and techniques described within standards for risk identification are descriptive and qualitative in nature, and very few tools are based upon statistical or mathematical techniques. Most standards address the issue of monitoring and controlling the effectiveness of risk treatment actions selected for implementation in the risk management process, but they are not concerned with managing and improving the risk management process itself.

Thus, standards appertaining to risk management have, in general terms, a high degree of commonality, given there are few, and minor, semantic differences among them. Where there are differences, these tend to be limited to the inclusion of additional elements such as communication, consultation and collaboration with stakeholders, links to the organization objectives and strategy, and guidance related to the adoption and implementation of a risk management system/function within the organization.

A source of variability among the standards is related to the scope of coverage of the standards themselves. Certain standards cover mainly, almost exclusively, the risk management process itself and ignore the aspects involved in establishing the organizational infrastructure required to apply the process. They also devote little, if any, attention to the aspect of managing the process as an organizational asset, including measuring the effectiveness of the process (as distinct from measuring the effectiveness of risk treatment actions implemented in a specific instance of the process), or generating lessons learned or in general continuous improvement of the process. Standards that offer greater coverage and that explicitly address the organizational issues involved in adopting and implementing a risk management process in an organization are of generally greater value.

The rationale behind the provision of an overview of those standards appertaining to operational risk management is that in the domain of cyber threat management, as well as risk management in general, there is a broad body of knowledge that can be leveraged for developing cyber threat management programs. The evidence, however, is that many organizations are either unaware of it, or choose not to utilize it. As an example of this lack of utilization, many enterprises run multiple, complex projects and programs, yet do not use generally accepted project management methods, such as PRINCE2 or PMI accredited methods. Utilizing such project management methods would lead to better project risk management, since this is a major component of such methodologies, and yet they are not implemented.

Logic dictates that, given that there is a business case for most projects/programs and a cost-benefit of so doing, all enterprises would wish to minimize project risks in order to better allocate capital resources. The issue then becomes one of why do organizations not use such external, but available knowledge. Following this overview of relevant information for risk/cyber threat management, the potential reasons are investigated.

AS/NZS 4360:1999 risk management standard

In November 1995, Standards Australia and Standards New Zealand published AS/NZS 4360: Risk Management, a generic risk management standard. This was succeeded in 1999 by a revised version.

By nature AS/NZS 4360 did not address the detail of the specific issues that risk managers working in specialist areas face in using the standard. Applying a generic standard in specialist technical areas often requires additional guidance. Therefore, the risk management technical committee had a program of preparing a series of explanatory guides or handbooks to assist practitioners. Since March 2001, eight guides based on AS/NZS 4360 have been published:

1. A basic introduction to managing risk (SAA HB 142: 1999).
2. Guidelines for managing risk in the Australian and New Zealand Public Sector (SAA/NZS HB 143: 1999).
3. Risk Financing (SAA HB 141: 1999).
4. Environmental risk management: principles and processes (SAA HB 203: 2000) (this is in fact joint and has been published in both jurisdictions).
5. Information security risk management guidelines (HB 231: 2000).
6. Guidelines for managing risk in outsourcing (HB 240: 2000).
7. Organizational experiences in implementing risk management practices (HB 250: 2000).
8. Guidelines for managing risk in the healthcare sector (SAA/SNZ HB 228:2001).

A further four were reviewed by the committees:

- Business Continuity Management
- Occupational safety and health
- Risk management and corporate governance
- 'Assurance'

Three further publications that are related to 4360 were:

- Emergency risk management: applications guide – reviewed and endorsed by the risk management standard committee, and published by Emergency Management Australia.
- Risk Management for Local Government (SNZ 2000) – published by Standards New Zealand but without reference to the Standards committee, and not endorsed by it.

- Using AS/NZS 4360: 1999 Risk management in Security Risk Analysis Author: Rick Draper ISBN: 1 876878 01 0

A structured approach to analyzing risks is essential for organizations to be able to make informed, defensible decisions about managing those risks. Without developing an understanding of the components of risk, it is almost impossible to implement the most appropriate and cost-effective mix of strategies.

In 1995, Standards Australia and Standards New Zealand published AS/NZS 4360: 1995 Risk management, and for the first time there was a publicly available, generic framework "for establishing the context, identification, analysis, evaluation, treatment, monitoring and communication of risk".

AS/NZS 4360 was subsequently reviewed and a new edition published in 1999. Most definitions and terminology were maintained between editions. However, there was an additional requirement included for communication and consultation during all stages of the risk management process. There were also changes to the qualitative descriptions used to communicate the level of risk.

The definition of risk remains unchanged between the 1995 and 1999 standards:

"[Risk is] the chance of something happening that will have an impact upon objectives. It is measured in terms of consequences and likelihood."

The important point to note in this definition is that, in order for a risk to exist, there must be some likelihood of the event (leading to the realization of the risk) occurring, and there must also be some negative consequences arising should that event occur.

Using the approach defined in AS/NZS 4360: 1999, risk management is not compulsory. However, it does represent a guide to sound risk management practice and, if used properly, provides a structured, defensible approach to risk analysis.

ISO 31000: 2009 Published November 2009

This standard is widely viewed as being a replacement for AS/NZS 4360:2004 (In the form of AS/NZS ISO 31000:2009). The main difference between the two is that the Standards Australia approach provided a *process* by which risk management could be undertaken, whereas ISO 31000:2009 addresses the *entire management system* that supports the design, implementation, maintenance and improvement of risk management processes.

Entitled *"ISO 31000:2009, Risk management – Principles and guidelines",* the standard "provides principles, framework and a process for managing any form of risk in a transparent, systematic and credible manner within any scope or context".

A major recommendation of ISO 31000: 2009 is that organizations should develop, implement and continuously improve a risk management framework as an integral part of their overall management systems.

Simultaneously, a revised and harmonized ISO/IEC Guide 73 was issued. ISO 31000 is set to become a family of risk management standards, building from the original AZ/NZS 4360 standard. As such, this standard is not industry-specific, but rather, provides the necessary general frameworks and methodologies for any organization to benchmark against what is set to become a best practice.

A further objective of ISO 31000: 2009 is to enable organizations to lift themselves out of the more usual 'silo' type of risk management operations by enabling, through implementation of ISO 31000: 2009, all strategic, management and operational tasks of an organization, throughout projects, functions and processes. All become aligned with a common set of risk management objectives.

A key point of this standard is that the intention is for existing risk management programs to be supplemented with it, rather than it having an overall replacement objective.

ISO/IEC 17799 information security management

The original version of the document upon which ISO 17799 is based (the "DTI Information Security Code of Practice") was much smaller in scope than the current standard, and identified 10 controls which were considered to be the most important, known as 'Key Controls'.

By the time the first version of ISO 17799 was published, in December 2000, these had been eliminated. However, the standard itself was still smaller than the present version, and comprised ten main sections, as opposed to the current twelve.

In addition to the new sections, the current version, which was published in June 2005, introduced new controls to cover new emerging issues. Changes were also made to make the standard more 'user friendly' and to harmonize it with other management standards.

Legislation

ISO 17799 identifies three controls as likely to be essential from a legislative perspective:

15.1.4	Data protection and privacy of personal information
15.1.3	Protection of organizational records
15.1.2	Intellectual property rights

Common Practice

The standard also identifies a further seven controls which it considers to be 'common practice' for information security:

5.1.1	Information security policy document
6.1.3	Allocation of information security responsibilities
8.2.2	Information security awareness, training and education
12.2	Correct processing in applications
12.6	Technical vulnerability management
14	Business continuity management
13.2	Management of information security incidents and improvements

ISO17799 is "*a comprehensive set of controls comprising best practices in information security*". It is essentially, an internationally recognized generic information security standard. Its predecessor, titled BS7799-1, has existed in various forms for a number of years, although the standard only really gained widespread recognition following publication by ISO (the International Standards Organization) in December of 2000. Formal certification and accreditation were also introduced.

The ISO 17799 standard comprises ten prime sections:

a) Security policy
b) System access control
c) Computer and operations management
d) System development and maintenance
e) Physical and environmental security
f) Compliance
g) Personnel security
h) Security organization
i) Asset classification and control
j) Business continuity management (BCM)

17799 is organized into ten major sections, each covering a different topic or area:

1. *Business Continuity Planning.* The objectives of this section are:
   a) To counteract interruptions to business activities and to critical business processes from the effects of major failures or disasters.

2. *System Access Control.* The objectives of this section are:
   a) To control access to information;
   b) To prevent unauthorized access to information systems;
   c) To ensure the protection of networked services;
   d) To prevent unauthorized computer access;
   e) To detect unauthorized activities;
   f) To ensure information security when using mobile computing and tele-networking facilities.

3. *System Development and Maintenance.* The objectives of this section are:
   a) To ensure security is built into operational systems;
   b) To prevent loss, modification or misuse of user data in application systems;
   c) To protect the confidentiality, authenticity and integrity of information;
   d) To ensure IT projects and support activities are conducted in a secure manner;
   e) To maintain the security of application system software and data.

4. *Physical and Environmental Security.* The objectives of this section are:
   a) To prevent unauthorized access, damage and interference to business premises and information;
   b) To prevent loss, damage or compromise of assets and interruption to business activities;
   c) To prevent compromise or theft of information and information processing facilities.

5. *Compliance.* The objectives of this section are:

   a) To avoid breaches of any criminal or civil law, statutory, regulatory or contractual obligations and of any security requirements;
   b) To ensure compliance of systems with organizational security policies and standards;
   c) To maximize the effectiveness of and to minimize interference to/from the system audit process.

6. *Personnel Security.* The objectives of this section are:
   a) To reduce risks of human error, theft, fraud or misuse of facilities;
   b) To ensure that users are aware of information security threats and concerns, and are equipped to support the corporate security policy in the course of their normal work;
   c) To minimize the damage from security incidents and malfunctions and learn from such incidents.

7. *Security Organization.* The objectives of this section are:
   a) To manage information security within the Company;
   b) To maintain the security of organizational information processing facilities and information assets accessed by third parties;
   c) To maintain the security of information when the responsibility for information processing has been outsourced to another organization.

8. *Computer & Operations Management.* The objectives of this section are:
   a) To ensure the correct and secure operation of information processing facilities;
   b) To minimize the risk of systems failures;
   c) To protect the integrity of software and information;
   d) To maintain the integrity and availability of information processing and communication;
   e) To ensure the safeguarding of information in networks and the protection of the supporting infrastructure;
   f) To prevent damage to assets and interruptions to business activities;
   g) To prevent loss, modification or misuse of information exchanged between organizations.

9. *Asset Classification and Control.* The objectives of this section are:
   a) To maintain appropriate protection of corporate assets and to ensure that information assets receive an appropriate level of protection.

10. *Security Policy.* The objectives of this section are:
    a) To provide management direction and support for information security.

AS/NZS 3931:1998 – risk analysis of technological systems

The objectives of this standard are to provide a basic model for analysis of risk; to provide guidelines for selecting and implementing risk analysis techniques, primarily for risk assessment of technological systems; and to enable quality and consistency in the planning and execution of risk analyses and in the presentation of results and conclusions.

It was intended as a step towards the development of a common methodology and understanding of the process of analysis of technological risk, thus providing a gateway across a range of countries and industries, and of applications such as design, quality and safety of technological systems. It introduced differences in terminology and application to those of AS/NZS 4360:

a) *Scope and application*: AS/NZS 3931 does not address the full process of risk management described in AS/NZS 4360.

b) *Terminology*: AS/NZS 3931 defines *risk* as a combination of the probability of occurrence and the consequences of a specified hazardous event, e.g. an event which can cause harm (physical injury, damage to health, property or the environment). It starts with an analysis of 'what can go wrong' and focuses on technological applications.

AS/NZS 4360 recognizes that risk is inherent in all activity, and that risk management may be as much about identifying opportunities as avoiding or mitigating loss.

Professional Body Frameworks and Guidelines

(COBIT) control objectives for information and related technology 2000

The COBIT framework was developed under the auspices of the formation Systems Audit and Control Association (ISACA), which is an international association for the support and improvement of professionals whose jobs involve the auditing of corporate and system controls.

The main theme of COBIT is business orientation. It was designed to be employed not only by users and auditors, but also, and more importantly, as comprehensive guidance for management and business process owners. Increasingly, business practice involves the full empowerment of business process owners so they have total responsibility for all aspects of the business process. In particular, this includes providing adequate controls.

The COBIT Framework provides a tool for the business process owner that facilitates the discharge of this responsibility. The Framework starts from a simple and pragmatic premise:

"In order to provide the information that the organization needs to achieve its objectives, IT resources need to be managed by a set of naturally grouped processes."

The Framework continues with a set of 34 high-level Control Objectives, one for each of the IT processes, grouped into four domains:

- Planning and organization
- Acquisition and implementation
- Delivery and support
- Monitoring

This structure covers all aspects of information and the technology that supports it. By addressing these 34 high-level control objectives, the business process owner can ensure that an adequate control system is provided for the IT environment.

IT governance guidance is also provided in the COBIT Framework. This provides the structure that links IT processes IT resources and information to enterprise strategies and objectives. IT governance integrates optimal ways of planning and organizing, acquiring and implementing, delivering and supporting, and monitoring IT performance. It enables the enterprise to take full advantage of its information, thereby maximizing benefits, capitalizing on opportunities and gaining competitive advantage.

In addition, corresponding to each of the 34 high-level control objectives is an *Audit Guideline* to enable the review of IT processes against COBIT's 318 recommended detailed control objectives to provide management assurance and/or advice for improvement.

The *Management Guidelines*, COBIT's most recent development, further enhances and enables enterprise management to deal more effectively with the needs and requirements of IT governance. The guidelines are action-oriented and generic and provide management direction for getting the information and related processes of the enterprise under control, for monitoring achievement of organizational goals, and for monitoring performance within each IT process. It also facilitates benchmarking of organizational achievement, enabling the mapping of an organization and where it stands in relation to the best in class in its industry and to international standards.

COBIT is intended to enable the development of clear policy and good practice for IT control throughout organizations, and is designed to be an IT governance tool that helps in understanding and managing the risks and benefits associated with information and related IT.

Whereas the *COBIT Framework* focused on high-level controls for each process, *Control*

Objectives focuses on specific, detailed control objectives associated with each IT process. For each of the 34 IT processes of the Framework, there are from three to 30 detailed control objectives.

Control Objectives align the overall Framework with detailed control objectives from 36 primary sources, comprising the de facto and de jure international standards and regulations relating to IT. It contains statements of the desired results or purposes to be achieved by implementing specific control procedures within an IT activity and, thereby, provides a clear policy and good practice for IT control throughout the industry, worldwide. Control Objectives are directed to the management and staff of the information services, controls, and audit functions and, most importantly, to the business process owners.

There are 302 detailed control objectives that provide an overview of the domain/process/control objective relationships and facilitate the translation of concepts presented in the Framework into specific controls applicable for each IT process.

(OCTAVE) operationally critical threat and vulnerability evaluation

The Operationally Critical Threat, Asset, and Vulnerability Evaluation (OCTAVE) is a framework for identifying and managing information security risks. It defines a comprehensive evaluation method that allows an organization to identify the information assets that are important to the mission of the organization, the threats to those assets, and the vulnerabilities that may expose those assets to the threats. By putting together the information assets, threats, and vulnerabilities, the organization can begin to understand what information is at risk. With this understanding, the organization can design and implement a protection strategy to reduce the overall risk exposure of its information assets.

It defines the essential components of a systematic information-security risk assessment. By following the OCTAVE framework, an organization can make information-protection decisions based on risks to the confidentiality, integrity, and availability of critical information assets. The operational or business units and the departments responsible for the information infrastructure, work together, to address the information security needs of the enterprise. OCTAVE thus gives the organization a comprehensive, systematic, context-driven approach to managing information-security risks.

OCTAVE examines organizational issues and technology issues to assemble a comprehensive picture of the information security needs of an enterprise. It contains the following phases:

- Phase 1, Build Enterprise-Wide Security Requirements
- Phase 2, Identify Infrastructure Vulnerabilities
- Phase 3, Determine Security Risk Management Strategy

Each phase of OCTAVE is designed to produce meaningful results for the organization.

During Phase 1, information assets and their values, threats to those assets and security requirements are identified using knowledge of the staff from multiple levels within the organization, along with standard catalogues of information. For example, known threat profiles and good organizational and technical practices are used to probe staff members for their knowledge of the organization's assets, threats, and current protection strategies. This information can then be used to establish the security requirements of the enterprise, which is the goal of the first phase.

Phase 2 of OCTAVE builds on the information captured during Phase 1 by mapping the information assets of the organization to the information infrastructure components (both the physical environment and networked IT environment) to identify the high-priority infrastructure components. Once this is done, an infrastructure vulnerability evaluation is performed to identify vulnerabilities. As in Phase 1, standard catalogues of information are used; for example, standard intrusion scenarios and vulnerability information are used as a basis for the infrastructure vulnerability evaluation. At the conclusion of Phase 2, the organization has identified the high-priority information infrastructure components, missing policies and practices, and vulnerabilities.

Phase 3 of OCTAVE builds on the information captured during Phases 1 and 2. Risks are identified by analyzing the assets, threats, and vulnerabilities identified in the earlier phases in the context of standard intrusion scenarios. The impact and probability of the risks (also called the risk attributes) are estimated and subsequently used to help prioritize the risks. The prioritized list of risks is used in conjunction with information from the previous phases to develop a protection strategy for the enterprise and to establish a comprehensive plan for managing security risks that are among the goals of Phase 3.

A Comparison with Certified Standards

Whilst there are standards that do not require certification, the rationale for firms adopting a standard may be similar and, in some aspects of the use or adoption of standards by multiple firms within the same sector, act in the same way is if there was certification.

Additionally, there are instances in which certification for a standard are based upon external influences beyond the control of an organization. An example of this would be where a large-scale organization requires all the suppliers in its' supply chain to have certified for a certain standard, such as one of the ISO 9000 series standards.

In order to provide an insight into why an organization may seek to certify for a standard that is not compulsory, nor pay a part in an overall risk management program, the ISO14001 standard has been used herein by way of example. It is necessary to understand those factor influencing standards compliance in conjunction with psychological effects on judgment and decision making in order to fully appreciate the complexity of why one enterprise may pursue a particular route in developing its' risk management program, whilst another heads in another.

Environmental Management System ISO 14001: The strategic decision of deciding to certify

14001 is an international standard for environmental management systems that was introduced in 1996. It gained wide recognition among businesses, much in the same way that 9000 has. As a result, managers in almost every organization evaluate whether the organization should be 14001 certified.

The standard's body, the ISO, had previously been successful in motivating organizations to systematically address and improve product and service quality with the 9000 series of standards. The United Nations Conference on Environment and Development (UNCED) envisioned a similar set of voluntary standards to encourage the systematic improvement of environmental quality.

14001 sets the criteria for an environmental management system (EMS). The EMS dictates requirements for the organization's structure, responsibilities, practices, procedures, processes and resources, so that responsible corporate environmental management is institutionalized in the organization.

In this respect, the standard is similar in the objectives of some sectoral regulations, in that it relates to the interaction between an organization's operations and the environment in which it is situated. An example here would be the Basel banking regulations that were intended to routinise and create harmonization of the global banking environment.

An 14001certification is based on the principles of continuous improvement: scope, plan, implement, check, and correct. It must be communicated, employees trained and empowered and procedures documented.

Case studies have found variances across sectors and positioning of organizations as a result of evaluating the costs of implementing an ISO 14001 program. In one case, the organization found large-scale cost savings following its commitment in implementing an environmental management system. In other cases projects within organizations found little or no savings generated by the program whereas. However, in others programs, larger than expected returns were experienced. Organizations can find that they are able to increase their competitiveness, even where it already had a low cost leadership position, within a competitive industry.

Further, organizations have found an additional bonus from implementing an ISO 14001 program in the form of key customers preferring 14001 certified suppliers as well as the social legitimacy earned from stakeholders pressuring for greener business practices.

While managers can estimate direct costs of certification, evaluating the intangible costs and benefits and the indirect impacts on the firm's performance is more difficult. However, academic research has concluded that organizations seek to certify for ISO 14001 since a good EMS will do two things.

First, it will allow the firm to uncover ways in which the firm can reduce its environmental impacts while simultaneously reducing costs or increasing productivity. *Secondly*, it will coordinate the environmental activities of the firm to achieve greater organizational efficiency and effectiveness. Additionally, such a program may shed light on other areas that managers were not previously aware of in terms of environmental impact, thus alerting them to potential liabilities.

More stringent accountability of company officers through national and international legislation (Sarbanes Oxley Act 2002 -USA; Loi sur la Sécurité Financière – France; Corporate Law Economic Reform Program (Audit Reform & Corporate Disclosure) Act 2004 – Australia, etc) resulted in the removal of previous defense of lack of knowledge of misdoings may therefore also have promoted the mapping and understanding of business operations in order to reveal potential risks to key management personnel.

In many cases, organizations that merely comply with existing regulations often fail to take into account recent changes in scientific knowledge, technical sophistication, or production economics on an ongoing basis. Thus these firms are under the constant risk of having to make radical changes to their processes if regulations change significantly. For employees, their acceptance of changes to processes is also greater due to their perception that it is due to externally imposed conditions.

Institutional pressure has certain effects on firms. Institutions are the structures and activities that provide stability and meaning to social behavior, and are present in the form of laws imposed by government and in the social norms or individual values that have developed over time. These may also be more important when there is uncertainty, as with the case of environmental performance metrics.

A broader conceptualization of institutions, of which government regulations are only a part, is that where individuals and groups impose norms of operating that define which business activities are deemed acceptable. To the extent that firms conform to institutional demands, they develop better stakeholder relationships. These stakeholders support the firm (or restrain their opposition). Conforming to institutional pressures helps protect firm performance by bestowing social legitimacy on the firm.

It has also been claimed that where a firm frequently fails to comply with institutional pressures, then it becomes subject to greater scrutiny, including from regulators. One way to conform to institutional pressures is to associate with acceptable signals. This includes conforming to widely accepted standards. The 14001 certification process required organizations to comply with documentation standards. Whilst a firm did not have to reveal such documentation outside of the certificating authority, the fact of its existence will satisfy some stakeholders.

An ancillary benefit to such conformity is the greater degree of accommodation by watchdog agencies and interest groups in the event of an incident. Given that watchdog agencies have limited resources, they prefer to focus their efforts on those organizations that have not historically shown due diligence.

Therefore, if a firm exceeds stakeholder expectations, it can enhance its reputation and gain a competitive advantage, thereby securing higher financial returns than its competitors. In building legitimacy, firms merely need to engage in the same behaviors as their competitors. To build a reputation, firms must differentiate themselves from their competitors, and standards certification exists to do both: certification provides legitimacy, whilst continuing new actions as part of continual improvement can help build reputation.

It may be possible to discern the contexts that encourage and reward type certification. While costs are real, the economic and institutional benefits are often long term, diffused, and sometimes invisible. Further, the benefits accrue not only from improved performance, but also from avoiding damaging impacts.

In the case of 14001, some industries have been exposed to greater pressure to certificate than others. Examples are those industries whose activities are heavily scrutinized, such as the mining, forestry and chemical sectors. Operating or working with firms in these industries creates the context in which the economic and institutional benefits are heightened.

Because of heavy exposure, some business to business customers are also likely to make certification demands on suppliers. These are firms that will not want to be perceived as outsourcing their environmentally sensitive activities to other firms that may have less regard for the environment.

Additional pressures for certification may arise from operations which spread across national borders. Even though domestic standards and customers may not require it, firms may discover that international partners and clients demand it. Firms with significant sales to foreign customers are generally more likely to be certified than those firms with primarily domestic customers. One explanation put forward for this is that firms are more concerned about their ability to monitor suppliers' activities and certification is a means of ensuring a standardized method of operating is maintained by suppliers.

Another context that may give rise to type certification is one in which a number of other firms have certified to the standard in the industry. Even in the absence of performance enhancing pressures for conformity, firms want to avoid the negative inferences that could come from stakeholders as a result of not being certified, that is to say, firms imitate each other in respect of the propensity to certify.

There are criticisms of standards certification however. One such is that although the standard requires firms to put into place the systems or structures for monitoring environmental aspects and reducing environmental impacts, there is no requirement that environmental performance actually be improved or that specific goals be met.

This can result in a company's environmental performance falling but remaining certified. Another criticism is that far from deflecting scrutiny, certification may attract additional scrutiny since certificated firms are expected to have a more complete paper trail. Additionally, any internal audit illustrating poor or failing practices, as part of the certification process, may alert external agencies to such operations and attract more detailed investigation on an ongoing basis. Consequently, firms that are most in need of certification are the least likely to seek it.

Best Practice Transfer of Existing Knowledge External to the Firm

Organizational leverage of best practice adoption

Although the new internet risk management environment requires organizations to identify, assess, quantify and generally manage operational risks in areas where there are difficulties in so doing, there is, as illustrated in part above, a large body of knowledge that lends itself to assisting in this task.

The question therefore is to what extent do organizations make use of such knowledge external to the firm in their strategic and operational cyber and general risk management programs? For example, a focus on cyber threats requires such organizations to fully comprehend the risks that underlie the existence and operation of computer networks and within this recognition is the acknowledgement of the lack of historical data upon which to develop effective risk management frameworks.

By referring to existing knowledge external to the firm, organizations can create robust model upon which to develop their individual risk management methodologies. Sources of knowledge vary from professional bodies, to the various supervisory bodies within specific business sectors. Equally, the range of knowledge varies from that with a high degree of specificity, for example technology risks, to more generalized information, for example, qualitative approaches to setting thresholds of acceptance of risks within organizations as a whole.

As a specific example of existing knowledge relating to the field of cyber threats for the banking sector, the following provide banks with suitable knowledge external to the firm.

Best practice transfer is distinct from the diffusion of knowledge within an organization, although frequently the two terms, transfer and diffusion, are often used interchangeably. 'Diffusion' is generally used in connection with the dissemination phenomena, in which attention focuses on the source and on a generic destination unit[2]. In such cases, idiosyncratic differences between individual recipient units are per-force relegated to a secondary role, if not completely ignored. By contrast, 'transfer' is typically associated with situations in which the unit of analysis is the objective, and attention in the analysis also spans the characteristics of the recipient organization.

Consequently, the word 'transfer' signals close attention to the individual characteristics of both the source and the recipient of knowledge. In cases of technological knowledge transfers, there may also be a distinction between 'point-to-point transfers' versus 'diffusion'; typically knowledge transfer is a distinct experience rather than one of gradual diffusion.

Table 3.1 Existing knowledge relating to network operational risk management

Title / Year	Author	Type	Focus
ISO/IEC17799 Information technology – Code of Practice for information security management	International Standards Organization	International Standard	Information Security
AS/NZS: 3931:1998 Risk analysis of technological systems – Application guide	Joint Standards Australian Standards New Zealand Committee MB/2	Standard	Technological System Risk Analysis
AS/NZS:4360:1999 Risk Management	Joint Standards Australian Standards New Zealand Committee OB/7	Standard	Risk Management
BIS. Sound Practices for the Management and Supervision of Operational Risk. February 2003	Basel Committee on Banking Supervision	Best Practice Guidelines	Operational Risk Management
BIS. Risk Management Principles for Electronic Banking. July 2003	Basel Committee on Banking Supervision	Best Practice Guidelines	Electronic Banking Risk Management
BIS. Management and Supervision of Cross-Border Electronic Banking Activities. July 2003	Basel Committee on Banking Supervision	Best Practice Guidelines	Cross-Border Electronic Banking Risk Management
BIS Trends in risk integration and aggregation. August 2003	Basel Committee on Banking Supervision	Best Practice Guidelines	Industry Patterns in Risk Quantification
OCTAVE The Operationally Critical Threat, Asset, and Vulnerability Evaluation	The Software Engineering Institute, Carnegie Mellon University, 2003	Best Practice Guidelines	Information Security Risk Evaluation
CobIT. July 2000. Control Objectives for Information and Related Technology	COBIT Steering Committee and the IT Governance Institute	Best Practice Guidelines	Information Technology Control Objectives
The Basel Committee on Banking Supervision Basel II: International Convergence of Capital Measurement and Capital Standards: a Revised Framework. June 2004	Basel Committee on Banking Supervision	Regulation	Capital Adequacy Revision; Risk Quantification
Computer Security Journal Volume XIX No.2 2003. Better Risk Assessment Using a Cascading Threat Multiplier	Computer Security Institute	Best Practice Guidelines	Quantification of Technology Risks

Best practice adoption by organizations has been proposed by several authors as a means of improving firm performance. However, the scope to do so may be limited by the specific regulatory frameworks within which an organization may be required to operate in. A particular mix of resources forms the basis of competitive positioning of individual firms, and firm resources are represented by means of assets, capabilities, organizational processes, firm attributes and information.[3]

Early studies of technological innovation assumed that new technology was instantly diffused across total capital. Similarly, early studies of international and domestic transfer of technology assumed that the transmission of technologies between and within countries was costless. However, it has subsequently been found that, in practice, many corporations still treat transfers and replications of advanced technology as relatively straightforward undertakings and therefore assign them to untested junior managers. In many instances therefore, the cost of transfers of best practice are in reality too high and often uncertain in terms of the success in it being transferred.[4]

Intra-firm transfers of best practice

The transfer of best practice has long been an important concern also for managers (Ford Motor Company 1913) with it becoming a central managerial responsibility in more recent times (Toyota 1978). What is far more difficult to ascertain is whether there are common elements to those organizations that openly *seek out* information and knowledge that will enable them to turn the uncertainties of a global economy and a multitude of risks to their own advantage.

Most research in the field of intra-firm transfers of best practice has highlighted the urgency for organizations to achieve "time compression", that is, the ability to accelerate the diffusion of emerging capabilities throughout the firm. Global price competition dictates the need in achieving annualized improvements in productivity, for example, in order to maintain competitive advantage

However, little advancement has been made in understanding the internal workings of organizations. It has been argued that one of the fundamental questions not yet satisfactorily answered is why is it so difficult for firms to imitate best practice even after it has been recognized for a considerable time.

---

[3] Daft, Richard L., & Weick, Karl E. (1984). "Toward a model of organizations as interpretation systems". *Academy of Management Review* 9 (2), 284-295.

[4] Teece, D. (1977) "Technology Transfer by Multinational Corporations: The Resource Cost of Transferring Technological Know-How." *Economic Journal* (87), pp 242-261.

The Appropriation of Economic Rents from Existing Knowledge

Inasmuch as it reduces organizational slack, transfers of best practice can be seen as a way to appropriate rents (profits) from existing knowledge. Barriers to the transfer of best practice can therefore be claimed to be barriers to profit appropriation.

The concept of rents, as opposed to profits, is one where the source of high profits is located in a firms' resource bundle, rather than in its membership in a collective, that is, an industry effect. It has therefore been claimed that when assets are specialized to the needs of the firm, or when their use otherwise involves significant transaction costs, the rent (profit) on that factor is not logically or operationally separable from the profits of the firm.

Because the profits realized by a firm originate in some form of scarcity, then the profit maximizing firm, in the resource based theory, is seen as a seeker of scarce, valuable, and costly to copy inputs for production and distribution. By accumulating resources with rent-yielding potential, a firm may increase the amount of generated rents and therefore its profits. Profits can only result from this activity if the costs of accumulating the resources are lower than the rents these resources can actually produce. To realize the rent-yielding potential of such resources, a firm also needs to be able to appropriate the rents (profits) that the acquired resources may generate.

Organizations are able to generate valuable new assets, such as knowledge and competence, which may be achieved through *environmental scanning*. Another means is by external *benchmarking*, where firms seek to improve their performance by learning from best practice. The firm's knowledge base may also increase through the generation of new applications from existing knowledge within the organization. However, an organization will realize above average profits from its superior asset endowment only if it can generate all potential rents by deploying these assets efficiently.

An organization may reduce or eliminate the rent yielding potential of assets as a result of the decision as to how to deploy those assets. A deployment decision may be injudicious to rent generation where managers make deployment decisions of strategic assets in a setting that is characterized by uncertainty, complexity and intra-organizational conflict. A firm may also dissipate part or all of the rent yielding potential of its superior asset during the process of asset deployment.[5]

In the resource based theory of the firm, assets must be deployed efficiently in order to guarantee rents. Investment decisions in information technology, for example in

[5] Ghemawat, P. (1991). *Commitment: The Dynamic of Strategy.* New York: The Free Press.

determining the infrastructure, support and operation for optimal cyber threat resilience, therefore depend upon them being deployed efficiently. Utilizing external knowledge in the deployment of such technologies can therefore lead to optimizing asset deployment (capital).

The adoption of best practice by an organization could be seen as a mechanism to enhance the appropriation of rents from an existing stock of knowledge (external to that organization). When the diffusion and incorporation of best practices is incomplete, valuable superior knowledge is not fully utilized in all parts of the firm. Consequently, those parts of the organization where best practice has not diffused will exhibit avoidable deficits in performance, i.e. organizational slack. Thus, in this way, adoption of best practices by the organization can be viewed as a mechanism to reduce organizational slack.[6]

In the context of a cyber threat and resilience program, acquiring knowledge external to the organization, whether through environmental scanning activities or best practice benchmarking, still requires optimal diffusion throughout the enterprise. A failure to so do can have two effects; operational risk is not reduced; a lack of reduced risk exposure impacts on the business case/cost-benefit of a risk management/resilience program and may halt further budget allocation to the efforts.

The four stages of knowledge transfer

Four stages exist in the process of knowledge transfer:

- Initiation
- Implementation
- Ramp-up
- Integration

Initiation comprises all events that lead to the decision to transfer. The order of the events may differ; it may be that a need is identified which triggers a search for potential solutions, leading to the discovery of existing superior knowledge. Alternatively, the discovery of superior knowledge may reframe as unsatisfactory a hitherto satisfactory situation.

As in the case of best practice benchmarking, the discovery of superior results will reveal how good is best and who is currently the best. More focused inquiry may follow

[6] Szulanski, G. (1996). "Exploring internal stickiness: Impediments to the transfer of best practice within the firm." *Strategic Management Journal* 17: 27-43.

into how those results are obtained and whether the transfer of best practices is feasible. This inspection often requires months of information collection and evaluation.

Benchmarking is more demanding when existing business operations are inadequately understood or when measures of performance or internal measurements are missing since benchmarking requires internal measurements. As such the ability of organizations to benchmark has *business process analysis and mapping* as a pre-requisite.

The implementation phase begins with the decision to proceed and implementation related activities cease or diminish after the recipient organization begins using transferred knowledge. Complex knowledge transfers may involve several participants in both the source and recipient organizations.

As well as effective multiple communications links being established, there will also be a technical gap that needs to be filled. The width of this gap depends upon what the recipient organization of knowledge has to do to in order to be able to effectively use the transferred knowledge. It may also be non-existent or insignificant if there is a pre-existing relationship between the parties. To effectively close the technical gap, the source's knowledge may be adapted to suit the anticipated needs of the recipient organization.

The eventfulness of the implementation stage depends upon how difficult it is to bridge the communication gap between the source and the recipient. Closing the technical gap may be difficult for a number of reasons. The recipient organization may deviate from recommended ways of implementing the use of transferred knowledge, because of unfamiliarity, to preserve pride of ownership and status, or as a result of hidden resentment (the well worn "not invented here" syndrome).

The ramp-up phase begins when the recipient organization starts using the transferred knowledge. This is often a period of intense and difficult adaptation requiring alterations and corrections to the way knowledge is put to use. In this way, the organization is concerned primarily with identifying and resolving unexpected problems that hamper its ability to match or exceed the post-transfer performance expectations. Modifications to the way new knowledge is put to use becomes increasingly difficult because routinization embeds unresolved problems into organizational practice and initial expectations are re-adjusted, based upon actual experience and thus temporary workarounds may become perpetual.

Unexpected problems may occur during the ramp-up phase as a result of insufficient training of personnel, or those who are trained then leave the organization, or are unsuited to the new environment. As a result, there may be delays in using the new knowledge and expertise, but this new knowledge is crucial in containing costs. Expertise may be available from outside sources, but in any case, if the transition to using new knowledge is gradual, rather than sharp, a duplication of effort and resources is more likely.

Integration begins after the recipient organization achieves satisfactory results after applying the transferred knowledge. Use of the knowledge becomes routinised and, over time, the use of new knowledge becomes incorporated into the regular activities of the organization and loses its separate identity.

The use of new knowledge gradually becomes habitualized and tends to persist, unless its appropriateness is explicitly questioned and re-evaluated, requiring an affirmative decision to continue, generally from the Board. This decision may be evoked by external or internal disruptions. External disruptions may result from variations in the environment where the knowledge has been put to use, or from the appearance of a clearly superior alternative.

Internal disruptions may occur due to individual lapses in performance due to inadequate training and repetition, or by the refusal to continue to use new knowledge because expectations are not being met. It may also be caused by a lack of clarity as to why it is necessary to use the new knowledge. In all cases, the maintenance of a comprehensive truce in organizational conflict determines the ability to sustain routine use of new knowledge. Organizational strategic decisions i.e. top-down or bottom-up are therefore crucial, that is, there must be Board support or a Board directive.

Successful replication of knowledge in a different setting may be compromised by idiosyncratic features of the new context in which the knowledge is put to use. In the case of transfers of highly technological sophisticated process knowledge, its reach into poorly mastered *process techniques* is such that, any substantial divergence of *process designs*, risks multiplying operational problems beyond manageable levels. The completeness of information technology security and general computer operation security is therefore important. Outsourcing of some operations may reduce an impact from a lack of internal competencies, but increases dependence upon the outsourced supplier for such skills.

Difficulty in a transfer of knowledge may also be the result of a perceived lack of reliability of the source.[7] When the source of knowledge is not perceived as trustworthy or knowledgeable, it is more difficult to initiate a transfer of knowledge from that

---

[7] Nelson, R. R., & Winter, S. G. (1982). *An evolutionary theory of economic change*. Cambridge, Mass.: Belknap Press of Harvard University Press.

source, and its advice and example will be more openly challenged and resisted. The degree of familiarity between the source and the recipient has also been found to affect knowledge transfers.

The motivation of a recipient to accept knowledge from an external source and engage in the activities necessary to utilize that knowledge may prove critical to ensure a non-eventful transfer. A lack of motivation may result in foot dragging, passivity, feigned acceptance, hidden sabotage, or outright rejection in the implementation of new knowledge. The lower the motivation of the recipient organization to accept external knowledge, the less likely it will be that a transfer of knowledge will be uneventful. Therefore if there is no mandatory requirement to certificate or for regulatory compliance, there may be a lower motivation for organizations to transfer existing knowledge.

The ability to exploit outside sources of knowledge is largely a function of the level of prior related knowledge. Critical prior knowledge includes awareness of the locus of useful complementary expertise within and outside of the organization and the stock of prior related knowledge determines the absorptive capacity. A recipient organization that lacks absorptive capacity will be less likely to recognize the value of new knowledge, less likely to assimilate that knowledge and less likely to apply it successfully to commercial ends.

With cyber threat risk management, and enterprise resilience being at the beginning of the life of these management disciplines, the skill set and knowledge stocks within organizations may not be at a sufficiently high level with the result that the ability to exploit existing knowledge external to the firm becomes limited.

The ability of a recipient organization to institutionalize the utilization of new knowledge reflects its retentive capacity. Maintaining the use of new knowledge is facilitated by extending that use to the full logical extent and, when it displaces old knowledge, by taking steps to eliminate the use of old knowledge. Without retentive capacity, an organization may discontinue the use of new knowledge and revert to the previous status quo. This is frequently the case in a post-I.T. security audit (and specifically when external consultancies are engaged for the purpose), whereby practices such as the writing down of logins/passwords is identified and outlawed by senior management, only to be rediscovered as a general practice in subsequent audits.

The contextual relationship between the source and the recipient organization of knowledge is dependent upon the pre-existing relationship between the parties. A transfer of knowledge is not a single event, but rather an iterative process of exchange. A recipient organization may require explanations of the nature of the source's knowledge in order to decide whether a transfer of knowledge could meet its needs. Once transfer commences, it may be necessary for the source to support the initial period of utilization of the new knowledge, and therefore the success of such an exchange depends upon the ease of communication.

Organizational learning via environmental scanning

Organizations seek to maintain or improve their competitive advantage through the *strategic planning* process. This in turn is reliant upon inputs in order for senior management to make informed decisions.

Environmental scanning is the acquisition and use of information about events, trends, and relationships in an organization's external environment, the knowledge of which would assist management in planning the organization's future course of action. Depending on the organization's beliefs about environmental analyzability and the extent that it intrudes into the environment to understand it, four modes of scanning may be differentiated:[8]

- Undirected viewing
- Conditioned viewing
- Enacting
- Discovery

Organizations scan the environment in order to understand the external forces of change so that they may develop effective responses which secure or improve their position in the future. They scan in order to avoid surprises, identify threats and opportunities, gain competitive advantage, and improve long-term and short-term planning.

It has been claimed that environmental scanning constitutes a primary mode of organizational learning, given that organizations are dependent upon knowing and interpreting external changes, albeit limited to each organization's ability to adapt to its outside environment.

Such environmental scanning includes both *looking at* information (viewing) and *looking for* information (discovery). Further, scanning is influenced by external factors such as environmental turbulence and resource dependency, organizational factors such as the nature of the business and the strategy pursued, information factors such as the

[8] Aguilar, F.J. (1967) *Scanning the Business Environment.* New York: McMillan.

availability and quality of information, and personal factors, such as the scanner's knowledge or cognitive style.

Scanning as a form of information behavior is composed of information needs, information seeking, and information use. In the context of environmental scanning, information needs often refer to the focus and scope of scanning and in particular the environmental sectors where scanning is more intense. Information seeking may require several resources that are used to scan the environment, and may be influenced by the organizational methods and system deployed to monitor the environment. It has also been claimed that it impacts in relation to decision making, strategic planning and in equivocality reduction.[9]

The Link Between Scanning and Performance

In attempting to answer the question as to whether environmental scanning improves organizational performance, several studies have concluded that it does. The intelligence-rationality factor, which comprises environmental scanning, controls, communication, adaptiveness, analysis, integration, multiplexity, and industry experience, has been found by researchers to be by far the most important factor in separating successful companies from the unsuccessful.

Scanning firms have historically significantly outperformed non-scanning firms, with the average annual performance of the scanning firms being consistently better than the non-scanning firms. Thus, environmental scanning and assessment has a positive influence on corporate performance.[10]

There is also a relationship between organizational strategy, environmental scanning and firm performance. Taking Porter's (1985)[11] now classical typology of product differentiation, low cost leadership, and niche focus, it has been found that strategy and environmental scanning has a substantial influence on the firm's return on assets and return on sales. High performing firms in both differentiation and low cost

---

[9] Choo, Chun Wei, and Auster, Ethel (1993). "Environmental scanning: acquisition and use of information by managers", in: *Annual Review of Information Science and Technology*, edited by M. E. Williams. Medford, NJ: Learned Information, Inc. For the American Society for Information Science.
[10] Newgren, Kenneth E., Rasher, Arthur A. & LaRoe, Margaret E. (1984). An empirical investigation of the relationship between environmental assessment and corporate performance. Paper read at *Proceedings of the 44th Annual Meeting of the Academy of Management*, August 12-15 1984, at Washington, DC.
[11] Porter, M.E., (1995), *Competitive advantage: creating and sustaining superior performance.* New York, Free Press.

strategies engage in significantly greater amounts of scanning than low performing firms in those two strategic groups.

The degree of scanning by chief executives of high performing organizations (measured in terms of a higher average return on assets employed) generally increase the frequency, intensity and breadth of their scanning as external uncertainty increase. In the case of cyber threat management therefore, with the new operating environment having created a high degree of equivocality and environmental uncertainty, organizations may be expected to increase their environmental scanning.

There may well also be a relationship between performance, (measured by profitability and growth), and advanced scanning systems: firms using advanced systems to monitor external events have demonstrated higher growth and profitability than firms that do not have such systems.

Information derived from environmental scanning is increasingly being used to drive the strategic planning process of organizations in most developed countries. Despite this, the practice of scanning by itself is insufficient to assure performance – scanning must be aligned with *strategy*, and scanning information must be effectively used in the strategic planning process. When coupled with the availability of information on external change, scanning can induce strategic, generative organizational learning.

Although all forms of scanning necessarily involve the seeking and use of information about the environment, different organizations operating in different environments may be expected to scan quite differently. Four modes of managerial scanning have been identified by researchers. A general model of organizational scanning based upon the two dimensions of environmental analyzability (the ability to analyze what is happening in the environment), and organizational intrusiveness (the extent to which an organization actively intrudes into the environment to collect information) have been proposed.

Organizational scanning is characterized by information needs, information seeking, and information use patterns. It is also affected by the sense-making, knowledge creation and decision making processes that constitute organizational scanning.

Organizations differ in their modes of scanning, depending upon management's beliefs about the analyzability of the external environment, and the extent to which the organization intrudes into the environment in order to understand it. Differences in perceptions of environmental analyzability are due to the characteristics of the environment combined with management's previous interpretation experience. Analyzability is closely related to the concept of perceived environmental uncertainty, defined as being the variable that measures the totality of the scanner's perception of the external environment's complexity and changeability.

Dimensions of the environment that determine its perceived uncertainty are factors of: the simple-complex dimension (the number of environmental factors considered in decision making) and the static-dynamic dimension (the degree to which these factors change over time). Decision makers in environments that are dynamic and complex experience the greatest amount of perceived environmental uncertainty.

However, the combined effects of a large number of external factors and actors, unclear cause-and-effect linkages, and the rapid rate of change, create the perception that the environment is un-analyzable. Further, besides environmental uncertainty, the level of knowledge and information available about the environment may also be an important factor in determining the perception of analyzability. In some sectors, the use of information technology has made it possible to efficiently amass and analyze data and trends and this, coupled with information availability, has lead to the perception that the environment is analyzable.

The extent to which an organization actively intrudes into the environment is where an organization allocates substantial resources for information search and for testing or *manipulating* the environment. A passive organization is one that takes whatever environmental information comes its way and attempts to interpret the environment with the given information. They hypothesize that the differences are due to the degree of conflict between the organization and its environment. A hostile environment increases scanning because of new problems and the need to identify new opportunities and, as such, organizations allocate more resources to scanning in such hostile environments, and vice-versa.

Where organizations are forced to respond to, adapt to or imitate the ebb and flow of normative and regulatory currents in their environments, it is generally regarded as being at the core of institutional theory. Institutional theory attends to the deeper and more resilient aspects of social structure. It considers the processes by which structures, including schemas; rules, norms, and routines, become established as authoritative guidelines for social behavior. It inquires into how these elements are created, diffused, adopted and adapted over space and time, and how they fall into decline and disuse. Although the ostensible subject is stability and order in social life, students of institutions must perforce attend not just to consensus and conformity but to conflict and change in social structures. [12]

---

[12] Powell, Walter W., & DiMaggio, Paul J., eds. (1991). *The new institutionalism in organizational analysis.* Chicago, IL: University of Chicago Press.

Researchers have labeled organization-environment relationships and these are described by verbs that carry the connotation that environments dominate or overpower organizations: change is imposed, authorized, induced, imprinted, and incorporated.

Table 3.2 Three Pillars of Institutions

	Regulative	Normative	Cognitive
Basis of compliance	Expedience	Social Obligation	Taken for granted
Mechanisms	Coercive	Normative	Mimetic
Logic	Instrumentality	Appropriateness	Orthodoxy
Indicators	Rules, laws, sanctions	Certification, accreditation	Prevalence, isomorphism
Basis of legitimacy	Legally sanctioned	Morally governed	Culturally supported, conceptually correct

In addition to the relationship with its environment, the organization's overall business strategy may be related to the sophistication, scope and intensity of its environmental intrusiveness. This in turn is affected by organizational size and inertia, organizational slack (defined as the availability of resources to allocate to active scanning), past experience with scanning and interpreting the environment.

An organization that experiences changes in its environment will seek to process information and make sense of it, creating new knowledge within the firm. Organizational sense making may be driven by beliefs or actions. In belief driven processes, people start from an initial set of beliefs that are sufficiently clear and plausible, and sew them as nodes to connect more information into larger structures of meaning.

Undirected Viewing

Undirected viewing takes place when the organization perceives the environment to be un-analyzable and so does not intrude into the environment to understand it. Information needs are ill-defined and much of the information obtained is non-routine or informal, usually gained through chance encounters. Since the environment is assumed to be un-analyzable, the organization does not seek comprehensive, hard data, and is satisfied with limited, soft information. The information use is primarily concerned with reducing high levels of environmental equivocality.

During undirected viewing, sense making is characterized by what has been coined "informal bracketing". Bracketing of external signals is informal in that what the organization notices is dependent upon what subjective clues observers happen to be attending to at the time. Partly because multiple observers with different frames of reference may be involved, many cycles of sense making are required to resolve environmental equivocality. Knowledge that is used in undirected viewing is based upon tacit beliefs that the complexity, opacity and dynamism of the environment are such as to render it un-analyzable.

Conditioned Viewing

Conditioned viewing occurs when the organization perceives the environment to be analyzable but is passive about gathering information and influencing the environment. Information needs are said to focus on a small number of relatively well defined issues or areas of concern, and are often based upon widely-accepted industry assumptions and norms. Information seeking makes use of standard procedures, typically employing internal sources, with a significant amount of data coming from external reports, databases, and sources that are highly respected and widely used in the industry.

During conditioned viewing, sense-making is belief driven, and there are fewer cycles of equivocality reduction. Over time, the organization develops a set of assumptions and beliefs about the environment and uses them to define a number of areas of particular interest to structure the scanning activity. Cultural knowledge supplies the assumptions and beliefs about the business and the environment that the organization is in. These may be part of the received knowledge that firms in the same industry share. They draw a frame of reference within which knowledge about the environment is created. Decisions are mostly programmed, following standard procedures and premises derived from past experience. Representation of the decision situation is simplified, and procedures are structured by rules and routines which may be adopted from standard industry practice.

Enacting

Enacting takes place when the organization perceives the environment to be un-analyzable, but then continues to intrude actively into the environment in order to influence events and outcomes. Information needs are those required for experimentation and testing the environment. Information seeking is from external sources and channels that the organization has created through its intervention. Enacting organizations construct their own environments, gather information by trying new behaviors, experiment, test, and stimulate, ignoring precedent rules and traditional expectations. Information use is focused on the actions that have been taken, and this information is used to reduce equivocality as well as to test existing rules and precedents.

During enacting, sense making is action driven. The organization intrudes actively into the environment to construct new features, then concentrates sense making on them. Tacit knowledge is important in enacting, since the types of enactments to be pursued depend upon individual intuition, while the interpretation of enacted information depends on personal insight and instinct. As the organization acquires new ways of viewing its environment, new tacit knowledge may be generated. Decision making processes tend to be phased and incremental, involving iterative cycles of design and trial-and-error. Overall, the modus of learning is for the organization to learn by doing.

Discovery

Discovery takes place when the organization perceives the environment to be analyzable and it actively intrudes into the environment to collect an accurate set of facts about the environment. Information needs are well-defined, broad, detailed and open ended search goals. Information seeking is for hard, formal, often quantitative data. The organization is likely to have its own scanning unit, whose staff systematically analyses data. Information seeking and use in conditioned viewing (as opposed to discovery) is restricted to a few issues: routinised, and based upon received knowledge. Decision making is based on logical, rational procedures, often including systems analysis and quantitative techniques.

During discovery, sense making is based upon formal, systematic scanning that is aimed at determining the objective facts of what is happening in the external environment, and can be both action and belief driven. Measurement, modeling, forecasting, trends analysis and other quantitative methods are employed to discover the true condition of the external environment. The organization believes that there is a stock of knowledge that it can draw upon for analysis and planning. Overall, the modus of learning in discovery is for the organization to invest resources in collecting information about and analyzing the environment and then to adjust its actions in the light of the new knowledge. The primary difference between conditioned viewing and discovery is that discovery requires significant resources for entering the environment to create new features and/or collect information. In addition, with discovery, scans are broad and comprehensive in order to determine true states of affairs, whereas conditioned viewing concentrates on selected areas/issues.

The different modes of scanning are compared overleaf.

Un-available	**Undirected Viewing**		**Enacting**	
	Information Needs	General areas of interest	Information Needs	Specific areas of concern
	Information Seeking	'Informal'	Information Seeking	'Testing'
	Information Use	'Noticing'	Information Use	'Experimenting'
Available	**Conditioned Viewing**		**Discovery**	
	Information Needs	Sensitized areas of concern	Information Needs	Detailed search goals
	Information Seeking	'Routinised'	Information Seeking	'Formal'
	Information Use	'Watching'	Information Use	'Discovering'
	Passive		**Active**	

Organizational Intrusiveness

Un-available	**Undirected Viewing**		**Enacting**	
	Information Needs	Waiting for important change	Information Needs	Create features in environment
	Information Seeking	Little pre-existing knowledge	Information Seeking	Tacit knowledge: learn by doing
	Information Use	Coalition/Political mode	Information Use	Anarchic / Process mode
Available	**Conditioned Viewing**		**Discovery**	
	Information Needs	Driven by norms and beliefs	Information Needs	Determine objective reality
	Information Seeking	Cultural knowledge: expectations, frames	Information Seeking	Explicit knowledge: hard data, formal models
	Information Use	Programmed/ Rational mode	Information Use	Process mode
	Passive		**Active**	

Organizational Intrusiveness

Fig. 3.2 Environmental Scanning as Information Seeking

(Aguilar, F.J. (1967) *Scanning the Business Environment.* New York, Macmillan.)

Using Information External to the Organization

From the above, it may be inferred that organizations have a wealth of external information from which to draw when developing its' cyber threat management program and building enterprise resilience.

Taking each element in turn, it is possible to summarize that organizations should seek to undertake environmental scanning in the four modes, that is, undirected viewing; conditioned viewing; enacting and discovery. This information should be analyzed and assessed to ensure that the enterprise's scanning activities are aligned with the strategic plans formulated for the organization.

As part of a cyber threat management program, internal measurements should be made, requiring the organization to execute a business process mapping and analysis program, since this is a pre-requisite for benchmarking activities and allows an oversight of both process design and process techniques utilized by the enterprise. This may lead to identification of areas of weakness and/or process improvements, increasing competitiveness.

Once these activities have been completed and maintained on a continuous basis, the information gathered should be transferred within the organization in order to facilitate best practice transfer. This would be comprised of internal and external information, as well as having standards, regulations, professional body practices and inter/intra sectoral best practice data. How and why this information is utilized is influenced by the various psychological factors that affect judgment and decision making within organizations and is addressed in the following chapter.

Chapter Four

PSYCHOLOGICAL EFFECTS UPON JUDGEMENT AND DECISION MAKING

Introduction

This chapter applies to organizations in illustrating the issues within the subject matter of the psychology of judgment and decision making. However, it may be considered differently according to the prevailing context facing companies operating in different sectors/countries and so forth. Additionally, it illustrates potential traps in that there are two different presentations of issues within organizations – those at a high level for the Board to understand, and those in detail for operational personnel. As such the attitudes and context may well be very different at the two levels within an organization and requires understanding in order to target the correct profile of the individual in assessing the impact of psychology on organizational decision making.

It also indicates a potential bias that may be present according to the historic data available to those vested with the authority to make decisions at all levels of an organization, as well as their pre-existing knowledge of the subject matter that relates to the decision to be made.

In recent times, there has been an increasing prominence in the publicity, awareness and commercial research surrounding internet attacks and the impact on all types of organizations, both commercial and governmental. The stage at which organizations are prepared, aware and managing such threats may impact on the understanding and

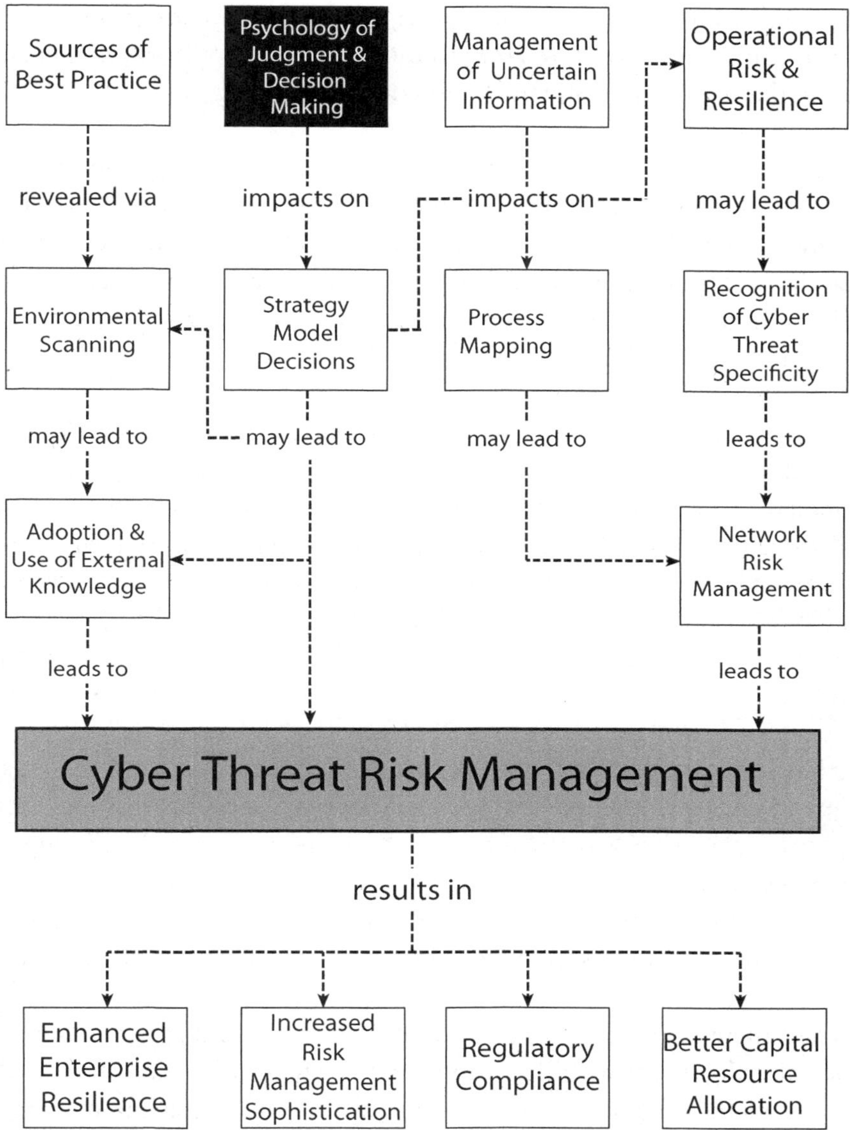

Fig. 4.1 Focus of Chapter 4

immediacy of information received by the recipient organization in respect of the strategic management of cyber threats i.e. data available may not be utilized to its' maximum capability.

The subject matter has been simplified in the extreme for the purpose of giving the reader a basic understanding of the core elements. For this reason it is divided here into the primary elements of perception, memory, context and how question framing affects answers. The second section appertaining to the psychology of judgment and decision making covers areas relating to models of decision making, heuristics and biases, and the social side of judgment and decision making.

As to why this aspect of cyber threat/risk management is so important, the recent (at the time of writing: August 2012) $2 billion risk exposure of one the world's biggest banks can be viewed as to the influences of psychology on judgment and decision making. In this instance, the bank's risk managers made fundamental mistakes based upon the notion that a hedge on credit exposures could reduce the bank's risk but simultaneously earn billions in profit.

The firm's chief investment officer was established in order to invest excess deposits and generate additional revenues, in much the same manner as most treasury units in corporations operate as a matter of course. Avoiding the technical actions behind the losses in detail, the issue was that the bank invested in credit-default swaps which were designed to mitigate the bank's risk exposure, but the positions they took in derivatives distorted the market. This in itself was due to the risk management team relying too heavily upon its value-at-risk modeling (which estimated the potential loss of a risky asset or portfolio over a given period) and led to a failure of understanding its' true risk exposure.

Taking this as a clear example of decisions made, judgment and biases, an organization took the view that its' trading actions would derive excess profits whilst not being improper or risky, despite them subsequently being viewed as being improper and having secondary risk exposures that were not accounted for by the risk management team, since their positions were so vast that the banks' actions moved the very instruments that they were seeking to utilize as the basis of its' hedging strategy.

The management of organizations has to determine the risk appetite, the mitigation strategies, the alignment with the corporate strategy in delivering shareholder value that meets market expectations, and numerous other decision making actions. Understanding psychological impacts upon such judgment and upon the decision-taking process is therefore critical in the formulation, not just of managerial decisions on a daily basis, but at all levels of the organization and their impact on risk/cyber threat management.

Cognitive Dissonance

The theory of cognitive dissonance states that people are usually motivated to reduce or avoid psychological inconsistencies. When there is inconsistency (dissonance-arousing) then people will find ways to rationalize the inconsistency to fit with their internal views, motivations, emotions and feelings.

It has also been found that people experience cognitive dissonance when they hold two thoughts that are psychologically inconsistent, that is, thoughts that feel contradictory or incompatible in some way.[13]

There is a proposition that people try whenever possible to reduce cognitive dissonance. Dissonance may be regarded as a "negative drive state" (an aversive condition) and as such is linked to motivational theory.

Self-Perception Theory

Researchers have proposed that cognitive dissonance findings can be explained by "self-perception theory". According to this theory, dissonance findings have nothing to do with a negative drive state; instead they have to do with how people infer their beliefs from watching themselves behave.

Self-perception theory is based upon two main premises:

1. People discover their own attitudes, emotions, and other internal sates partly by watching themselves behave in various situations.

2. To the extent that internal cues are weak, ambiguous or uninterpretable, people are much in the same position as an outside observer when making these inferences.

The difference between self-perception theory and cognitive dissonance theory is that self-perception theory explains classical dissonance findings in terms of how people infer the causes of their behavior, whereas cognitive dissonance theory explains these findings in terms of a natural motivation to reduce inner conflict (dissonance).

Cognitive dissonance influences a wide range of judgments and decisions. Most dissonance arousing situations fall into one of two general categories: *predecisional* or *postdecisional*. In the first type of situation, dissonance, or the prospect of it, influences the decisions people make. In the second kind of situation, dissonance, or its prospect, follows a choice that has already been made, and the avoidance or reduction of this dissonance has an effect on later behavior.

---

[13] Festinger, L., and Carlsmith, J.M. (1959). Cognitive consequences of forced compliance. *Journal of Abnormal and Social Psychology,* 58, 203-210a.

Examples of such attempts to reduce predecisional dissonance are those where the person acts in a way that is excessive in an attempt to offset a particular view of them that is at odds with their own view of self. Researchers Sherman & Gorkin[14] used a scenario with subjects that sought to identify sexism in the target group. Those found to hold sexist views, whilst professing to be non-sexist, subsequently took strong liberal views towards a set of questions that formed a positive view towards women at work. In other words, after displaying traditional sex-role stereotypes, the target group members tried to reduce their dissonance by acting more liberated; a means called "bolstering". This method of dissonance reduction has been exploited commercially and in promoting concepts and ideals such as energy conservation.

By contrast, postdecisional dissonance that follows a decision rather than precedes it has been found to result in an increase in a belief held before a decision was taken. Knox & Inkster[15], for example, found perhaps bizarrely that people who gambled on a horserace held stronger held belief in their likelihood of winning directly after placing a bet. Similarly, following on from the work of Knox & Inkster, Frenkel & Doob[16] used the same methodology to explore the question of whether voting for a political candidate increased the confidence in the candidate winning an election. The findings confirmed the earlier work, with voters believing more strongly that their candidate would win immediately after voting than before they had voted.

Although it is known that changes in attitude can *lead* to changes in behavior, research on cognitive dissonance shows that changes in attitude can also *follow* changes in behavior, since the pressure to feel consistent will often lead people to bring their beliefs in line with their behavior.

The implications of this, when relating to risk management, is the degree of initial belief in either data accuracy; the evaluation of the probability of an event occurring; in the degree of independence of items; and in the valuation of expected loss arising from the impact of an event occurring.

---

[14] Sherman, S.J., and Gorkin, L. (1980). Attitude bolstering when behavior is inconsistent with central attitudes. *Journal of Experimental Social Psychology,* 16, 388-403.

[15] Knox, R.E., and Inkster, J.A. (1968). Postdecision dissonance at post time. *Journal of Personality and Social Psychology,* 8, 319-323.

[16] Frenkel, O.J., and Doob, A.N. (1976). Post-decision dissonance at the polling booth. *Canadian Journal of behavioural Science,* 8, 347-350.

Memory and Hindsight Biases

There has been a view that the memory is akin to a storage chest, where information is stored until called upon, and sometimes the location of the information is lost and so therefore is the memory of an event or object, where we are said to have forgotten. However, research has shown clearly that memories are not copies of past experiences recalled, but rather are constructed at the time of withdrawal.

Experiments by academics[17] further strengthen this view of memory being reconstructive. In a series of experiments, wording changes were used, either in conjunction with video footage and memory tests subsequent to viewing, or presenting lists of sentences to subjects. The results were similar in both series, in that the form of a question, even when changed by one word, can markedly affect how people reconstruct their memory of an event. Additionally, experiments have shown that people do not memorize sentences or specific listed items, but rather they construct and memorize a general scenario. Once one piece of information is integrated with others, it is sometimes difficult to remember which information was new and which was already known.

Hindsight bias is the tendency for people to have difficulty in telling how they are affected by information about an outcome. An example of this phenomenon is when people are asked to estimate in retrospect how likely they once thought the results were to occur, they assign higher probabilities than do people predicting the experimental outcome in advance. It is the tendency to view what has already happened as relatively inevitable and obvious – without realizing that retrospective knowledge of the outcome is influencing one's judgments.

Hindsight bias has been shown to be manageable in terms of its reduction through having people stop to consider reasons why the results of an experiment or event may have turned out differently. It has been found that informing people about hindsight bias and encouraging them to avoid it is not sufficient to eliminate it, but when subjects were asked to consider carefully why outcomes occur, hindsight bias was still present, but to a much lesser degree. Since memory is highly reconstructive, the only means to eliminate hindsight bias when decisions are being considered is through thorough and accurate records at all times.

As such, organizations may be better placed in their risk management programs in some sectors than others in reducing the influence of hindsight bias in assessing risk

---

[17] Loftus, E. (1980). *Surprising new insights into how we remember and why we forget*. New York: Ardsley House.

and probabilities, since the audit and supervisory requirements are higher in certain industries than others – banking, aviation, nuclear power, railways for example. These regulatory requirements often mandate the detailed recording of a large number of operational details.

Context Dependence

The effect of a stimulus is context dependent, that is, decision makers do not perceive and remember information in isolation, but rather they interpret new information in light of past experience and the context in which the material occurs. In the area of judgment and decision making, there are four main effects of context dependence:

1. Contrast effect,
2. Primacy effect,
3. Recency effect and;
4. Halo effect.

Contrast Effect

Early studies in psychology concerned perceptual judgments, such as temperature or color discrimination and weight estimation. Sherif, Taub & Hovland[18] published an article on the contrast effect, illustrating this effect by having subjects lift weights. They found that when asked to first lift a heavy weight, then lighter ones, the subjects rated relatively light weights as lighter than they actually were; this is the contrast effect. Further experimentation proposed that the contrast effect only occurs when the contrasted stimuli are similar to one another.

Therefore, an organization may be more advanced in its' operational risk development if it has experienced negative impacts arising from risk events occurring. That is, the weighting given to developing enterprise risk management may be higher within those organizations. To assess this possibility, organizations could be assessed and questioned as to whether they have experienced network attacks. Where this has been the case, if the principles of the contrast effect hold true, it might be expected that those organizations who affirm their experience of attacks, would have developed more robust operational risk management programs than those who have not.

---

[18] Sherif, M., Taub, D., and Hovland, C.I. (1958) Assimilation and contrast effects of anchoring stimuli and judgments. *Journal of Experimental Psychology,* 55, 150-155.

Primacy Effect

The classic study of this effect was published by Asch[19] which was a study of impression formation. In most of his research, he asked subjects to give their impressions of a hypothetical person who had certain traits. Asch found that that characteristics appearing in each series influenced impressions more strongly that the characteristics appearing later. This pattern is known as the primacy effect.

Further studies found that the primacy effect is not merely a product of the first entry in a series. Instead it is a general relationship between the position an entry occupies and the effect it has on judgments. Thus, first impressions are the most important, but second and third impressions still show a significant primacy effect.

The primacy effect occurs not only when people form impressions of each other, but in a great many situations involving the evaluation of sequential information. For example, a primacy effect sometimes occurs when people are exposed to opposite sides of a controversial issue. In many cases, people are more influenced by the first presentation of an issue than by subsequent presentations.

The Recency Effect

The recency effect counters the primacy effect in that in some instances, the final presentation has more influence than the first presentation. The recency effect often occurs when people are able to remember the last presentation more clearly than the first one.

Researchers Miller & Campbell[20] asked the question as to which effect is the strongest. For example, if a choice was available to speak first or last at a public debate, which should be selected? They edited the transcript of a court trial and rearranged the proceedings so that all the material for the plaintiff appeared in one block of text, and all the material for the defendant appeared in another block. They then recorded the proceedings with different people reading parts of different characters. Each recording lasted about forty-five minutes and the communications were presented in one of eight different ways (see below). In some conditions, subjects rendered judgments immediately after hearing back-to-back communications (pro-con or con-pro), and in other conditions, a one-week delay separated various phases of the experiment.

---

[19] Asch, S.E. (1946). Forming impressions of personality. *Journal of Abnormal and Social Psychology,* 41, 258-290.

[20] Miller N.H., and Campbell D.T. (1959). Recency and primacy in persuasion as a function of the timing of speeches and measurements. Journal of Abnormal and Social Psychology, 59, 1-9.

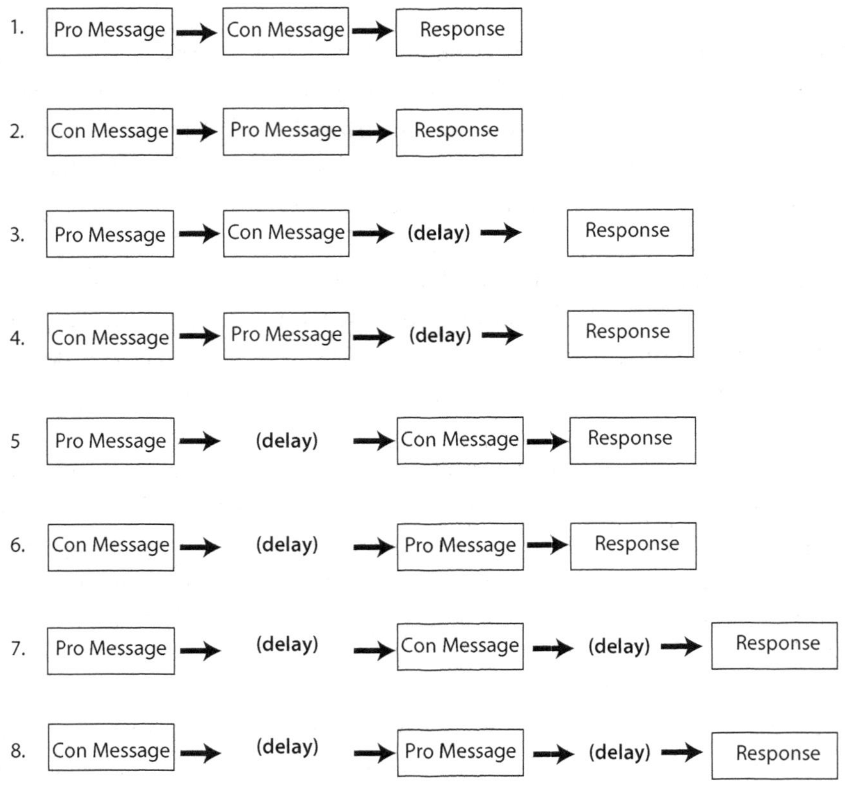

Fig. 4.2 Recency and Primacy in Persuasion as a Function of Timing of Communication (Miller & Campbell 1959)

What Miller & Campbell found was a primacy effect in some cases and a recency effect in others; that is, they found that in some conditions people were more persuaded by the first communication, and in others, they were more persuaded by the second communication (regardless of whether the communication was pro or con). When subjects were asked about the case one week after hearing back-to-back presentations (conditions 3 & 4), a primacy effect occurred. When communications were separated by a week and subjects were asked about the case immediately after the second communication (conditions 5 & 6), a recency effect occurred. The first two conditions and the last two conditions did not result in significant primacy or recency effects.

Miller & Campbell also found evidence that recency effects were a function of differences in recall. Subjects in condition 5 tended to recall more factual material about the con communication than about the pro communication and subjects in condition 6 tended to recall more factual material about the pro communication than the con communication.

Essentially the same results have been experienced in experiments on how people make predictions. People were asked in one case to generate reasons why a future event might occur (pro-reasons) and reasons why the event might not occur (con-reasons). For some events people listed pro-reasons first and for others they listed con-reasons first. A strong primacy effect was found when people generated both sets of reasons back-to-back, but a recency effect when people worked on a three minute task between listing pro and con reasons.

As such, the recency effect may also affect the outcome of the risk assessment process within the overall risk management development, where a higher weighting or value is placed on events which have occurred more recently than those which may in fact have had a higher potential impact but occurred longer ago.

Halo Effects

Both the primacy and recency effects show that the same stimulus can have a different effect on its context and order of presentation. The halo effect is another example of context dependence. Thorndike investigated the effect and concluded that "even a very capable foreman, teacher, employer or department head is unable to treat an individual as a compound of separate qualities and to assign a magnitude to each of these in independence of the others."

Many pioneering experiments were undertaken by Asch in investigating the effect and found that when there was the inclusion of a central characteristic such as "cold" or "warm" into a series of characteristics of a person's character, then a halo was formed. Contextual factors strongly influence how people respond, whether it relates to shape, form, personality, argument or inanimate object; that is, there is no stimulus without a context.

Therefore, in the subjective analysis of threats and their potential impact, a risk management team must be careful not to include factors creating context dependence, through labeling threats or events with words or terms that manipulate the assessment process.

Plasticity

The context and wording of questions has a strong influence on judgment and decision making. Experiments with risk scenarios have found that most people are "risk seeking" when it comes to loss options; that is, they prefer to risk a relatively large loss rather than suffer a sure loss with the same expected value.

If this was correct in all forms, then insurance companies would be unable to write any business aside from statutory cover. The insurance industry is based upon people's willingness to pay a premium, which is a "sure loss" in order to avoid a larger, but uncertain loss.

When people are presented with an additional option of a "sure loss" but couched in terms as an insurance option, 65 per cent of people have been found to prefer the sure loss. However, it has been proposed that in such research the use of the term "insurance" may have highlighted the potential for large losses, or perhaps the term invokes a social norm to act prudently.

It is clear therefore that the same choice leads to a different preference when it is cast in terms of insurance. When it is presented as insurance, people become "risk averse" as opposed to "risk-seeking". Other research has indicated that this phenomenon occurs across a wide range of situations.

Similarly, the term risk management, as well as the universal requirement to undertake such an activity within the banking sector, may have a plasticity effect, in that banking organizations may undertake risk management actions, with an attributed cost, to effectively manage potential downside risks which have a higher degree of improbability of occurring.

Order Effects

People are also influenced by the ordering of questions or response alternatives. Usually these effects are small, but in some cases they can be substantial. Where for example two questions are posed and there is a need for consistency on the part of the respondent, then answers to the second question can be pulled in the direction of the first.

Answers can also be influenced by the order in which response alternatives are presented, although these response-order effects are usually slight and rarely occur when the choice involves very brief dichotomous choices such as "agree or "disagree", or where there is a large choice set of alternatives. One of the most common response-order effects is a recency effect, in which the same answer is chosen more frequently when it appears as the last alternative in a series.

Pseudo-Opinions

Although context and order can significantly influence the way people answer questions, responses are "plastic" only to a certain point. When people are familiar with an issue, variations in context and order typically produce marginal changes of less than 30 per cent.

However, when people know little about a subject or issue, they are more easily influenced by these variations. When they know virtually nothing about an issue, a certain percentage shows the ultimate form of plasticity by offering an opinion on the issue when they have no real opinion. Such opinions are called pseudo opinions.

Survey researchers have increasingly used filters which are designed to remove respondents who have no opinion on a given topic. There are several ways in which filtering may be accomplished and are generally effective in screening out pseudo opinions, although in some cases they run the risk of creating a bias in the survey results. Schuman and Presser[21] conducted a number of experimental polls comparing filtered and unfiltered questions. Based upon their findings, they concluded that most filters shift at least 20 per cent of the respondents from expressing an opinion to that of "don't know"; do not significantly affect the relative proportion of respondents who give a particular answer; and do not strongly affect the correlation between answers to one question and answers to another.

Plasticity in choices and opinions is closely related to attitudinal inconsistency. Whereas plasticity usually refers to a discrepancy in how people answer two versions of the same question, inconsistency refers to a discrepancy between two related attitudes (attitude-attitude inconsistency) or between an attitude and a corresponding behavior (attitude-behavior inconsistency). Research has found that attitudes about abstract propositions are often unrelated to attitudes about specific applications of the same propositions. When it comes to specific applications, there are invariably complicating factors: situational constraints, other principles that present conflicts, etc.

Research on attitude behavior inconsistency suggests that abstract attitudes bear little relation to specific actions. It has been found in further research that the correlation between attitudes and behavior is almost exactly zero. However, what did correlate significantly was the performance of the subjects (who were students, tested for their attitudes towards cheating and actual behavior of cheating in an examination). Whether or not a student cheated, depended in much greater part upon how well they had prepared for the examination than upon any opinions they had stated about honesty in examinations. Additional research raised the question of whether attitudes and behaviors are usually heavily discrepant, with findings that suggested the answer is yes.

---

[21] Schuman, H., & Presser, S. (1981) *Questions and answers in attitude surveys: Experiments on question form, wording and context.* Orlando, FL: Academic Press.

Studies have concluded that it is considerably more likely that attitudes will be unrelated or only slightly related to overt behaviors than that attitude will be closely related to actions. However, later work proposed that it might be desirable to abandon the idea of attitudes. Following on from this view, a revisionist school was born and argued that attitudes are consistent with behavior, provided certain conditions are met.

If the attitude-behavior concept holds true, then it may be expected that in responding to questions relating to cyber threat management and enterprise resilience, the degree to which an organization has fully developed its' operational risk management program may influence the way in which responses are made.

Decision Making

Decision making is an activity that lies at the heart of management. The assumption of a management role places an individual in an organization's decision making activity, with authority to make decisions and to organize and develop the organization's decision-making capability.

Decision making bears the connotation of being decisive, yet many decisions are taken over long periods of time in which there are many stops and starts to the development of the issue and its resolution.

Those involved in the process often fail to perceive how the decision was made. This is partly through not being involved in all elements of the process that lead to the decision. Some political aspects of a decision will be inaccessible to most members of an organization. Participants will also have a biased view of the activities they have been engaged in.

The problems facing organizations differ in certain respects in that some decisions are only made once in the life of the company, whereas other decisions are required on a frequent basis. To a degree, decisions form a hierarchy, with the differences implying a topology for problems and their consequent decisions, with a classification scheme to highlight the differences between types of decisions. To the extent that decisions are repetitive, routine or a definite procedure has been established for making the decision, the decision can be described as programmed. Decisions are non-programmed to the extent that they are novel, unstructured and consequential. These decision types form extreme polar types, end points on a continuum of decisions.

There may be few decisions that are entirely programmed or non-programmed. All managers develop ways of dealing with problems, some of which can apply to novel situations. Even a non-programmed decision such as a strategic decision, may have some familiar elements in its structure.

A decision may move away from being a programmed decision to a non-programmed one. The most important decisions facing organizations may be described as being closer to non-programmed than programmed. The problems involved have a considerable degree of ambiguity. They may be continually refined and highly interdependent with other important problems. Information concerning such problems is usually incomplete and a number of individuals and groups are likely to influence the decision. The decision itself may extend over a considerable period of time.

Normative Model

The normative model of decision making provides a logical means for making a decision. It is a model typical of those proposed in the decision-making literature of corporate planning and management science. A normative model describes how decisions should be made, rather than how they are made.

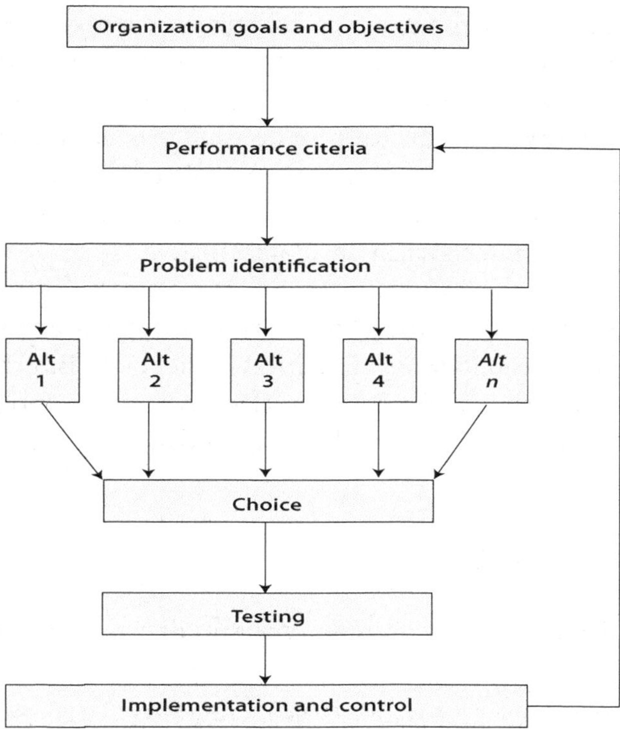

Fig. 4.3

The Normative Model of Decision Making[22]

The model is a proposal of how ideally to make a decision. The ability of this decision-making process to deliver the best decisions rests upon the activities that make up the process and the order in which they are attended to. The normative decision-making process is based upon the organization having a set of goals and objectives. These can be developed to provide criteria, clear definitions of how the objectives are to be measured so that the organization can assess its progress in achieving the objectives is has set. The criteria become a part of the means by which problems can be identified. A comparison the target to actual and potential performance identifies the performance gap in a gap analysis.

Identification of a problem is followed by a search for alternative solutions to the problem. Solutions may be found by a number of means. The decision maker may use memory, through viewing the current problem with others that have been solved in the past. Such a search process may extend to the active participation of other organizations and may include using consultants who are regarded as specialists in the problem area. Original solutions may also be developed through dedicating resources, both individual and group.

However, following such a process can be difficult since it may be extremely difficult to define objectives for an organization that are sufficiently specific to be useful in diagnosing problems. Frequently there may be intangible aspirations between groups and individuals. Information is the basis for decision making, and whether it is being used to identify and develop situations or to monitor the effectiveness of a decision, the information requires collection, processing and evaluation. There are clearly resource limitations upon the availability of information.

In view of these issues, it is difficult to envisage an organization adhering to the normative model of decision making. Empirical studies of decision making have been undertaken and have shown that the actual process of decision making within organizations varies significantly from the normative model.

Strategic Decision Making

Mintzberg[23] studied 25 strategic decision processes drawn from a wide spectrum of

---

[22] Plous, S. (1993) *The Psychology of Judgment and Decision Making.*McGraw-Hill. New York.

[23] Mintzberg, Henry, Raisinghani, Durum & Theoret, Andre (1976). "The structure of 'unstructured' decision processes". *Administrative Science Quarterly,* 21 (2), 246-275.

organizations. This study, along with the literature provides a basic structure or shared logic underlying the decision making of organizations in their handling of "unstructured" decisions. The three main decision-making phases can be defined as:

- Identification
- Development
- Selection

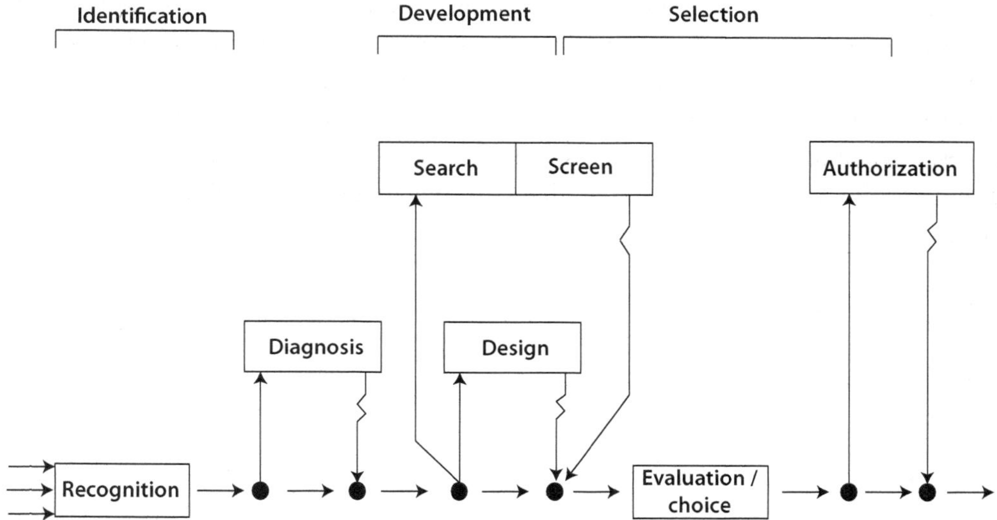

Fig. 4.4 A General Model of the Strategic Decision Process

Development

Mintzberg's' study found that the greatest amount of activity was concentrated in the development phase of the decision process. This phase leads to the development of one or more possible solutions to meet the problem or crisis, or elaborates the choice of ways that are available for exploiting an opportunity. The development phase contains two basic routines: a search routine for locating ready-made solutions and a design routine to modify those solutions that have been found, or to develop custom-made solutions.

Within certain sectors, such as banking, the choice is simplified through the criteria for complying with various regulatory requirements, the selection effectively being prescribed. The main decision therefore is whether to seek to meet the regulatory mandates or not and by which means. The issues surrounding such a decision are more complex than a single economic cost-benefit analysis or opportunity cost, given the concurrent requirement to manage risks as part of a competitive advantage. Additional factors such as peer pressure, supervisory oversight, and reputational enhancement have also to be factored according to Mintzberg's' framework.

Selection

In general, it is not appropriate to describe selection as a single and final step in the decision process. Frequently, the decision phase requires the decision to be factored into a series of sub-decisions, each requiring a selection step. Selection may be intrinsic to the development phase of a decision. Typically, selection is a multi-stage process, involving progressive deepening of the investigation of the alternatives. Mintzberg identified three routines that together make up the *selection phase* of the decision process:

- Screening,
- Evaluation-choice, and
- Authorization

Time

Typically the decision process in Mintzberg's study spanned long periods of time, with 17 of the 25 decision processes taking more than one year, and 6 more than 4 years. Mintzberg stated that the process of decision is "recursive and discontinuous, involving many difficult steps and a host of dynamic factors over a considerable period of time, a situation in which almost nothing is given or easily determined".

Time therefore becomes an issue in terms of how it is used when decisions are being made. In part, the time is taken to operate the information and communication processes that make up the seven routines described in the diagram above. It is also used to manage the politics of the decision, to gain the involvement and support of those who can influence the politics of a decision and believe that they will be affected by the decision. The political context of a decision requires the development of a solution that accommodates political interests in and around the organization.

Incrementalism

Other studies to those of Mintzberg confirm the lengthy nature of the process, but focus on the process as one using time in order to gain knowledge and commitment through a prolonged process of exploration and learning. Two approaches have been proposed that may be adopted in making decisions, a rational comprehensive method (*the root approach*) and a method of successive limited comparisons (*the branch approach*).

The root approach to decision making is similar to the normative model. Under this approach, the decision maker is assumed to have extensive knowledge of a range of alternative solutions that are relevant to the problem, together with a detailed knowledge of the consequences of those choices. On the basis of this knowledge, large numbers of alternatives are compared and the alternative selected which will provide the highest level of overall goal attainment.

On the basis of considering decision making in public administration, an alternative method of decision making has been proposed, with a method of successive limited comparisons or branch approach. Following the branch approach, the decision maker identifies few alternatives and those that are identified are not radically different from the organization's present policies and experience.

The branch method has been considered to be a workable approach to decision making, and also an approach that recognizes the decision maker's limited ability to identify and evaluate a wide range of alternatives, especially if some of those alternatives are far removed from present experience.

Not only does the root approach assist the decision maker by limiting the need for search and analysis, it is also less reliant upon a full understanding of goals. Instead of requiring the decision maker to be able to specify all relevant goals and the trade-offs between those goals before considering alternative solutions, the branch approach relies upon the act of choosing between alternatives to highlight the relevant issues concerning goals.

When considering the normal activities of organizations and the many regulatory requirements of current commercial environments, the branch approach may be regarded as being the most appropriate approach to decision making, given the sameness of the activities. It can be proposed that a number of regulations simply extend what enterprises ordinarily should already be doing.

However, the method has been questioned in terms of its dynamism, since the series of decisions that the organization adopts may not keep up with the rate at which a changing environment poses new issues for the organization.

Logical incrementalism

A study by Quinn[24] identified a decision-making process that is similar to the branch method but provides a more proactive approach. The study was based upon interviews with executives from a range of large companies that had recently made important strategic changes, non-programmed decisions. Strategic decision making was found to be a process directed and developed by a number of executives of companies in a conscious and purposeful manner.

In the companies studied, the decision centers on an executive who has a broad vision of what he is trying to achieve through the decision. The decision is being made in a context where significant information necessary for making the decision does not exist. The novelty of the decisions that are being made ensures that much information concerning future markets, the operation of technologies and the costs structure that will be incurred cannot be predicted with certainty or even given probabilities. Consequently the precise form that the decision should take cannot be determined at a single point in time but has to be developed over time through the building up of experience. There is not only a lack of information available to the decision maker, but they must also consider the political context of the decision, and the need to win support for developments that may involve other individuals or groups who have power to influence the decision.

The executive uses time to refine their understanding of the proposed development. Through this process a solution emerges and is developed over a considerable period of time, often three to ten years. The decision takes the form of a series of actions that explore and develop the solution while building a greater commitment and consensus to support the development. The decision to become committed to a particular strategy is in fact delayed while issues involved are explored through feedback and the solution refined.

Compared to the normative model, logical incrementalism lacks a clear structure and does not involve a series of discrete stages. Rather, progress is made through a developmental activity that shapes the solution and builds understanding and acceptance. The decision process is primarily concerned with that phase of decision making which is described as solution development and is achieved through the phased implementation and testing of the solution.

In the context of logical Incrementalism, evaluation and choice are implicit in the development of the solution. The logical incremental process of decision making in effect only provides a single alternative. The selection phase of decision making is

[24] Quinn, J.B. (1980). *Strategies for change: Logical incrementalism*. Homewood, IL: Richard D Irwin.

therefore a question of whether the solution continues through development and the timing of full commitment to the decision. This final act is delayed either until sufficient understanding and acceptance of the decision has been built, or until events, such as competitive pressures or regulation, precipitate full commitment and implementation.

It may therefore be argued that an incrementalist approach is more likely to be adopted by those within sectors facing new regulatory regimes/environments in developing their preparedness for compliance, given the similarity of the variables, the timeline, and the environmental changes within the sector.

Framework for Shorter Term Decision Making

There are types of decision made within organizations that are either short term or urgent. The shorter the timescale in which a decision is made, the more responsive the organization has to become. Further, the shorter the timescale, the more likely that decisions have to be made by the lower management structure of an organization.

Fig. 4.5 Management levels and decision making

The time span of the decision decreases the further down the management structure that the decision has to be taken. The modern pattern of managerial control is that senior management deals with strategic matters; middle management deals with tactical planning and lower management deals with operational control. However, the traditional pyramid structure of organizations has been replaced by a flatter structure, with autonomous units being more responsible for their own decisions. As stated elsewhere, this new organizational structure is particularly the case in risk management, with representation of several organizational levels comprising the risk management committee.

The ideal pattern of control and monitoring is that strategic decisions obtained from the corporate objectives are formulated by the organization's board of directors in conjunction with senior management. These strategic directions are evolved into tactical plans by middle management, who then expect lower management to execute the by developing and implementing courses of action which make up the tactical plans.

Fig. 4.6 Strategy Evolution Process

However, the framework requires the operational plan to be executed in a manner that aligns with the strategic and tactical plans. In the case of network operational risks, the lack of historical data, as stated elsewhere, may result in errors in the degree of belief, leading to an undermining of the strategic plan. Only with an upward information flow, over a period of time, can the strategic and tactical plans be re-visited; that is, the operational plan prescribes a major part of the tactical and strategic plans.

Decision Making Under Chaos

The theory of chaos has profound and wide-ranging implications for business decision making. Its impact can be felt from high order strategic decision making to day-to-day decisions. According to chaos theory, the smallest decision can have dramatic consequences, and make long-term strategies difficult to sustain in a chaotic environment.

If it is accepted that chaos theory does impact on strategic decision making, then a radically different approach to decision making is required. Methods and attitudes which can cope with the realities of chaos are needed, however, the full implications of chaos for strategic business decision making has yet to be fully explored and there is little in the literature at this time that is directly applicable to networks and cyber threats in relation to managing such risks.

The implications for decision makers in the frame of reference for strategic management of chaos theory are wider than use of a range of mathematical and statistical techniques. There is a need for the decision maker to adopt new and radically different frames of reference, a new perspective where the old methods and certainties are gone. They have to be replaced by a less secure world requiring a high tolerance of ambiguity and a capacity for imaginative, flexible and speedy responses.

Chaos theory indicates that long-term forecasting is a futile exercise and therefore there needs to be recognition of the fact that decisions taken with the long-term in view are likely to be flawed. Attention is better given to short-term decisions where chaos theory suggests that there may be a chance of making the right decision.

One such example is with weather forecasting. While the weather system has been identified as the archetypal chaotic system, the recognition has led to improvements in short-term weather forecasts. This involves looking at the general weather situation at the present and find similar situations from the past i.e. pattern matching.

In the business sphere, transferring such methods could result in competitive advantage through having better short-range forecasts. For the strategic management of new technology risks, similarly, taking a series of short-term assessments will be preferable to attempting long-range forecasting of the risks given a lack of historical data upon which to pattern-match.

Recognizing the unpredictability of events will thus enhance the importance of contingency planning. It is insufficient to have a single strategy and set of tactics. To cope with uncertainties it is necessary to develop a whole set of plans and fall-back positions. Although organizations do this already to some extent, chaos theory makes the activity of contingency planning more central to management's task. It cannot be regarded as of secondary importance and undertaken as an afterthought to the strategic planning process.

Applicability to Cyber Risk Program Development

In addition to the influences upon judgment and decision making, psychological factors will come into play during the development of any internal questionnaire to be used as part of a cyber threat/risk management program.

It is critical to the understanding of the mode of questioning, the format and structure of the content of each question, as well as the scaling utilized in measuring responses that psychological factors must be accounted for. In the absence of this, the danger lies in measuring inappropriate responses from respondents who may/may not have undue influence on the outcome of the results of a survey through position, perceived knowledge or any other factor.

Once the potential for skewness of data arising from psychological impacts upon responses/measurements have been accounted for, there still needs to be a clear recognition of the subsequent influences placed upon the project team members, both in the analysis of the data and in the interpretation and reporting of it. The combination of obstacles to the implementation of best practices, allied to factors affecting the environmental scanning capabilities and activities of an organization can lead to programs delivering up the expected outcome of a cyber threat/resilience program, rather than being derived from data.

One problem facing risk management teams is the dependency upon data. Information provides the inputs required in order to evaluate and judge, with decisions supported by it. The factors affecting information and how it may impact upon risk management team's reliance upon it in deriving a cyber threat/enterprise resilience program is covered in the following chapter.

Chapter Five

MANAGING UNCERTAIN INFORMATION

Uncertainty in Information

Intrinsic within the risk management process is the requirement to make decisions based upon information, both within and external to the organization. The proposition has been made that organizations engage in environmental scanning, map their business processes, and acquire information external to the firm. As such, a large body of information is available as part of the decision making process. However, the assumption is that such information has a high level of certainty and confidence level attached to it.

Organizations have always operated and made decisions on the basis of uncertain information: to rely only on that which was certain would be impossible. Strategic and operational decisions must be taken constantly within firms, simply in order for the full functioning of the roles of Boards, business units, operational units, down to individual personnel fulfilling their roles.

Examples of how organizations rely upon uncertain information abound, with each element of the organization using such information without recognition in many instances of the uncertainty within the information used. Take the following examples for banking institutions:

- Marketing departments rely on statistical and textual information in order to develop its market segmentation models and products, through identifying market behavior.

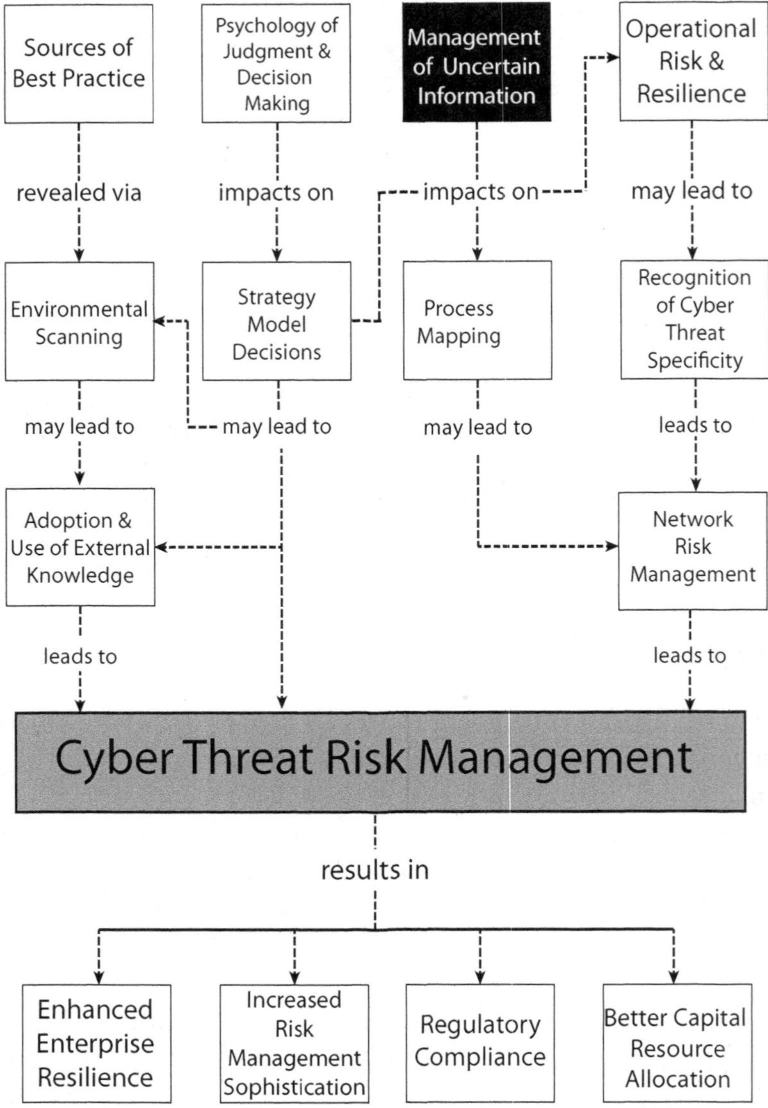

Fig. 5.1 Focus of Chapter 5

- Within the trading operations of the bank, key information on economic, corporate and market indicators is received from third parties, analyzed and used to predict future performance of investments. This in turn is used to base judgments on strategic decisions relating to the overall investment strategy of the organization upon and the relative profitability and shareholder worth.

- Within the corporate communications division, the textual and graphical information received from the many sources within the organization requires a heuristic approach in order to quantify and collate it in order to create coherent communications strategies for the bank.

- The information technology department constantly works to assess new or evolving technologies that may facilitate a differentiation strategy or competitive advantage for the bank over its competitors. With development and implementation processes for underlying technologies requiring long lead-in times, these departments must rely upon uncertain information upon which to base their purchasing decisions or in briefing the Board of the bank.

- The legal and tax departments receive claims from clients or must undertake tax planning for private banking clients or corporate users. Their judgments as to jurisdictions optimizing funds flows, asset management locations and other activities are based upon information that is uncertain due to constantly changing regulatory regimes as well as Governments which change and address the same issues in a different manner.

Decision support tools, systems and frameworks are available to decision makers, but these can only enhance the ability to make correct decisions where there is a transparency in the manner in which such tools operate. If there is opacity in the way the tools operate, whether computer-based systems or a framework proprietary to an organization, then there cannot be confidence in the output, since the reasoning within the tool is not explained and such reasoning may be fatally flawed. Therefore, a range of tools for handling uncertain information is needed.

Without recognizing what they are doing, departments and individuals within an organization draw upon information theory in their attempts to model some aspect of the real world that applies to their day-to-day strategic and operational decision making activities. Examples of the theories they are using are those of fuzzy logic, possibility and probability theory, and recourse to Bayes theory.

The nature of uncertainty in information is complex and many factors affect the types of uncertainty and the degrees of uncertainty. In the subliminal use of these underlying theories, users adopt many strategies for aggregating factors in order to minimize the potential negative effects of operating under conditions of uncertainty and organizations have become highly adept at using uncertain information.

Handling such uncertain information, is carried out mainly by humans within the organization, rather than having recourse to computers and other information systems in making strategic decisions. Banks for example have a high level of utilization of information technology and information systems, but its use under conditions of uncertain information in making decisions is primarily at a low level. Uncertainty handling must be incorporated into any system that attempts to provide a substantive model of the real world.

Commercial pressures have led to increasing demands for people to be able to handle more complex information, more quickly, more reliably and, in particular, in a more natural and intuitive fashion. This has inevitably led to ongoing development of models for handling and seeking to analyze, quantify understand uncertain information within information systems, since it is the only means by which such demands can be met. A good example here is that of search engine developments over the past decade. Initially these were developed for end users for searching the internet followed by rankings according to payments. More recently however, there has been a shift towards search engine capability for the retrieval of data internal to organizations and this will continue.

Although the concept of uncertainty is widely accepted, there is no formal classification of the term, since it is linked with a number of different fields, such as linguistics and recognition, although many have attempted to classify the term without success.

Information is assumed as being composible, that is to say, it is capable of existing in one subject, is consistent or capable of being true together as an entity. For some items of information, other items of information can be generated. For example, a database record for a past client of an organization is composed of information regarding their name, address, order history and any other relevant details such as personal preferences.

Increasingly, with the massive growth in the use of social networking, coupled with commerce sites that record user behaviors, this composibility has created vast amounts of data that may or may not be of future use, thereby requiring tools capable of modeling multiple potential usages of information. Without the capability to handle and reconcile data, the usefulness of it degrades through error rates such as false positives/negatives, which, in the case of risk/cyber threat management are critical.

Further, some information may be described as correct, according to some measure and that some can be described as incorrect. For example, for the same database record, a client may be asked whether their name and address have been entered correctly within the organizations' client database.

There can though be expectations about information, such as the presence of certain information. For example, for a database on a client, it would be expected that there is information on name, address and order history for each client. Of note here that the expectation is that the information *exists*, rather than that it is known *what* the actual information is.

Information Classification

Taking the above assumptions as given and being correct, information may be classified as being one or more of the following:

Accurate: Information is accurate when all expected information is present and correct and it is error free.

Incomplete: Information is incomplete when all the information present is correct but some expected information is absent. This could occur because the information is open to multiple interpretations, under-specified, vague or just deficient. The classic example of this is where the ambiguous statement is one such as "this food is hot", which could be interpreted as "this food is very spicy" or "this food is very warm". Therefore, if from this one statement, one is expected to be able to ascertain which of the two interpretations hold, then the ambiguity means the statement is incomplete.

Incompatible: Information is incompatible when there is conflict between correct and incorrect information present. An example of this would be, if in the staff records there is a record indicating a promotion for an employee a year after the retirement date. There is an inconsistency with the common-sense knowledge about people being promoted after their retirement.

Approximate: Information is approximate when some expected information is missing and possibly there are conflicts between the correct and incorrect information. For example, it could be believed that it is likely to rain soon because there are dark clouds in the sky. However the reasoning is incomplete because the reasoning relies on a general rule that does not take account of all relevant information. Furthermore, the inference of rain made from the general rule could be incompatible with other information available, such as the barometric pressure rising sharply.

Table 5.1 Classification of information according to presence/absence of expected information and presence/absence of incorrect information (Hunter 1996)[25]

	All expected information is ***present***	Some expected information is ***absent***
All incorrect information is ***absent***	Accurate	Incomplete
Some incorrect information is ***present***	Incompatible	Approximate

There are informal relationships between different kinds of uncertainty. For example, where the more focused information is, the more likely it is that it will be incorrect. This is known as the maximality principle. It can be partially explained by viewing the principle as stating there is a pay-off between completeness and correctness. By using the above classification meanings for certainty and uncertainty can be delineated:

Certainty: The information is believed and used with certainty when it is accurate, that is, certain information is a synonym for accurate information.

Uncertainty: Uncertainty exists in information when it is incomplete, incorrect or inaccurate.

It is clearly extremely difficult to define words for uncertainty so that they are appropriate for all users or all contexts. However, when certain formal assumptions are adopted, then some classifications become much more meaningful and useful. This is important in the context of cyber threat management, given the constant and rapid evolution and launching of various attack types. A process may appear, for example, to be a normal command seen in operating systems, may in fact be an exploit masquerading as normal code. In this instance, if the exploit is regarded as certain and permitted to run by security systems, the consequences may be catastrophic.

Types of Uncertain Information

Uncertainty in information is not a homogenous concept. Rather, there are clearly diverse types that require distinct means for handling. The following are specific types of uncertain information[26]:

[25] Hunter, A., (1996). *Uncertainty in Information Systems, An Introduction to Techniques and Applications.* McGraw Hill.

[26] Krause, P., and Clark, D., (1993). *Representing Uncertain Knowledge: An Artificial Intelligence Approach.* Intellect.

Probabilistic Information

People use probabilistic information, with various degrees of frequency. They reason very effectively with complex tasks of assessing probabilities and predicting values by various strategies.

Such information is widespread and examples abound – the existence of databases of information facilitates the extraction of useful probabilistic relationships from such information in cases such as credit scoring of individuals. However, it does not always require large amounts of information in order to generate probabilities. Most concepts used in human reasoning are to some extent vague (fuzzy), and many are useful because, depending upon the context, they can be delineated.

Inconsistent Information

Frequently, the situation can occur that some information and its contrary appear and in some cases this can be useful in determining inconsistencies such as insurance fraud schemes. In other cases it can be undesirable, since it can have severe adverse affects, such as in financial accounts reconciliation.

It is not always possible or feasible to maintain consistency of information, since this depends upon the ability to resolve any inconsistency. There can also be the case where, even if it is possible to resolve the inconsistency, the loss of data in so doing would be more harmful than retaining the inconsistency.

An alternative to resolution can come from using it to support different views during an interim period. This involves the ability to represent the information, reason rationally with the information, to diagnose the likely cause of the inconsistency, and to propose necessary actions in response. An example of such a case would be where there are two databases within an organization, both supplying information on a single subject, but each with different (inconsistent) information. In such cases, the contradictory information is not rejected, but rather it is retained and used in conjunction with strategies which support the information until an informed selection is made.[27]

Default Information

This is loosely defined as information that is used in the absence of a better alternative and covers a wide variety of information including heuristics, hypotheses, conjectures, null values in data, closed world assumptions for databases, and some qualitative abstractions of probabilistic information.

[27] Smets, Ph. (1992). Imperfect Information: Imprecision and Uncertainty. In Smets, Ph., and Motro, A., editors, *Uncertainty Management in Information Systems.* Kluwer, 1992.

Thus, inconsistent information is a form of incompatible information. Probabilistic, fuzzy and default information are forms of approximate information when certain information is absent. In general, approximate information can be obtained from subjective evaluations or derived from past experience, and as such it is an estimate that can conflict with the behavior of the thing it models.

Levels of Uncertainty

Uncertain information can be used in many roles and it is useful to develop appropriate strategies for such information by adopting the terms "object-level" information and "meta-level" information, and defined as the following:

*Object-level Information: w*ithin an organization, the purpose of an information system is to handle information for some benefit to the organization. Object-level information is that which an end user is using. The user is aware of the existence of object-level information in the system. Queries to, and answers from, the system are in terms of the object-level information. For example, this is where an organization company has a database of information relating to personnel, departments and functions.

Meta-level Information: in order for an information system to handle object-level information, there is a need for extra information about the object-level information, and about the possible users of that information. This extra information is meta-level information. Whilst meta-level information is used to facilitate the information system meeting the end user's needs, it is not actually seen or used directly, by the end user. For instance, meta-level information can be used to increase the amount of information given in answer to a query, whereas the answer is actually object-level information. An example here is in word processing software, where the end user designates a file name and saves the file to disc. To retrieve the file, a search can be run on the PC, which uses meta-data in the file to recognize and retrieve it for the user.

Decision support tools have been used extensively for quite some time for organization tasks such as credit scoring, financial trading, risk modeling, administration, and network optimization (electricity, water, and gas companies). Two main approaches to decision support systems are rule-based systems and case-based systems.

Rules based systems use "rules" to represent information ranging from definitions and regulations to heuristics and rules conjecture. In these uncertain information is predominantly object-level.

Case-based systems use "cases" to represent information, such as comparative instances upon which decisions relating to a current problem relate. A user will load cases of interest by delineating the type of case of interest. Keywords are often used in such systems for case retrieval. As such, there can be both the object-level and the meta-level uncertain information.

Historically, decision support systems used formal approaches to handling uncertainty and this aspect reduced the value of such systems. However, this has been followed by a continued growth in the development of causal probabilistic networks (Bayesian belief networks) as a means of handling uncertain information. The rate of growth of information has outstripped the ability of models to keep pace and this applies in particular to cyber threat security systems, in that if such systems were to model every piece of data, the ability of I.T. systems and networks to work as intended becomes severely compromised in terms of their speed of operation.

Although the uses of information systems are diverse, and thus addressing uncertainty in such systems is equally diverse, there are a number of common themes in addressing the core issue of uncertainty in information and this requires a series of formal techniques.

Modeling uncertainty involves a significant dilemma however, in that in order to minimize the mistakes from using uncertain information, there is a need to adopt a rich and powerful model, but conversely, information systems usually need simple and efficient representation and reasoning facilities.

Formal Approaches to Uncertainty

A need to be able to handle uncertain information requires a sufficiently expressive means to represent it. Adopting ad hoc approaches to handling of uncertain information can easily become counter-productive. A task assigned often has the assumption behind it that the delegator has confidence about the nature of the outcome from the delegate.

With handling uncertain information, the behavior of uncertain data sets can be difficult to predict. Therefore in handling uncertain information, only within the context of well-understood principles should there be any degree of confidence in the outcome.

There are many constraints on the ability to handle uncertain information. Within the organization, there is a limitation on the ability to capture and store all available information. The environment within which the information is given may result in incomplete information and this will increasingly be the case as cloud computing and remote access capabilities continues. It may therefore be approximate in one or more ways. The information may also be changing over time, with differences in the life of the accuracy of the information.

If there is opacity in the way decision support tools, systems and frameworks operate (the so-called black box model of operation), whether computer-based systems or a framework proprietary to an organization, then there cannot be confidence in the output, since the reasoning within the tool is not explained and such reasoning may be fatally flawed. This approach utilized within risk management has been attributed to the recent banking and financial institutional failures, in that the modeling and complexity was far beyond the capabilities of the Regulators in understanding the underlying risk exposure.

Classical Formalisms and Uncertain Information

The proof theory of classical logic can be automated so that if a set of propositions implies a particular preposition, then a proof for that preposition can be found in a finite number of steps. For *prepositional logic* and for *predicate logic*, the testing of the consistency of a set of propositions can also be automated. This means that it is possible to use classical logic as the basis for information handling. Expert systems, risk management systems, programming languages and database systems are all based directly on classical logic.

Whilst classical formalisms are appropriate for certain kinds of uncertain information, they are significantly limited for addressing certain key important kinds of uncertainty, such as probabilistic, fuzzy, default and inconsistent information.

In general, there are many design considerations for formalizing uncertainty including the expressiveness of the language and the strength of the system for manipulating statements of the language. If an insufficiently expressive language is adopted, then it cannot represent all the information that will be potentially available.

Similarly, if the power of the reasoning system is weak, then potentially some inferences will be lost. Historically, using more expressive languages and using more powerful reasoning systems used to render the mechanization less computationally viable. However, with the steep increase in processing capabilities at a low cost, this is less the case than in earlier computing periods. To be practical the algorithms that mechanize the reasoning should be computationally viable, otherwise the system will be too frequently paralyzed by indecision. To delineate this problem, there are extensive mathematical analyses of computational properties of many of the proposals for handling information.

Probabilistic information is widely used in a number of ways. Reasoning with it can be intuitive and provide a powerful means of overcoming uncertainty. Such information is pervasive within organizations and is usually in the form of approximate information. It can also arise from subjective analysis of situations, for example where experienced personnel may draw upon historic experience in their evaluation of plans and targets and is the case for risk management and business continuity teams in their day-to-day working.

Whilst there are an increasing number of statistical software packages available that facilitate complex statistical analyses of detailed bodies of data, such as those utilized for client data-mining for sales and marketing, there are fewer instances of the automation of probabilistic information for *reasoning* within organizations. However, the use of techniques for computer based probabilistic reasoning has increased in recent years, with the main techniques being embedded within probability theory, incorporating Bayesian networks, fuzzy information, the use of default information, and in managing inconsistent information.

Probability Theory

Probability theory is well established and provides an intuitive and powerful formalization for handling likelihoods. Conditional probability is the probability of a particular event, given the probability of another specific event. Within information systems, conditional information can be used to represent contingent information. However, using conditional probabilities directly is problematical since much information is required.

One of the key objections to using probability theory is that the complete specification of a total distribution requires many conditional probability statements, or equivalently joint probabilities. It is however sometimes possible to ameliorate this problem by adopting assumptions about certain propositions being mutually independent.

Two ways in which probabilistic information can be acquired are described as *subjective* and *objective*. In the objective approach, a number of examples are used to calculate the frequency that an event occurs out of the possible events.

By contrast, the subjective approach is based on the *belief* that the user has in an event occurring. The degree of belief a user has in a proposition is context sensitive. Taking the example of two dice, if the user knows that they have a weight bias of some manner, then they would take this into account in offering a probability as to how many times a particular side of the dice would fall face-up given a certain number of throws of the dice.

By assuming independence between some of the propositions, it is possible to decrease the number of conditional probability statements required. However, as stated elsewhere, where information is used as part of an enterprises' risk assessment, that relating to network risks cannot be viewed as having a high degree of event independence. As such, probability theory cannot be justified for cyber and network risk assessment.

Bayesian Networks

These are an approach to using conditional probabilities in information systems which augment the use of conditional probabilities with extra structural information and are more efficient for representing and reasoning with probabilistic information. In particular, they incorporate assumptions about which propositions are independent of other propositions, thereby simplifying the computations. They are used to model situations in which causality or influence is prevalent, but in which there is only a partial understanding, hence the need to model probabilistically.[28]

Since probability theory is well established, for a variety of approaches there is much data that can be used to generate useful, reliable conditional probability statements. Additionally, probability theory can be applied to a wide range of uncertainty including ignorance (or missing data), linguistic vagueness and linguistic ambiguity.

However, for some applications there may be problems with obtaining reliable probabilities due to there not being enough known, or through inherent complexity, for example in the case of cyber threats, which multiply, mutate and change with high degrees of frequency and also change in terms of their targeting and dispersal. They can also be difficult to expand, given the sensitive nature of interdependencies in probabilistic information. There may also be questions about desirability, with much information not coming in a probabilistic form and thus not necessarily best handled by forcing such information into a probabilistic form.

The appropriateness of probability theory for capturing diverse kinds of uncertain information has been debated for some time. Nevertheless, Bayesian networks are

[28] Heckerman, D., and Wellman, (1995). M. Bayesian Networks. *Communications of the ACM,* 38: 27-30.

nowadays being used in a variety of applications, including decision support systems for diagnosis, planning and information retrieval.

In the case of organizations undertaking risk assessment programs, utilizing probabilistic information in conjunction with a Bayesian belief network would align it with the methodology expounded within the international standards, where an initial confidence level is attributed to information and enhanced over time, drawing upon the accumulated historical data to improve the degree of confidence. This is applied in a subjective risk assessment where there is little or no historical data upon which to base a decision.

Fuzzy Information

Most concepts used in human reasoning are to some extent vague or fuzzy, but despite this they can often be useful because, depending on the context, they can be delineated. A good example of this is in the parking a car, where most people can do it relatively easily. This is because the final position of the car and its orientation are not given precisely in advance of the operation. However, if it were specified precisely, then the difficulty would rise sharply with the degree of precision, until it would be unmanageable for humans and only achievable with recently implemented self-parking systems in cars. Therefore, a task is easy for humans when specified imprecisely and yet difficult to solve by traditional formal methods because such methods do not exploit the tolerance for imprecision.

Other examples of this phenomenon are distorted speech, such as slurring through inebriation; poor quality handwriting, nuances of natural language, walking in a heavily crowded shopping area and in general making day-to-day decisions, in an uncertain environment and without the need for precision for the outcome.

Thus, the importance of fuzzy reasoning lie in the ability to handle fuzzy concepts, that is to say, the ability to understand terms such as short women, high costs of living, etc. When the same concepts are addressed by classical logic, a high degree of difficulty arises and recourse to other systems, such as fuzzy logic is necessary.

Possibility Theory

Using the difference between possibility theory and probability theory, possibility theory has been proposed as a formalism for representing and reasoning about ignorance or incompleteness. Its proponents argue that in probability theory, ignorance is incorrectly interpreted as randomness, where outcomes are equally probable. However, the state of knowledge where there is an equal lack of certainty about all events that are liable to occur cannot be expressed by a single probability measure. By contrast, possibility theory captures states of knowledge from complete information to total ignorance.

Possibilistic Logic

Possibilistic logic is for reasoning with uncertainty. There are propositions that are true or false, but due to a lack of precision of the available information, in general it is only possible to estimate to what extent it is possible or necessary that a proposition is true. This contrasts with fuzzy logic, where the information is vague or incomplete, but not incorrect. The vagueness leads to propositions with intermediary degrees of truth.

The Use of Default Information

Organizations rely much more on exploiting *general* rules (not universal laws), or defaults, than on a myriad of individual facts. Defaults however do tend to be less than 100% accurate and so have exceptions.

It can be intuitive and advantageous to resort to defaults and therefore allow the inference of some useful conclusions, even if it does entail making some mistakes, as not all exceptions to defaults are necessarily known. Furthermore, it is often necessary to use defaults when there is insufficient information to allow specification or use universal laws. For example in the case of cyber threat management, a default can be that all inflows of data to the security perimeter are to be regarded as unsafe until they have been assessed and the threats quantified.

Using default information requires non-monotonic reasoning. For example, "if a holds, then b normally holds as well". It is called non-monotonic because, as more information is acquired, an exception may arise, hence the inference would have to be withdrawn. Again taking cyber threat management as an example, the exception can be where the inflows of data are from a trusted source, such as a remote office. By contrast, with monotonic reasoning, if an inference is drawn from data, that inference remains, whatever further data is added to the database. Thus, non-monotonic reasoning allows for inferences to change if new information suggests it should, whereas monotonic reasoning is committed to its original inferences.

Non-monotonic reasoning is diverse and is used in dialogue, storing information, learning and many other areas of cognition. It has significant implications for engineering intelligent systems, and in particular natural language interfaces and user modeling techniques and more recently has been used by Japanese corporations such as Honda in its Asimo robot projects.

In all aspects of cognition, the issue of efficiency is central to the role of non-monotonic reasoning. However, non-monotonic reasoning involves a degree of uncertainty. Default assumptions are not always valid because of exceptions; therefore efficiency comes at some risk. The key problems facing the use of non-monotonic reasoning are the trade-off between efficiency and accuracy and are impacted by:

Qualification Problem: when making a decision, it is not the normal practice to check every relevant aspect prior to making the decision. Similarly, not every aspect of a plan is checked for its ability to be realizable before executing it. It is a problem of restricting reasoning only to information that is directly relevant. Therefore to formalize non-monotonic reasoning, problems of what to check become the main issue, without having to check every conceivable exception for every situation. Clearly there are major implications in the management of data inflows and cyber/enterprise resilience in relation to exception rules.

Ramification Problem: when reasoning about a plan, there are many ramifications possible. However, it is likely that only a small proposition of them will have any significance. Therefore the ramification problem is that of restricting consideration of the ramifications to those that are directly relevant. In the case of cyber threat management, the ability to identify and understand the importance of, say one type of threat versus another (viruses versus targeted attacks) and assign the correct level of significance is extremely difficult.

In reasoning about a plan, when an action is undertaken, if every item in a state has to be specified whether it remains constant when moved to another state, then the reasoning process becomes inefficient. Therefore, the ramification problem is one of ascertaining the important items that do change and the important items that do not change for any given action, without explicitly listing them all. This is also called the *frame* problem.

This applies to organizations in their determining operational risks in general, as well as to network risks. The volume of exceptions in the case of the latter creates a ramification problem, in that the level of embeddedness and interdependence created by networks results in items changing their state according to their placement relative to other items. For example, changing nodes in a network will change the threat level for each item that has some form of interaction with other items via that node.

Default Reasoning

Using default or defeasible information and using inconsistent information are two inter-related problems. A significant part of reasoning with default rules is resolving inconsistencies. Similarly, many problems of inconsistencies in information arise from the use of default information.

There are experimental implementations of automated reasoning systems for default logic and related logics. These include systems that compute extensions and systems that provide credulous and skeptical query answering, including search engines and database retrieval software. Applications in information systems currently have a particular focus upon enhancing information retrieval, information filtering, merging information, and in information routing. Central to reasoning with different perspectives is the handling of inconsistencies. Maintaining absolute consistency is not always possible or not even desirable, due to the constraints resulting in the loss of important information.

The means by which inconsistencies are formalized in the reasoning process cannot necessarily be done by eradicating inconsistency, but rather by supplying logical rules specifying what actions are required when they appear. In this way, it can be viewed as a shift from a classical view of information being either true or false, to a view where it is accepted that there may be a number of perspectives on information and that these perspectives may contradict each other.

The common example used to demonstrate inconsistency and its commercial utilization by many authors is that of a hotel booking system. A hotel will oversell available rooms, even though it is not possible logistically to accommodate the additional numbers. The system supports the inconsistency because it knows that only a certain percentage of customers will actually take up their room reservations each day, thereby ensuring a high utilization rate for every room in the hotel.

On the other hand, there are applications and systems in everyday life that see inconsistency as an undesirable trait, such as accountancy and stock market trading. Once inconsistency or uncertainty of any form is permitted into a system, it must also be accompanied by some form of reasoning component to derive answers from the more general information available. To design that component, it is necessary to build upon an appropriate formal model of deduction.

What is required is a logic that does not support trivialization of data, with proposed solutions to the problem including data revision and paraconsistent logics. The first approach effectively removes data to produce a new consistent data source. By contrast, the second approach leaves the data inconsistent, but prohibits the logics from deriving trivial inferences. The above sections have attempted to illustrate the issues and problems arising from the various types of information that are available to organizations, individuals, applications, systems and methodologies.

For most business sectors, defining the types of information and placing labels as to type and the degree of confidence in that information are extremely problematic. Whilst the process of labeling may be informal and unstated, the use of multiple methodologies in the risk assessment and risk analysis phases, drawing upon both quantitative and qualitative methods, would seem to indicate that such categorizing of information is actually occurring. Various sectoral professional bodies and the national and international standards best practices all clearly specify the use of multiple methods of data analysis in formulating risk frameworks.

As with many large-scale organizations around the world, the use and functions performed by technology has increased to the point where the very existence of the organizations has become dependent upon it. The pervasiveness of computing and associated technologies can been seen by reference to the areas in which it either supports controls or informs:

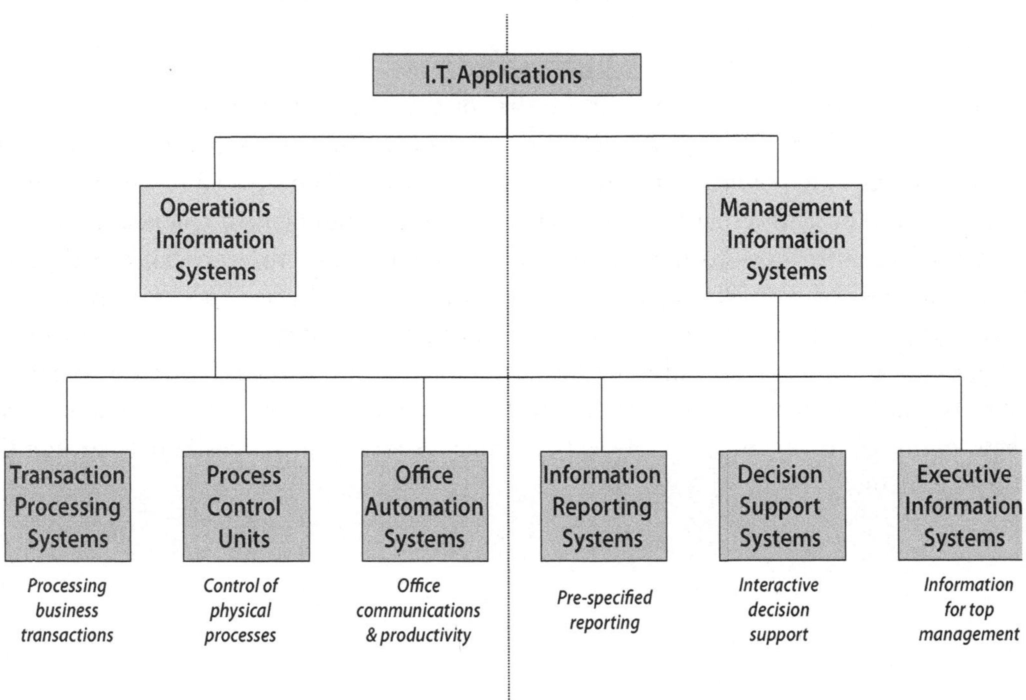

Fig. 5.2 Common I.T. Systems and Functions

From the above diagram, it is possible to understand the degree to which organizations reply upon information for all aspects of operations and in the decision process at all levels. An understanding of what factors require accounting for in the evaluation, assignment, ranking and utilization of data is therefore of prime importance.

Further, the pervasiveness of information and the flows of it are similarly critical to the ability of an enterprise to execute the functioning of the business and in the absence of this over a sustained period, can result in business failure. Business continuity planning and management has grown up around disruptions to operational capabilities of organizations and has been superseded in part in more recent times by the concept of enterprise resilience.

Resilience programs have a similar level of reliance upon information, data flows and the handling of it. Regulatory pressures have created further reporting requirements that entails acquisition of information, interpretation and modeling of information, with the Regulators in turn needing to understand, model and interpret such information.

An asymmetry in the mode and means of handling information can lead to undesirable outcomes, such as regulatory bodies not concurring with an organizations' assessment of its' financial risks, requiring them to hold additional risk capital and diminishing their level of competitiveness.

A more dangerous outcome would be that of cyber threats and the modeling and assessment of them being regarded as being overstated in their scope for damage by senior management when presented with reporting from specialist I.T./network security units or by risk management divisions. Understanding inconsistencies, validity, and options as to how to handle information/data is therefore crucial during the development of any risk/cyber threat/continuity program. This requires risk management teams to utilize the data in such a manner that the output from analysis aligns with how the organization wishes to manage its' operational risks. Ensuring that the risk management strategy aligns with the corporate strategy therefore becomes a key component in the overall cyber threat/risk/enterprise resilience program development.

Chapter Six

STRATEGY; DEFINITIONS, MODELS, THEORIES AND PERSPECTIVES

Strategy and Managing Risk

In order for a cyber threat/risk management/enterprise resilience program to develop, integrate and be usable within an organization, it is necessary that it has a good fit to the entity as a whole. However, of particular relevance is the strategic fit to the management of corporate risks in general, of which technology risks are but one. The rationale for this assertion is that without understanding the strategy type, the planning characteristics and implementation, plus the predominant model utilized by the organization, even prerequisites such as being able to set the enterprise's risk appetite are not possible.

In the specific case of technology/cyber risk management, understanding the corporate strategy, how it is formulated and implemented within the organization is key when combined with other factors affecting the risk management strategy formulation, since a psychological factor affecting the decision making level of an organization may limit the scope or type of program envisaged as being optimal for that particular organization by the risk management team.

Additionally, there may be a greater focus upon one type of strategy by senior management where there is a high degree of complexity, disruption or volatility at any particular time that requires an emphasis on the "what business should we be in" rather

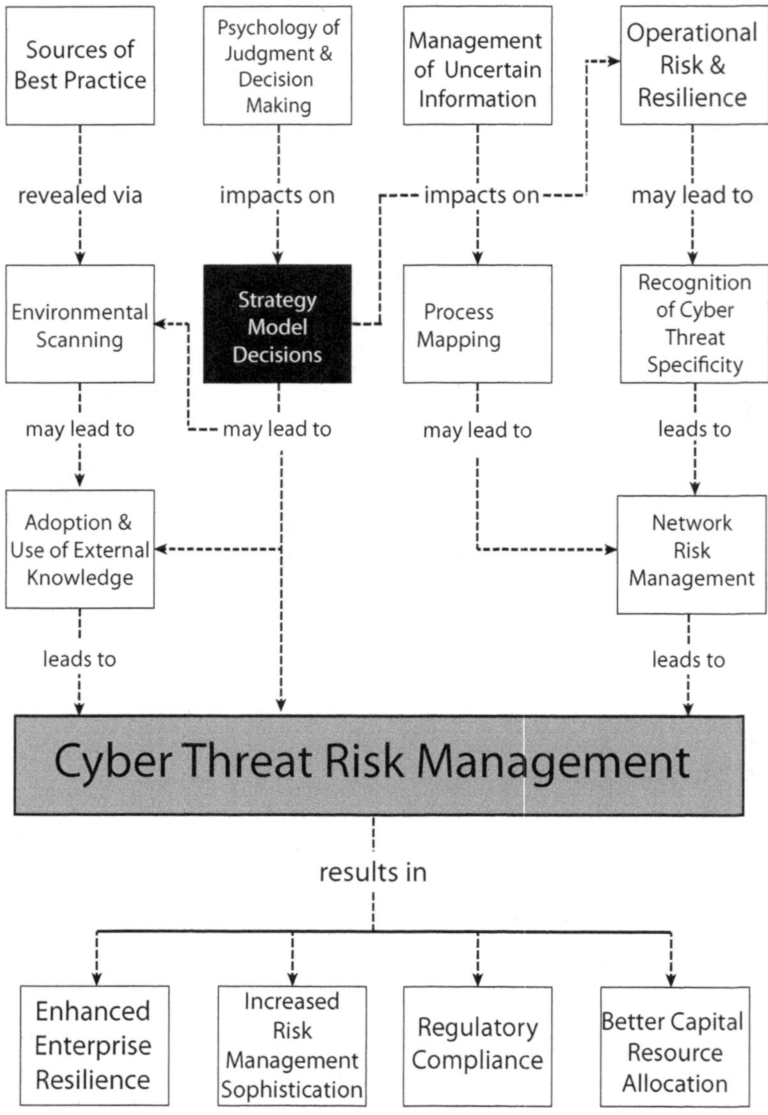

Fig. 6.1 Focus of Chapter 6

than the "how do we compete in this environment". In such circumstances, operational risks may have a lower level of precedence over other factors, or have a more limited budget available, making a business case for cyber threat/risk management more difficult to achieve.

Understanding the types of strategy, how it is formulated, what characteristics are embodied by each option and which is the most appropriate for a risk management program therefore is a necessity for good I.T./cyber threat/enterprise resilience strategy formulation in itself.

Strategic Planning

There is a broad base of academic and professional literature that makes the proposition that technological competencies and technical skills and knowledge developed within companies have a positive influence on the performance of companies.

Further, research has shown that multi-business companies with commonalities based upon shared capabilities and know-how have a higher economic performance than those that do not. Equally, it has been claimed that a common element in firm performance is the importance of a proven track record in terms of well-developed skills in related technologies, leading to a certain degree of technological specialization.

More recent theories on resource based competition and company performance focus upon the efficient use of unique firm capabilities. The resource-based view (RBV) combines the internal analysis phenomena within companies, with the external analysis of the industry and the competitive environment and can therefore also be viewed as being linked with other activities, such as environmental scanning performance and external information utilization.

Six dimensions of planning systems have been proposed as being:[29]

(i) use of techniques;
(ii) attention to internal facets;
(iii) attention to external facets;
(iv) functional coverage;
(v) resources provided for planning; and
(vi) resistance to planning.

Alternative dimensions for strategic planning systems have been proposed as:

(i) planning implementation;
(ii) market research competence;

[29] Ramanujam, V., N. Venkatraman, and J.C. Camillus. (1986). "Multi-Objective Assessment of Effectiveness of Strategic Planning: A Discriminant Analysis Approach." *Academy of Management Journal* 29: 347-372.

(iii) key personnel involvement;
(iv) staff planning assistance; and
(v) innovativeness of strategies.

However, others have proposed, by way of contradiction, that in fact planning is an *attitude* and a *process* concerned with the future consequences of current decisions. Formal strategic planning links short, intermediate and long-range plans. Contrary to risk management actions, strategic planning does not, however attempt to make future decisions or forecast future events. There is evidence that there is low or little impact and applicability in the case of small firms in relation to formal strategic planning. Overall, planning is said to improve the fit between the organization and its external environment.

Further, it has been argued to aid the identification of future marketing threats and opportunities, elicits an objective view of managerial problems, creates a framework for internal communication, promotes forward thinking and encourages a favorable attitude to change.

Four *roles* of formal strategic planning have been stated as being:

(i) the public relations role, intending to impress or influence outsiders;

(ii) the informational role, providing input for managerial decisions;

(iii) the group therapy role, increasing organizational commitment through the involvement of people at all levels of the organization in strategic planning, and;

(iv) the direction and control role, fulfilled when plans serve to guide future decisions and activities toward some consistent ends.

Whilst formal planning may or may not improve firm performance, it promotes long-range thinking, reduces the focus on operational details and provides a structured means for identifying and evaluating strategic alternatives. As such, there is a correlation between formal planning in respect of strategy and risk management programs, since each requires a degree of decomposition of risk and cost-benefit analysis of alternative actions.

There is a clear distinction between those firms that are reactive to changes in their competitive environment and those that are reactive, each having a distinct impact on the satisfaction a firm measures regarding its strategic planning approach. Competencies can be acquired from external sources, and it is therefore of particular importance if the view is taken that there is a relationship between core-competencies and economic performance.

Three Models of Strategy

Although the term strategy is freely used by researchers and practitioners, there is no consensus on its definition. It has been suggested that this inconsistency is due to two factors. First, strategy is multi-dimensional. Second, strategy must be situational and, accordingly, will vary by industry.

For the purposes of this book, strategy encompasses both the overall business strategy of an organization, and specific foundational areas including that of cyber threat/risk management strategy. Strategy can be regarded as a general discipline, as well as being composed of multiple elements, perspectives, actions and models.

The term also refers to three distinguishable mental models, rather than the single model that most discussions assume. The basic premise of thinking about strategy concerns the inseparability of organization and environment. Strategy uses it to deal with environmental changes, which offers novel combinations of circumstances to organizations. It has, by definition, to remain unstructured, non-repetitive and with no routine in order to cope with change. This is of particular relevance for cyber threat management, where attack types vary, mutate and change with frequency, precluding repetition in terms of threat management approach. Strategic decisions are considered to be important enough to affect the overall welfare of the organization.

Theorists who segment the strategy construct implicitly agree that the study of strategy includes actions taken, or the content of strategy and the processes by which actions are decided and implemented. They agree that intended emergent and realized strategies may differ from one another.

Further differentiation comes by dividing the categories of strategy into corporate strategy ("What business shall we be in?") and business strategy ("How do we compete in each business?"). There is concurrence that strategy formulation involves conceptual as well as analytical exercises, with most of the conceptual work undertaken by the leaders of the organization.

Beyond these definitions, differences in point of view are rarely recognized. There are multiple definitions of strategy. Further analysis of the literature indicates that it is possible to cluster the various *definitions* of strategy into three distinct groups. Although it is possible to assign a name to each model of strategy which represents its main focus, each model also includes many variations of its central theme and they are not independent of each other.

Linear strategy

This model focuses upon planning and is labeled linear due to the connotation of methodical, directed, sequential action. According to the linear view, strategy consists of integrated decisions, actions or plans that will set and achieve viable organizational goals. Both goals and the means of achieving them are the results of strategic decisions and, in order to reach them organizations vary their links with the environment. Terms associated with the linear model include strategic planning, strategy formulation, and strategy implementation.

Fig. 6.2 Resilience Strategy Organogram

Since the linear model is a sequential one, if the planning process by this means is to be achieved, the organization needs to be tightly coupled, so that all decisions made at the top can be implemented throughout the organization. With this model, the planning process is forward looking and in order for the decisions made in the present to be regarded as valid moving through time, the environment must be assumed to be relatively predictable or that the organization is well insulated from the environment.

Since the 1970's there has been a move away from the linear model, due to the strategic problem being viewed as increasingly complex, involving several dimensions of the managerial problem and the process, as well the variables of technical, economic, informational, psychological and political in their nature.

Adaptive strategy

The classic definition typifying the adaptive model of strategy characterizes it as being concerned with the development of a viable match between the opportunities and risks present in the external environment and the organization's capabilities and resources for exploiting these opportunities.[30]

[30] Hofer, C. W. (1973) Some preliminary research on patterns of strategic behavior. *Academy of Management Proceedings*. pp. 46-59.

In the adaptive model, the organization is expected to continually assess external and internal conditions. Assessment then leads to adjustments in the organization or in its relevant environment that will create satisfactory alignments of environmental opportunities and risks, as well as organizational capabilities and resources.

The adaptive model therefore requires organizations to engage in a high degree of environmental scanning and an optimization of capital resources through risk management in order to exploit opportunities and increase competitive advantage.

The adaptive model differs from the linear one in that monitoring of the environment and making changes are simultaneous and continuous functions in the adaptive model. The time lag for planning that is implicit in the linear model is not present. Additionally, the adaptive model does not deal as emphatically as the linear model with decisions about goals, but instead focuses on the manager's attention on '*means*' and the '*goal*' is represented by co-alignment of the organization with its environment.

Another difference between the two lies in the lack of importance attached to advance planning in the adaptive model. Strategy is less centralized in the top management, more multifaceted and generally less integrated than in the linear model. In terms of the environment in the adaptive model, the boundaries are seen as highly permeable and the environment is a major focus of attention in determining organizational action. In this regard, the case may be made that this particular form of strategy is best suited to the cyber threat/technology risk management domain, whereby the speed of change and the rate of reassessment required makes other forms of strategy less suited to this particular activity.

Adaptive strategy rests upon several assumptions in that the organization and its environment are assumed to be more open to each other than that implied in the linear model, and the organization must change with the environment rather than deal with it. As such, the model attempts to take more variables and propensity for change into account than does the linear model and can therefore handle greater complexity.

Interpretive Strategy

Development of interpretive strategy parallels interest in corporate culture and symbolic management outside the academic strategy literature. Although the parameters of the model are still unclear, there is a recurring theme, suggesting that the model is based upon a social contract, rather than an organismic or biological view of the organization, that fits well with the adaptive model.[31]

---

[31] Chaffee E. E. (1985) Three Models of Strategy. *Academy of Management Review,* 1985, Vol.10. No.1. pp.89-98.

The interpretive model of strategy assumes that reality is socially constructed and is not something objective or external to the perceiver that can be apprehended correctly or incorrectly. Rather, reality is defined through a process of social interchange in which perceptions are affirmed, modified or replaced according to their apparent congruence with the perceptions of others.

It has been contended that the interpretive model might be defined as orienting metaphors or frames of reference that allow the organization and its environment to be understood by organizational stakeholders, who are motivated to believe and to act in ways that are expected to produce favorable results for the organization.

Rather than emphasizing changing with the environment, as is true of the adaptive model, interpretive strategy mimics linear strategy in its emphasis on dealing with the environment. The main difference though is that the linear strategists deal with the environment by means of organizational actions that are intended to affect relations instrumentally, whereas interpretive strategists deal with the environment through symbolic actions and communication.

Governmental institutions have embarked upon various programs in an attempt to understand the context and environment surrounding cyber threats and the perpetrators of attacks. Their work is embodied in a large number of programs globally that are collaborative in nature, seeking input from commercial, academic and NPO's in respect of their views on cyber threat management.

In this way, such governmental organizations may be viewed as employing an interpretive strategy in their attempts to affect the environment and cyber threat and regulatory developments. A large number of regulations (in the U.S. in particular) have been shaped by collaborative work with external organizations and in the establishment of joint ventures with commercial organizations who have provided technology infrastructure for cyber threat management programs run by governments.

Interpretive strategy, like adaptive strategy, assumes that the organization and its environment constitute an open system. However, in the interpretive strategy the organization's leaders shape the attitudes of participants and potential participants toward the organization and its outputs; they do not make physical changes in the outputs. This attitude change seeks to increase credibility for the organization or its output and in this regard overlaps with the adaptive model of strategy.

A final distinction between the adaptive and interpretive models of strategy may be the way each conceptualizes complexity. Adaptive strategy arose from and attempts to deal with structural complexity, notably conflicting and changing demands for organizational output. Interpretive strategy emphasizes attitudinal and cognitive complexity among diverse stakeholders in the organization.

Four Approaches to Strategy

In 1996, Michael Porter asked the question, "What is strategy?" and then went on to give his definition of what is and what is not strategy.[32] However, until fairly recently, whilst it has been difficult to quantify what strategy is and how to develop a strategy that encompasses all businesses and countries, it has been possible to identify four generic *approaches* to strategy:

(i) classical;
(ii) evolutionary;
(iii) processualist and;
(iv) the systems approach.

A possible fifth option, that of an organic perspective and approach has been proposed, which differentiates between the two main approached to strategy: the *mechanistic* and the *planned* approach.[33]

Taking the traditional four approaches, these can be roughly divided into those concerned with outcomes of strategy, and those involved with the processes by which it is made:

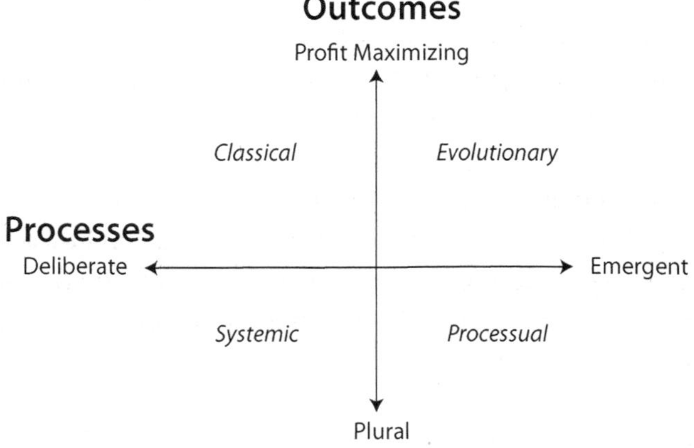

Fig. 6.3 Four Approaches to Strategy[34]

---

[32] Porter, M. (1996). What is strategy? *Harvard Business Review.*

[33] Farjoun, M. (2001).Towards an organic perspective on strategy. *Strategic Management Journal,* Wiley. July.

[34] Mintzberg, H. (1989). Strategy Formation: Schools of Thought, *Management Science.*

In the diagram, the vertical axis, the degree to which strategy either produces profit-maximizing outcomes or deviates to allow other possibilities to intrude, is measured. The horizontal axis considers processes, reflecting how far strategies are the product of deliberate calculation or whether they emerge by accident.

Thus, the *Classical* and *Evolutionary* approaches see profit maximization as the natural outcome of strategy making, whereas the *Systemic* and *Processual* approaches are more pluralistic and see other possible outcomes aside from profit as being possible.

The pairings are different with regard to processes, however. In this event, the Evolutionary and Processualist approaches see strategy as emerging from processes governed by chance, confusion and conservatism. For the Classical and Systemic approaches, theorists view strategy as being deliberate, even though in the two different approaches there may be differing outcomes.

The model is indicative of generic perspectives, but each approach may have a number of different perspectives on strategy positioned along the axis, sometimes with such perspectives overlapping into different quadrants.

Of note here is that outcomes may change over time where there is alignment with longer term objectives. An example here are technology startup companies in search and social networking, where the initial objectives were market share and/or subscribers, in order to later maximize profits.

Each approach to strategy has different conceptions of what strategy is about and how to actually do it. The theories provide the basic grounding for behavior and these assumptions have been called theories of action.

The importance of strategic theories in the current context is that without understanding what they are and how to use them, management actions could be deducted from use of supposed commonsense approaches to management that may simply be based upon ill-informed, half-forgotten, pseudo-scientific nostrums peddled to management in their early careers.

This also has applied to how senior management has regarded internet security and the threats posed to their organizations, that is, with little or no interest and even less understanding. As the integration and use of technology has evolved however, those in senior management roles have had to account for cyber/technology risks as part of the overall risk management doctrine in their respective companies and more recently, due to regulatory frameworks making them accountable for operational losses arising from technology failures/cyber attacks.

It has been claimed that nothing is more dangerous than to leave underlying assumptions hidden. Until implicit "theories of action" are revealed, they cannot be tested for their accuracy and amend them to the conditions of the day. Further, it is said that managers who do not actively confront their underlying assumptions may be condemned to be prisoners of their own theories. Each theory holds a different view on the capacity to think rationally and act effectively. They diverge widely in their implications for strategic management.[35]

Classical theory

For classicists, profitability is the supreme goal of business and there is reliance upon the rational planning methods dominant still in strategy textbooks. The question of what is strategy is viewed as being a rational process of deliberate calculation and analysis, designed to maximize long-term advantage.

This view proposes that if the effort is made to gather information and apply appropriate techniques, then both the outside world and the organization itself can be made predictable and shaped according to the plans of the management.

The measures and means by which strategic plans for the corporation were developed became detailed, leading to the first real measures of returns on investments as part of an overall profit-oriented goal of strategy, with policy being removed from operations.

Subsequently, all the characteristics now identified as belonging to the classical school of strategy emerged, these being: the emphasis on the long-run, the explicit and deliberate conception of goals, and the logical cascading of actions and resources from original objectives. Strategy thus became the determination of the basic, long-term goals and objectives of an organization, with the adoption of courses of action and the allocation of resources necessary to achieve those prescribed goals forming part of classical strategy.

The major difficulty was viewed as being how to build organizational structures that would allow top management to focus on their strategic responsibilities and remove them from the day-to-day operational requirements of an organization. Thus, strategy formulation and control was regarded as being the role of the top management of an organization only, with the strategy implementation being the responsibility of the operational managers in the divisions. This theory of strategy could be argued to fit to

---

[35] Argyris, C. (1997) Double loop learning in organizations. *Harvard Business Review,* September-October: 115-125.

cyber/risk management, in that the senior management gives input in the formulation of the risk appetite of the organization and the role of the risk management team/division is to formulate an appropriate risk strategy that aligns with this.

Others have argued that economics have supplied the strategy field with many basic techniques and concepts, such as the industry structure analysis and the concept of transaction costs in business organization.

However, it is also argued that the most pervasive contribution of economics to strategy is undoubtedly the philosophical core of assumptions within the ideal type of the rational economic man. The concept effectively provided for a solitary decision taker as a proxy for the firm and in this way it was possible to ignore the internal organizational complexities. Thus, reduction of the firm to a single individual permitted the sequence of mathematical calculations necessary to follow through the logics of the game.[36]

Commentators differentiate implementation as being a distinct phase in the strategy making process, only coming after the earlier phase of explicit and conscious formulation and that the actual carrying out of the orders is not problematic. Thus, the classical approach to strategy emphasizes the readiness and capacity of managers to adopt profit-maximizing strategies through long-term planning.

Evolutionist theory

Evolutionists propose that strategy in the Classical sense of rational, future-oriented planning is often irrelevant, since the environment is typically too unpredictable to be able to anticipate effectively and this is clearly the case for cyber threat management.

Additionally, the evolutionist approach is less confident about top management's ability to plan and act rationally. The expectation instead is that markets secure profit maximization. Rational planning methods are not excluded, but rather, whatever methods management selects, the evolutionists argue that it will only be the best performers that survive. Managers need not be rational optimizers, since evolution is nature's cost-benefit analysis.

Evolutionist theory often makes an explicit parallel between economic competition

---

[36] Hollis, M., and Nell, E J. (1975). *Rational economic man: A philosophical critique of neo-classical economics.* Cambridge: Cambridge University Press.

and the law of natural competition. This has been attacked by a number of commentators, who see such a view as being too abstract and unrealistic.

Business practice has been regarded as being far from that prescribed by the ideal of the rational economic man: not only did managers fail to set output at the theoretical profit-maximizing level i.e. where marginal cost equal marginal revenue, but they had no idea what their marginal cost and revenue curves were. Consequently, economists allowed for this by seeking to allow the markets be the determining factor. An evolutionary theory of the firm that downgraded managerial strategy and emphasized environmental fit followed on from this.[37]

The evolutionist perspective has a paradox however, in that the dynamic, hostile and competitive nature of markets means not only that long-term survival cannot be planned for, but it also ensures that only organizations that find profit-maximizing strategies will survive. This can be viewed as being articulated as a sort of Darwinian influence where there is survival of the fittest within a given market and the market is beyond the scope of influence of managers.

In this way, the markets are the key and not managers of organizations. Rather, the survival of the fittest is determined by those managers who are able to read the market conditions and shape and change their own organizations to be best placed to exploit it.

Evolutionist theorists doubt the capacity of organizations to achieve differentiation and adaptation in a deliberate and sustainable way. They emphasize the limited capacity of organizations to anticipate and respond purposively to shifts in the environment. This is exemplified by technology shifts that subsequently result in the demise of brands that formerly dominated the sector.

Theorists have proposed that environmental fit is more likely to be the result of chance and good fortune, or error, than the outcome of deliberate strategic choice, often through simply being in the right place at the right time.

It has also been proposed that investing in long-term planning can be counter-productive. Organizations maximize their chances of survival in the short term by achieving perfect fit against their current environment. In a competitive environment, flexibility is evolutionarily inefficient. Strategy is too expensive, in that the longer term investor in strategies of innovation and diversification can always be undercut by the short-term, inflexible, low cost producer. Therefore, organizational selection processes

[37] Alchian, A.A. (195) Uncertainty, evolution and economic theory. *Journal of Political Economy* 58: 211-221.

favor organizations with relatively inert structures, i.e. organizations that cannot change strategy and structure as their environments change.

Not only do the theorists state that markets are typically too competitive for expensive strategizing and too unpredictable to guess, but they are also too inefficient to permit the creation of any sustainable advantage. In a competitive environment, elaborate strategies can only deliver a temporary advantage, since competitors will be quick to imitate and erode any early benefits.

Of note here is that there is a proposition from other strategy theorists and economists that within some sectors, and in particular the banking and financial services sectors, sustainable competitive advantage is derived from optimizing network capabilities. This view is founded upon the cost compression advantages of network and transactional capabilities and ongoing shifts towards more cost-effective means of processing transaction, such as straight through processing and IP based rather than closed circuit networks. This capability through networks and data processing somewhat contradicts the views of the theorists and could be argued to favor cyber threat/technology risk management divisions given the dependence of an organization on networks for their competitive advantage and thus resilience.

Evolutionists therefore propose that strategy is a delusion. With the exception of those firms with large market power, economy would appear to be the best strategy, with the only comparative advantage being through relative efficiency. Since deliberate strategizing is ineffective, overall efficiency can be best secured by ensuring a steady stream of new entrants into any organizational population, from which the relatively ill adapted, will be selected out.

The evolutionist theory of strategy is therefore a less than positive one, with only differentiation being held to be a sound principle and even this is unlikely to be achieved permanently or deliberately. The approach proposed by the theorists is to focus on business efficiencies, implement numerous initiatives and let the markets determine the strategy.

Processualist theory

In agreement with the evolutionist theory of strategy, is the processualist perspective of strategy, which also views long-range planning as being futile. The proponents, however, see that environmental fit is not the determining point of survival. Their view is that the processes of both markets and organizations are rarely sufficiently perfect for either the strategizing of classical theory, in that markets do not ensure profit-maximizing outcomes, or the survivalist approach of the evolutionists.

Instead, processualists see the world as being a mess and sticky in some circumstances, where there is much confusion and strategies emerge in small steps. Indeed, they argue that it is the very imperfections of markets and organizational processes that managers owe their strategies and competitive advantages to. The foundation of the Processual approach focuses upon the internal complexity of organizations and comprises two of the themes that have since become fundamentals of Processual thought: the *cognitive limits* on rational action, and the *micro-economic politics* of organizations.[38]

The theorists aim for a more psychologically realistic theory of human behavior and emphasize the limits of human cognition. By this they mean that people are unable to consider more than a few factors at a time and will not start searches for relevant information. Rather, there is a bias in interpretation of data and a tendency to accept the first satisfactory option that appears, rather than seeking out the best option. As a consequence, they assert that the environmental scanning, data analyses and calculated comparison of strategic options advocated by the classical theorists tend to be flawed and incomplete and part of normal human nature.

The micro-political environment formulated, recognized the individual interests that exist in every enterprise and that firms are not united in optimizing a single utility, such as profit. Rather, they are coalitions of individuals each of whom brings their own personal objectives and cognitive biases to the organization.

In this respect, the interests of various business units or departments can be viewed as having this component in their make-up, with territories closely guarded and networks within the organization being built as high a level as possible.

Organizational members bargain between each other to arrive at a set of joint goals more or less acceptable to them all. The bargaining process also involves what are termed "policy side payments" in return for agreement. Thus strategy is the product of political compromise, not profit-maximizing calculation.

In this respect, the internal politics of an organization, allied to the affects of psychological factors upon the judgment and decision making processes can be viewed as playing an important role during the development of a cyber threat/risk management program, in that the composition of those who may be viewed as gatekeepers in the decision process need to brought on-side if such programs are to progress and be sustained.

The combination of political bargaining and bounded rationality strongly favors

[38] Cyert, R. M. and March, J.G. (1956).Organizational Factors in the Theory of Monopoly. *Quarterly Journal of Economics* 70 (1): 44-64.

strategic conservatism. The need for change will only be imperfectly recognized and is regarded with suspicion since it is a portent of renewed internal political fighting until a new dominant "coalition" is created.

Strategic behavior therefore tends to become entrenched in the routines and standard operating procedures imposed by political requirements and cognitive limits. Organizations opt for adaptive rationality rather than perfectly rational strategies. Further, as conditions and circumstances change, plans are liable also to change and thus strategy merges more from pragmatic processes of learning, compromising and changing than from a rational series of jumps forward.

Organizations simply opt for adaptive rationality, adjusting routines gradually as environmental factors impact on managers and forces recognition of the need to change. This ability of organizations to be able to live with slow reactions is contrary to the views of the evolutionists, and is put down to the proposition that markets are quite tolerant of underperformance. Firms are often able to build sufficient organizational slack to be able to buffer them against the need for organizational change, delivering sufficient profits to maintain the status quo.[39]

In this way, an emergent strategy does not have to be optimal since no other organization knows what the optimal strategy should be anyway and nobody would stick to it. Thus, it is proposed by the theorists that a failure to devise, implement and action the perfect strategic plan will not result in the demise of an organization.

Clearly, more recent events in the global banking system, from both the perspective of the actors and the regulators, would appear to undermine this particular proposal. There was no laid out plan to acquire distressed assets without understanding their composition and the regulators failed by not having a strategic plan for the events post Lehman Brothers.

In practice, strategy makers do not aim to achieve optimal solutions, but rather satisfy themselves with established routines of the organization. Strategy statements themselves can become routinised heuristics that constrain opportunities and lead decisions into established paths.

The regular procedures and precise quantifications of strategic planning become rituals. Instead, what is important is that the strategies give confidence to managers and it is not so important that they are right or wrong. This confidence gives them a sense of

[39] Nelson, R. R., & Winter, S. G. (1982). *An evolutionary theory of economic change.* Cambridge, Mass.: Belknap Press of Harvard University Press.

purpose to act, gives direction and acquires experience to make their own opportunities.

Such a process is a reversal of the classical one of strategy formulation first, followed by implementation. Here, strategy is discovered in action and the distinction between policy creation and policy execution is diminished. It may therefore also be argued that this form of strategy formulation is best adapted to cyber/technology risk management given that the environment shifts continuously and is so complex that a rigid strategy at the outset is inappropriate.

Many researchers have doubted the ability of top management to prescribe effective strategies and propose the metaphor of crafting of strategy, where the process is one of continuation and entangles with implementation, rather than a single-shot development for long-range planning.

Whilst this picture of strategy is far from the classical theorist's picture of careful development of a strategy, and seems more akin to muddling through to make the best of a situation, this muddling through has been claimed to be a science in itself, involving cautious comparison of successive options and careful maintenance of consensus.

A gradual adaptive approach has its own rationality, which has been termed "logical incrementalism".[40] This reflects the view of the strategist that they are unable to think through every aspect in advance, but rather impose their own bounds of rationality and therefore commit to experimentation and learning.

The incrementalist approach is not necessarily a tactical one. It may be informed by underlying logic, or "strategic intent", that is both sufficiently clear to provide some sense of direction and sufficiently broad to allow flexibility and opportunism along the way.

Some academics have gone further and proposed that the underlying strategic logic may be perceived only after the event. Strategies are often emergent with their coherence accruing through action and perceived in retrospect.[41] In the case of risk management and cyber threat management in particular, this strategic approach may therefore appear to be ill-suited for effective planning.

---

[40] Quinn, J.B. (1980). *Strategies for change: Logical incrementalism.* Homewood, IL: Richard D Irwin.

[41] Mintzberg, H., and Waters, J.A. (1985). Of strategies, deliberate and emergent. *Strategic Management Journal* 6(3): 257-272.

The Processualists who emphasize the stickiness of external markets reinforce this incrementalist approach. The resource-based strategy theorists argue that market imperfections inhibit the opportunity-maximizing strategies proposed by the Classicists, since the resources with which firms compete are not all bought and sold in markets according to opportunities and threats.

Resource based theories of the firm stress how a firm's resources include tacit skills, patterns of co-operation, and intangible assets that take time and learning to evolve. These resources cannot be traded, changed or copied with any ease and the origin of a firm's competitive advantage therefore lies in what is unique and embedded in its resources (the core, distinctive competencies).

Within the areas of risk management, technology and professional services in particular, strategy is as likely to emerge bottom-up as it is top-down, since it is at the bottom where the knowledge lies and is continuously recreated.

Thus, in the view of the Processualists, even where markets are attractive, entry may be limited to those organizations that have the correct resources for a successful market entry and will also fail if it underestimates the difficulty of acquiring the requisite competencies externally.

Systemic theory

From this particular perspective, strategy does matter, but not in the manner that Classical theorists think. Systemic theorists are much less pessimistic than Processualists about people's capacity to conceive and carry out rational plans of action and more optimistic than Evolutionists about their ability to define their strategies in defiance of market forces.

Where they differ from the Classicists is in their refusal to accept the forms and ends of classical rationality as anything more than historically and culturally different phenomena. For them, the rationales underlying strategy are peculiar to particular sociological contexts. The pillar of systemic theory is that decision makers are not simply detached individuals interacting in purely economic transactions, but rather, they are embedded within interwoven social systems.

It has been proposed that the notion of social embeddedness that captures the sense that economic activity cannot be placed in the sole context of impersonal financial calculation. In practice, people's economic behavior is embedded in a network of social relations that may involve their families, the state, their professional and educational backgrounds, and even their religion and ethnicity.[42]

These networks influence both the means and ends of action, defining what appropriate and reasonable behavior is for their members. Behavior, which might appear irrational or inefficient to the Classical theorist, may be perfectly rational according to local criteria and modus operandi of the particular social context.

Thus, according to the Systemic theorists, organizations differ according to the social and economic systems in which they are embedded. They are not therefore perfect profit-optimizers. Compared with the Classical approach, they should choose profit maximization as their goal, the Evolutionist theory argues that they are obliged to be profit maximisers, and they are not just organizational idiosyncrasies and the product of internal limits and compromises as in the Processual approach.

According to Systemic theory then, the norms that guide strategy derive not so much from the cognitive bounds of the human psyche as from the cultural rules of the local society. The internal contests of the organization are influenced by the external context as well.

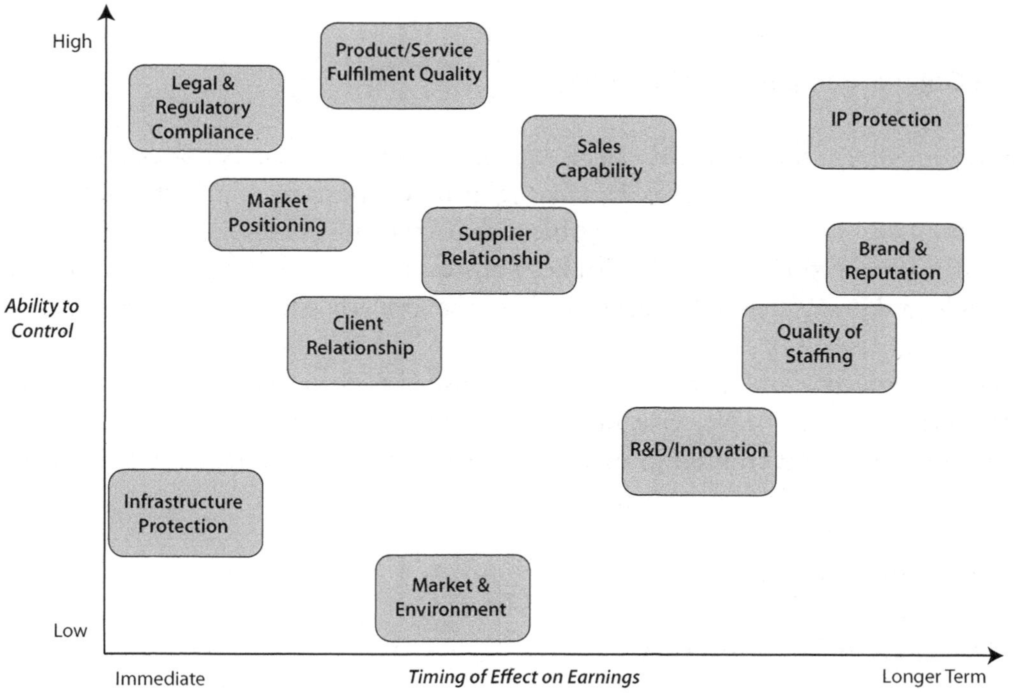

Fig. 6.4 Strategy Factor Impacts

[42] Granovetter, M. (1985). Economic action and social structure: the problem of embeddedness. *American Journal of Sociology* 91 (3): 481-510.

Therefore, key points in the Systemic approach are the differences between different countries' social systems and changes within those countries' social systems. The prevailing forms of business are widely known to vary according to the local interplay of state, familial and market structures.

When regard is made to the effect of social and cultural factors then upon strategy formulation, implementation and objective in the Systemic approach in respect of cyber/risk management; clearly the interaction between State and organization plays an important role. In other cases, market structure impacts upon ownership and control of organizations, which in turn affects the profit objectives of enterprises i.e. a listed company, may have a shorter term imperative to create profits for shareholders, whereas a mutual or family owned business may take a longer term view.

The influence of this upon cyber/risk management programs is therefore clearer to understand where capital allocation to programs may be influenced by ownership and control and the Systemic approach to strategy seeks to view the profit objective as being subservient to cultural and social influences and these in turn may influence how risks are managed.

The Organic Perspective of Strategy

It is claimed that strategy theory can be segregated into two distinct progressions, these being the mechanistic approach and the planned posture approach. A further development towards a more organic perspective on strategy, away from the mechanistic approach as a result of strategy process research, evolutionary and process models, and interactive and integrative views has similarly been proposed.[43]

The hard aspects of the strategy construct are pushed aside in favor of the soft variables that portray a more complex view of causality, which represent a shift in the underlying epistemological underpinnings of Classical strategy theory. Three key shifts exist according to Organic strategy theorists;

- the view of time
- the directional view
- the differentiated view

With a change to the view of time, in the mechanistic approach, there is a focus upon

[43] Farjoun, M. (2001).Towards an organic perspective on strategy. *Strategic Management Journal,* Wiley. July.

a single occurrence of a set of givens at a particular point in time. As such, there is a static viewpoint that disregards historic or future points. By contrast, an Organic view of time is that which is incessant, where concepts and relationships are part of a continuous process, with iterated sequences.

For the case of risk management and in particular cyber threat management, such a perspective is the advised one, shifting away from a static assessment and quantification of something that is accepted as transitional by nature, as threats and operational shifts require a dynamic viewpoint.

This contrasts with the mechanistic perspective which often presents a linear and sequential view of events and causality, and highlights deterministic causes of behavior and therefore pays less regard to interaction, feedback and multiple, reciprocal endogenous influences. Further, an Organic strategy perspective proposes an integrated approach of problem-centered, multi-level and relational view of strategy, phenomena and concepts.

As such, the advantages of an organic approach to strategy are through having a greater appreciation of the complexity and interdisciplinary nature of strategy. It also builds continuity since it builds on and not rejects lower level mechanistic conceptions. In addition, as changes, conflict and interdependence are chief concerns of modern firms and strategy itself, organic assumptions hold natural appeal.

A summary of the four types of mechanistic approaches to strategy may be defined as: the structure-conduct-performance (SCP), the strategy-structure-performance (SSP), and the resource-based-view (RBV).

Collectively, these different models of the mechanistic perspective see firm performance as affected by the environment and by firm strategy and other internal attributes. Internal firm attributes and those of the environment are seen as affecting strategy itself.

Developments towards an Organic perspective on strategy have come through a different orientation to process and time, the former being more accepting strategy in more dynamic and process terms. A change to strategic approaches has been the shift from *what* determines strategy and performance to *how* they are determined.

As such, the new models examine how initial conditions, timing, managerial choices, decisive moments, learning, and path-dependent processes enable and constrain current states and in turn provide platforms for future developments.

An addition of feedback loops has in effect been added to the mechanistic approach to strategy, with a new focus on strategic (external) interaction models that view capabilities, competition and performance as both *affecting* and being *affected* by strategy, whilst being less concerned with the differential contributions of resources and environment to performance.

Reciprocal causality in the design model of the strategic management process has led also to the notion of dynamic fit, and has influenced the views of formulation and implementation. The renewed interest in internal firm attributes, such as organizational structure, culture and decision processes are seen as having important influences on, rather than derivatives of, strategy formulation.

Resources and technology are those elements that provide the capability to accomplish the firms' goals and provide their distinctive competencies. These are subdivided into resources, relationships and work flow technology. Resources are those financial, physical, informational organizational and human assets within the organization.

Relationships are said to be such items as contracts, trust, loyalty, legal rights and social capital that bind the organization with various actors and stakeholders. Work flow technologies are said to be the various activities and operations in which resources are employed and the manner in which work is executed.

In an Organic perspective, greater emphasis is placed upon processes such as formulation and emergence, by which strategies are created, realized and managed and the processes, by which information is acquired, developed and maintained, organized, disseminated, transmitted and communicated.

Firm performance is claimed to indicate the quality of a organization's continuous co-alignment with the environment. The representation can be by measurement of a number of factors, such as growth, profitability, survival and other standard indicators and may also include multiple levels of analysis, such as at business unit level. In the case of risk management, benchmarking may be utilized as a proxy method of measurement where there may be too great a complexity for accurate measurements to be acquired.

As such, performance is measured not solely at a particular point in time, but rather it requires capture of development and changes over time and reflect different time scales. Static efficiency may lead to maladjustment in the long run and in the short term there may be a misfit to what is needed to attain long-term dynamic fit.

Therefore firm performance may have short and long term conflicting alignments and must reflect both the quality of the firm's ability to exploit current resources as well as its capacity to generate new ones. In the organic model, firm organization, firm environment, firm strategy and firm performance are causally related to each other.

The Organic model assigns particular importance to history in the way it defines constructs and relationships by accounting for the fact that history influences but does not determine current and future states of each variable. The context is defined both in space and time since systems are distinguished not only from events outside them but also from events occurring prior to them and subsequent to them. This viewpoint clearly aligns with cyber risk management and enterprise resilience activities to a greater extent than with other strategic models.

Therefore the model assumes too that agents intend to act and choose rationally, with actions being both prospective and purposive. However, it recognizes deviations from rational behavior, such as those stemming from agents' cognitive limits and other constraints on efficient adjustment, such as inertia for example. Thus, there is an acceptance of cognitive, affective, social and political influences on rational, planned actions.

The Organic model views the process of strategic management as a progression which includes the sequence of events and activities over time. Strategic management is viewed as consisting of a one-time mode, i.e. dealing with a particular strategy or a single strategic decision, plus a recurrent mode, i.e. dealing with a continuous stream of strategies and decisions.

Understanding the Organic perspective of strategy may be difficult to conceptualize in the context of a particular organization. However, if the view is taken that the modern business environment is highly complex, interrelated globally, constantly shifting, with low barriers to entry and exit, then this perspective may be viewed as the most appropriate for the current times.

Further, it may be argued that the Organic approach is already the dominant form of strategy perspective, since without the concepts proposed being understood and implemented, many of the new businesses that have emerged in recent times may not have appeared, such as social media companies, online sales outlets and digital rights management for DVD's and music. If this is the accepted view, then similarly, the Organic view of cyber threat/technology risk management strategy may also be the most appropriate for the current times, due to the interconnectedness, inter-dependency, constant evolution and shifts that occur on an ongoing basis.

The Effect of Strategic Decision Speed and Firm Performance

Theorists have identified a positive association between fast strategic decision-making and firm performance. However, contrary research examined the association and found no correlation except among firms in biotechnology, a high-velocity industry. The proposition of the strategic decision process theory is that decision-makers' cognitions are motivated and constrained by their business environment, organizational structures, and resources. It has subsequently been proposed that *environmental velocity* is a moderator of the decision speed to financial performance.[44]

From the perspective of the strategist, or managerial decision-maker, the deliberate rational decision-making process involves five intertwined cognitive stages:

1. Give attention to a problem or opportunity;
2. Collect information;
3. Develop an array of options;
4. Value the options using expected costs and benefits;
5. Select the option with the greatest utility.

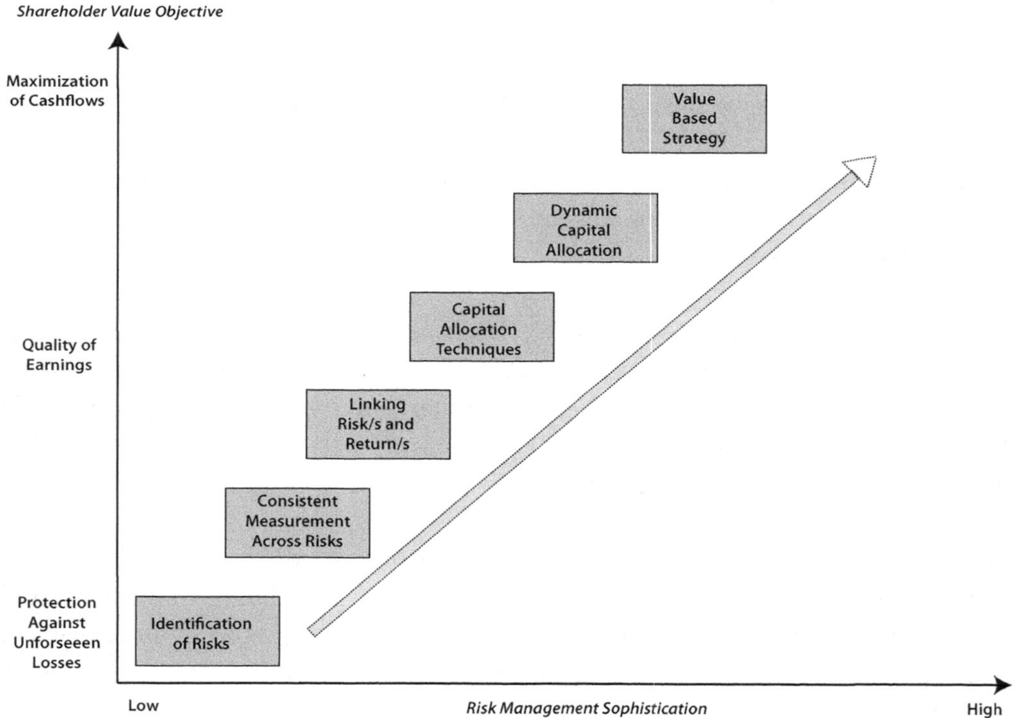

Fig. 6.5 Risk Management Objective V Sophistication

[44] Bourgeois, L. J., and Eisenhardt K. (1988) Strategic decision processes in high velocity environments: four cases in the microcomputer industry. Management Science 34: 816-835.

This would accord with the steps encompassed in risk management mitigation strategy development, however, some researchers claim that this synoptic explanation is an incomplete description of real decision processes. This is because decision mistakes are caused by misunderstanding probabilities, personal biases and failures of memory (see Chapter 4 in relation to the latter influences).

It is claimed that fast decision speeds may improve competitive performance because fast strategic decisions lead to early adoption of new products or improved business models that provide competitive advantage. It may also lead to pre-emptive organization combinations that enable economies of scale and knowledge synergies, as well as early adoption of efficiency-gaining process technologies.

The contra argument, that fast strategic decision-making may produce bad decisions and bad performance, has been blamed upon the sacrificing of comprehensive information gathering in favor of higher decision speed. However, fast decision-making does not necessarily signal cursory processing: decision-making in the most successful companies has been found to be fast and comprehensive. Other researchers have also found that decision-makers may keep pace with fast-moving environments by engaging in comprehensive *scanning*, research, and analysis (see Chapter 3). Fast decision-making is appropriate then in situations where delay does not yield useful information.[45]

Dynamism refers to the level of environmental predictability and is manifested in the variance in the rate of market and industry change and the level of uncertainty about forces that are beyond the control of individual businesses. Dynamic environments are similar to, but not the same as, 'high-velocity' environments. The latter involve fast-paced changes in demand, competition, and technology which may result in instability, turbulence and unpredictability.

Researchers have indicated that configurations of strategy and structure are important for the conclusions about the effects of environment upon firm performance. For example, informal, adaptable, loosely controlled firms have better performance in dynamic environments than mechanistic firms, and mechanistic ones have better performance in stable environments.

Centralization refers to the concentration of authority and power in a firm, with more centralization leading to less widespread decision-making power with regard to policy

[45] Glick, W. H., Miller, C.C., and Huber, G. P. (1993). The impact of upper echelon diversity on organizational performance. In *Organizational Change and Redesign: Ideas and Insights for Improving Performance,* Huber, G. P., Glick W. H. (eds). Oxford University Press: New York; 176-214.

and task performance. There are two types of organizational centralization: strategic decision-making and operations decision-making. Low strategic centralization (decentralization) involves widespread employee participation in strategic decisions. Low operational centralization involves behaviors usually associated with self-managed teams. This can be seen within risk management divisions and in particular cyber threat/technology risk management units, where the highly specialized knowledge required vests in personnel often at great distance from the upper echelons of organizations' managerial hierarchy.

The beneficial effects of decentralization of operations management is claimed to be enhanced by employee motivation, loyalty, creativity and improved responsiveness to market conditions. Conversely, centralized strategic decision-making creates valued strong leadership, and financial performance improves when leaders clearly define business strategy and resolve power and communication hierarchies.

Decentralized operations management yields front-line environmental information that may be useful in strategic decisions. The importance and accuracy of this information is not universally held and may be displaced by information from ERM and and other MIS. Nevertheless, decentralized operations management is seen as a positive force for decision speed. With an increasing reliance upon data and the ability to analyze it for all aspects of organizational operations, it can be seen that its' protection, along with infrastructure has become of prime importance to all entities.

Formalized organization structures are characterized by explicitly articulated and written firm policies, job descriptions, organization charts, strategic and operational plans and objective-setting systems. In highly formalized systems, little flexibility exists to determine who may decide to act or how to act and in the IT security domain, this is the norm. There is disagreement as to whether high levels of formalization detract from organization performance, but clearly it is a pre-requisite within any cyber risk management program.

Dynamism (instability or unpredictability) is an important challenge in the strategic decision-making process because it increases the degree of difficulty in understanding markets and environments. Many dynamic markets are increasingly caused by new/disruptive technologies and new business models, with strategic decision-makers in such environments reacting quickly in order to gain first mover advantage. Consequently, less time is taken on research since little benefit is perceived to be gained from such an activity. By contrast, decision-making in munificent environments is said to be less challenging than in low-munificence environments because the risk, or penalty, for selecting the 'wrong' option may be lower.

Historically, it may have been reasonable to expect most commercial organizations to have profit maximization as their objective and therefore either a Classical or Evolutionary strategic approach to be employed. However, when the velocity and degree of munificence within various sectors are taken into account, along with the the effect of decision speed, the expectation may not be met.

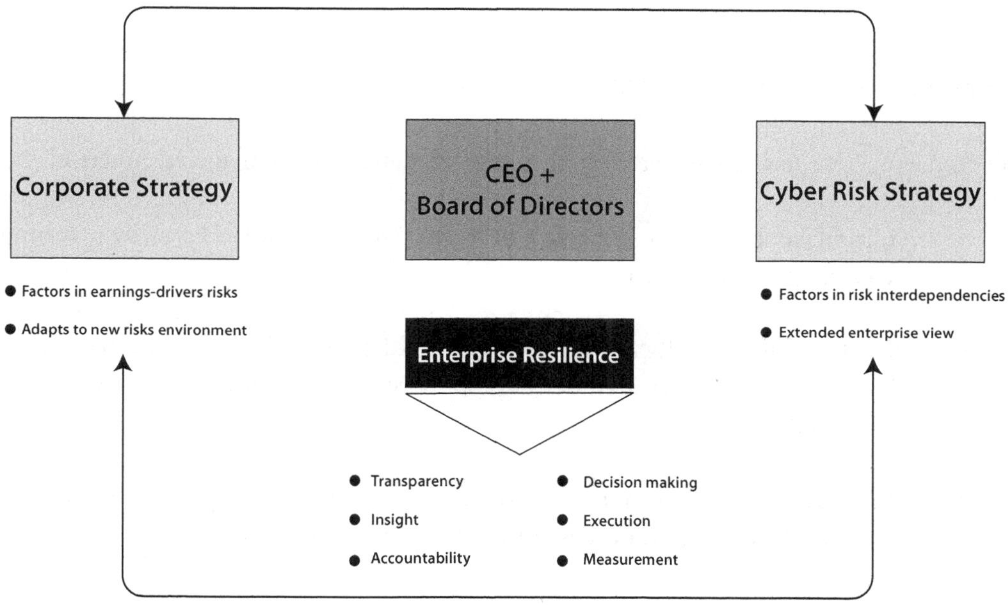

Fig. 6.6 Corporate and Risk Strategy Cycle

Similarly, the risk management process is prescribed as a highly planned process, undertaken with deliberate steps, pointing towards the Linear strategy model, whilst requiring enterprises to draw upon knowledge external to the firm, itself requiring a high degree of environmental scanning, indicating a more adaptive model .

Additionally, the risk management process requires organizations to draw upon historic data and project this forward in order to determine a hierarchy of risks. In this respect, taking a diachronic view of time within the strategic approach is more closely matched to an Organic perspective, rather than the static view of the other perspectives.

By contrast, the mechanistic perspective of the risk management process, presenting a linear and sequential view of events, by necessity, varies fundamentally with an Organic perspective of strategy. Strategy has shifted from determining firm performance within a given environment and set of internal firm attributes, to a position where it is the environment and internal firm attributes that affects strategy itself.

In this way, for the majority of business sectors, in relation to the prescribed means of operating within the modern networked global economy, a new, common environment has been created, offering opportunities for improved firm performance for those organizations that are best able to optimize their risk management operations. Thus it is the interaction with the environment, guided by the risk management process that affects firm performance, which in turn influences strategy.

Summary of the Theories of Strategy

Each perspective has its own strategy and how it matters for managerial practice.

- Classicists broadly see strategy as a rational process of long term planning, vital to securing the future.

- Evolutionists usually regard the future as far too volatile and unpredictable to plan for, and warn that the best strategy is to concentrate on maximizing the chances of survival in the present.

- Processualists also doubt the value of long-range planning and view strategy as being an emergent process of learning and adaptation.

- Systemic theorists argue that the forms and goal of strategy making are dependent upon the social context and that strategy should therefore be undertaken with sociological sensitivity.

In this way, the approaches of *evolution* and *process* both see strategy as not being that of rational planning since plans will be overwhelmed by events or error. What becomes apparent too is that the impact of exogenous factors and consequent actions sometimes result in a mixture of approaches.

In respect of cyber risk management, it can be seen that formulating a strategy to cover all eventualities, over a sustained period of time, which also is co-aligned with the organization's corporate strategy is not an insignificant task. Even where the organization concerned operates in a non-volatile or dynamic environment, the rate of technology evolution, adaptation and usage results in a separate operating environment with a large number of variables. Understanding how and what forms of strategy are available to both risk management teams and their Board's is important in determining how risks are managed and what level of risk appetite is appropriate for any specific entity.

Chapter Seven

RISK MANAGEMENT OPERATIONAL RISK AND ENTERPRISE RESILIENCE

Risk Management – Introduction

Risk management has been historically linked mainly to credit and market risks, with a number of models being developed and used for the management of these risks. Operational risk is concerned here with adverse deviation of a firm's performance due to how the firm is operated, as opposed to how the company is financed. In very recent times, failures of models and in the supervision of risk by Regulators led to a very public implosion of the banking sector, with a global impact which carries over today.

Risk management is said to be a strategic business process, where an organization's management assesses whether the company's business activities are consistent with its stated strategic objectives and how risk management is linked to investment and growth decisions.

Risk can best be understood in terms of its two main elements: 'stake' and 'uncertainty', where each element usually has a gain and a loss potential. The stake may be a financial gain or loss; an improvement or deterioration in strategic position; an improvement in or damage to reputation; a threat to a company's existence; or an increase or decrease in its sense of security.

Various definitions have been attached to the term risk management, with one such

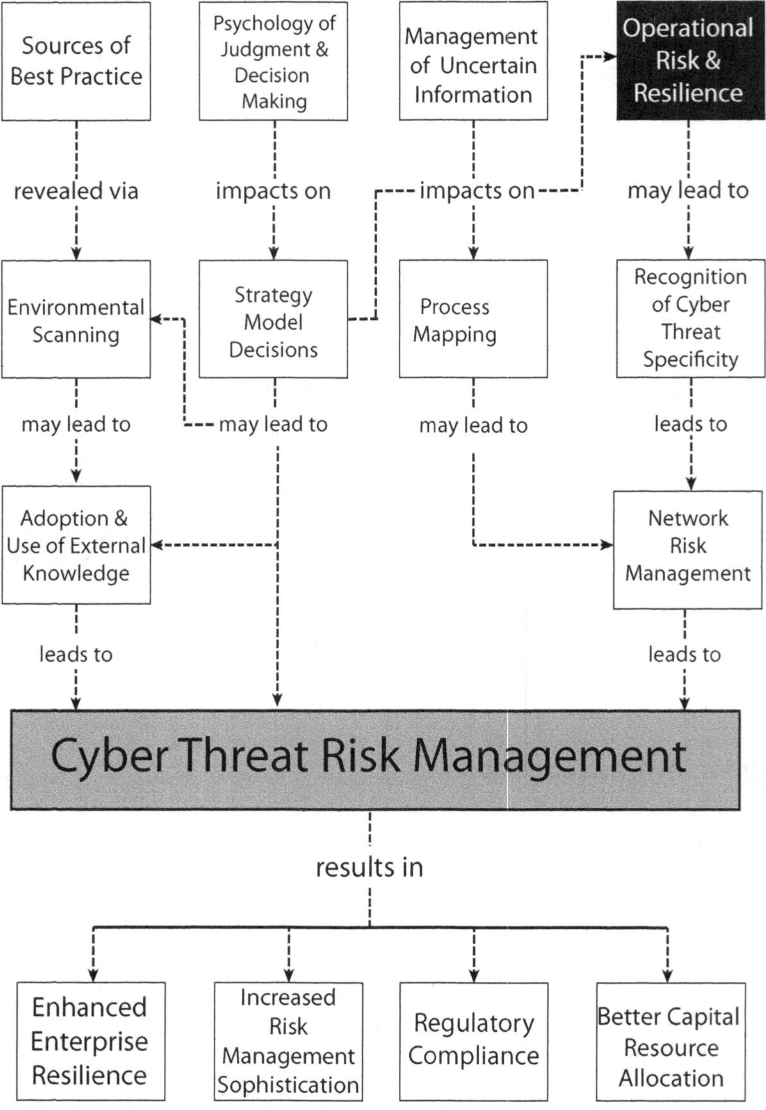

Fig. 7.1 Focus of Chapter 7

being the measure of the link between a firm's business activities and the variation in its business results. The general approach has been to add the capability of increasing value by reducing the variability or risk of earnings, thereby reducing the risk adjustment for valuation through the reduction in performance variability. Strategies adopted by enterprises that seek to increase earnings without addressing the related risk may not lead to those sought after increases due to the actions also increasing risk.

Understanding the causes of risk to earnings and their relationship to the business activity allows management of the trade-off between risk and return. The primary benefits of managing risk are:

- Avoidance of unexpected losses and improvement of operational efficiency – understanding risks allows management to focus on ways to reduce or eliminate loss and improve efficiency.

- Efficient use of capital – since organizations are obliged to allocate capital reserves based on expected earnings, managing risk optimizes the use of an organizations' capital.

- Satisfy stakeholders – this includes regulators and credit agencies – operations are part of risk management and a major contributor to:

  - Earnings volatility and thus value of the enterprise

  - Regulatory compliance – national and international corporate governance recommendations and statutory requirements view risk management as a Board level responsibility

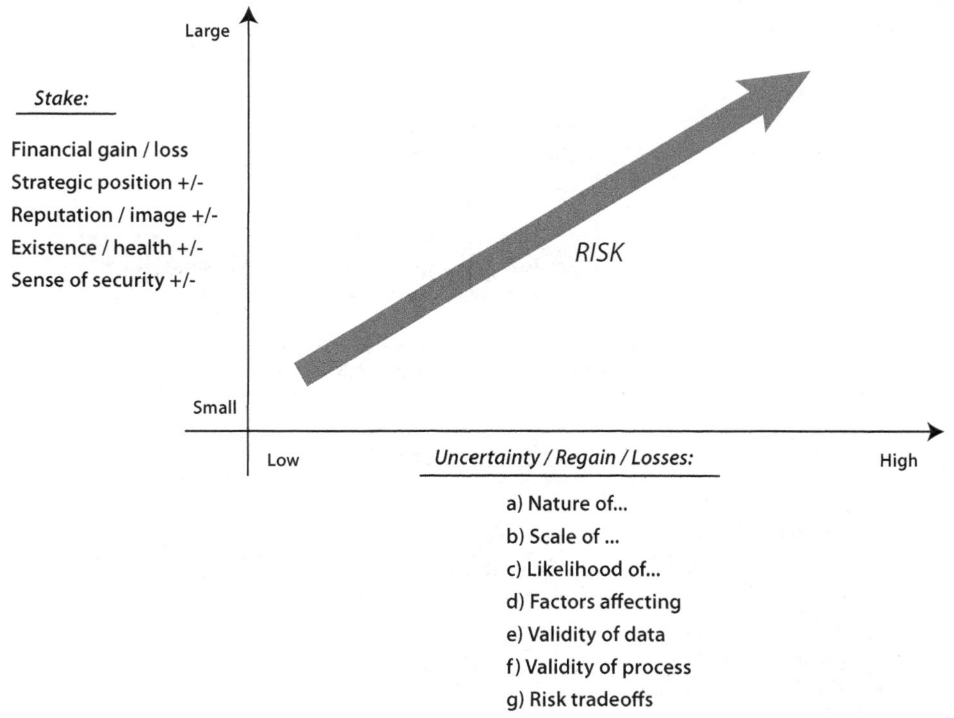

Fig. 7.2 Operational Risk Map

Traditional risk management responsibilities and responses are typically fragmented as a result of their differing origins. The roots of risk management have their origins in a number of unrelated disciplines. Military risk analysis led to the evolution of operational research. Personal and commercial risks generated the insurance and actuarial approach to risk management. Strategic risk analysis and the recognition that the future may not be the same as the past gave rise to scenario planning.

Another alternative to this is the use of option pricing theory to view different alternatives. Currency, interest and credit risks generated a banking approach to risk management and various hedging instruments. Operational and environmental risk management gave rise to contingency planning approaches, whilst computer and technology risks have spawned their own management science.

As a result of this, within organizations, different departments address different risks, using different approaches, often at a very low level. An example would be where insurance focuses on hazard risks such as fire and theft; financial derivatives assist in managing commodity, currency and interest rate risks; credit products are used to safeguard against operational setbacks; and historic databases are used for forecasting. Whilst some of these are primarily for financial risk management, it may be argued that only a holistic approach can give an enterprise-wide understanding of risk and, without it, management fails to adequately manage risks for the company's advantage.

Fig. 7.3 Organizational Operational Risk Structure

Risk management has become a critical issue as a result of globalization and the continued financial market pressure placed on organizations for greater returns. Whilst most companies now view risk as a key strategic issue, risk is typically still treated tactically and piecemeal. An integrated approach allows companies to consistently deliver superior performance while proactively managing risks.

With an increase in the potential for unplanned events to occur, there is an increasing acceptance of the need for an integrated approach to strategic risk management, enabling companies to consistently deliver superior performance while proactively managing risks. However, frequently the benefits of such an approach are not maximized due to management focusing purely upon potential negative consequences of certain actions or posed by certain risks.

The Strategic Benefits of Managing Risk

Enterprise security can provide not only security, but improved competitiveness. A US study on competitiveness focused upon the balance between competitiveness and security in five industry sectors: chemical, electric power, financial services, oil and gas, and pharmaceutical.[46]

Two key questions posed were:

1. Is it inevitable that security be a drain on productivity and corporate profitability?
2. Can a business case be made for investment in security and resilience?

The study concluded that whilst the business case for anti-terrorism was weak, the case for security was strong. It highlighted that the globalization of supply chains, IT interdependencies and technological complexity, political instability, and concentration of sources of supply have increased the potential for disruption in every sector studied.

The trend within organizations in recent years has been towards enterprise resilience, as a result of regulation. Previously, security was viewed as a sunk cost, whereas regulatory regimes have changed the way it is perceived. Previously, when a company's results were good, the regulatory bodies assumed that the company was managing its risk effectively. In the light of corporate failures, the same regulators now require

[46] Van Opstal, D. (2006). Cutter IT journal May 2006, Cutter International LLC.

organizations to demonstrate how such results were achieved, to ensure it was not through luck.

Further, management needs to develop a risk management vision and strategy based upon the risk environment and stockholder's risk appetite. The overall strategy for risk management should include the risk management philosophy and organizational responsibility. A case may be made for the existence of a continuum with two different policy choices as the ends, ranging from a highly centralized 'controller' model (such as financial institutions) to a highly decentralized and autonomous risk policy (such as large corporations e.g. Fortune 500 companies).

Companies can attain significant competitive advantage from superior risk competencies. These include risk processes, culture, incentives, training and organization. For example, compare financial services and banking, to stable industries, such as food, and it can be shown that companies are more accepting of the need to reconsider risk management holistically. Regulation and globalization are drivers for companies to shift from an 'avoid risk' culture to a 'think risk' one.

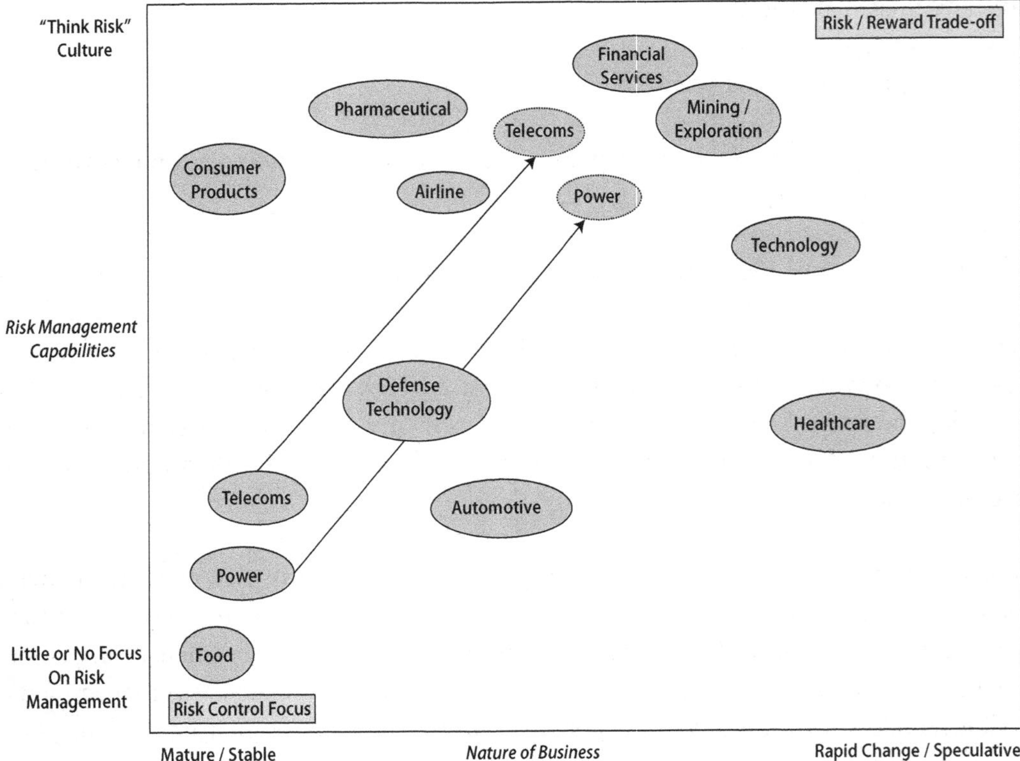

Fig. 7.4 Risk Cultures and Attitudes

Most companies are exposed to more than one type of risk, but many fail to recognize and manage the relationship between different types of risk. Furthermore, actions taken to address one type of risk have the potential to increase exposure in other areas.

Companies vary in their management of risk management sophistication, from poor to benchmark best practice. The differences range from simple risk assessment and a segregation between risk management and shareholder value, to consistent measurement across risks, to linking risks and returns. At the high end of the spectrum, companies are able to demonstrate the strategic inter-relationship between risks, returns and shareholder value.

It has been claimed by academics that, in order to create competitive advantage via risk management, each company must vary its risk management style according to their strategy, and that a failure to do so will result in them lagging behind the competition. However, there is also a strong argument in favor of implementing a common risk management framework that is able to deliver protection for the company against catastrophic losses and support superior risk returns performance and shareholder value growth.[47]

Were these propositions to hold true, organizations which vary according to business/product lines, geographical differences in fields of operation, and information technology use, would still be able to draw upon such common frameworks. A generally accepted methodology is illustrated below and has been applied across other, but related disciplines, such as business continuity and project management.

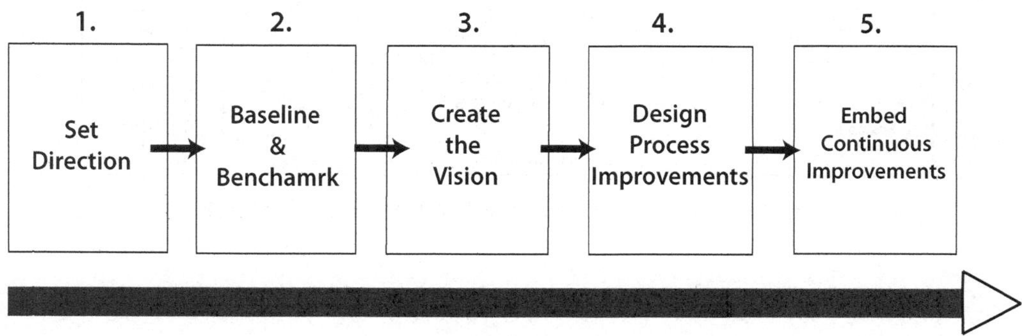

Fig. 7.5 Structured Risk Management Methodology

[47] Clarke, J., and Varma, S. (1999). Strategic Risk Management: the New Competitive Edge. *Long Range Planning*, Vol.32, No.4, pp 414 – 424.

Step 1. ***Set Direction***

This involves developing an understanding of both the company's and its stakeholders' risk concerns and in identifying the major areas of risk, such as operations, enterprise, events, and market risks. The key objective is to identify and aggregate the risks facing the enterprise and the risk issues perceived by management and stakeholders. This generally begins with a thorough review of the infrastructure, decision-making channels and operating systems. The risk appetites and cultures of the management and stakeholders are identified. Risks are prioritized through looking at the stake, the uncertainty and the quality of risk controls and processes already in place.

As an example of how an organization might map its' major areas of risk, the diagram below illustrates the case for a banking organization:

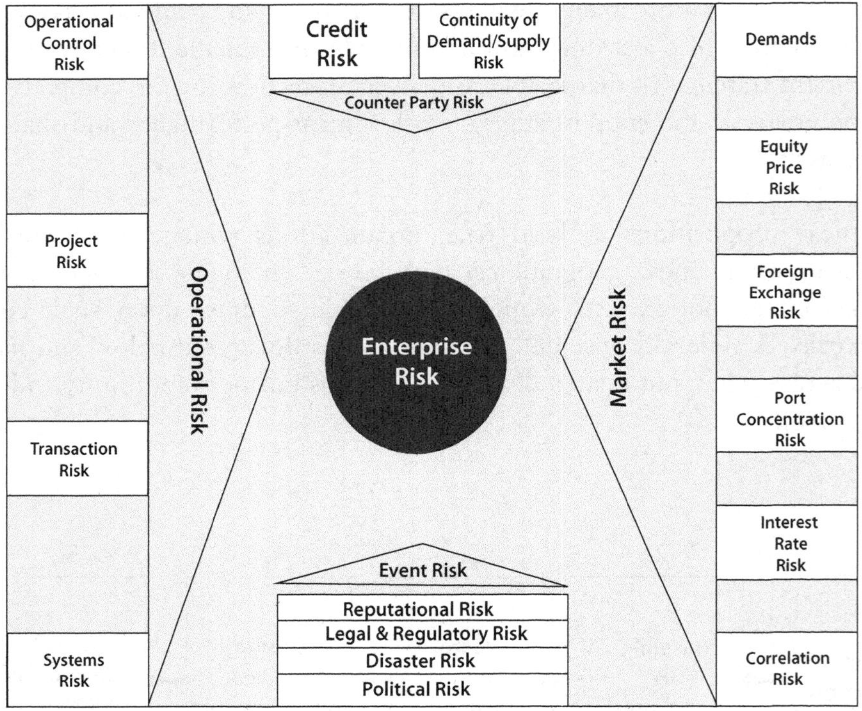

Fig. 7.6 Example of Mapping Major Areas of Banking Risk

Step 2. ***Baseline and Benchmark***

Major risk elements and priorities are quantified, risk drivers are analyzed and the current processes mapped. For some operational risks such as safety and technology risks, quantification may require assumptions to be made. Risk processes and risk performance are benchmarked against global best practice.

Whilst a common framework emphasizes the importance of benchmarking, and recognizes that technology risk quantification requires assumptions to be made, it falls short of recognizing the specificity of risks and in particular those embodied within computer network operations.

Step 3. ***Create the Vision***

The vision of management should be to scan the environment and identify quantitative and qualitative opportunities and threats and to determine the most appropriate response, depending upon stakeholders risk sensitivity. A risk management vision is created, comprising the three key elements of measuring, managing and monitoring.

This stage proposes a stage of environmental scanning, but rather than in the context of acquiring knowledge, it focuses instead upon the creation of a management vision based upon the threat landscape.

Step 4. ***Design Process Improvements***

Based upon the data gathered in the earlier steps, management decides on the most appropriate improvement options. This includes designing processes and documentation policies. Designing process changes occurs in four areas:

- Strategy and policy changes: a clear risk management strategy must be articulated by top management in the visioning phase and this is converted to a risk management policy document and training plan in the design phase.

- Management endorsement and commitment provides a mandate for the risk management program. Review of the organizational structures that will support risk management by management is also required.

- Risk measurement changes need designing. Tools to facilitate this task need crafting. An example is a type of dashboard that allows top management to be apprised of the status of all risks.

- Design changes must also focus on the operations and systems of the company, including changes to the IT infrastructure, internal controls and operating guidelines.

Step 5. ***Implement Change***

Implementation requires the involvement and commitment of senior management and employees. The working teams responsible for enterprise-wide change must be balanced in their composition and include corporate staff, risk experts for complex risk areas, process champions and line managers. The entire program must be driven by a management committee made up of key decision makers from across the enterprise.

Similarly, the descriptions of the further stages within the framework align with the best practice guidelines within the standards. As such, with risk management frameworks espoused by regulatory and international standards organizations concurring as to the optimal approach to risk management, it would be logical to expect that most major organizations would have such structures in place.

Process implementation is normally undertaken in steps, with a focus upon the development of a common risk management language understood by all. Training and communication are an essential element of roll-out.

Step 6. *Embed Continuous Improvements*

Continuous improvements must be embedded; compliance is monitored, and results measured against plans; risk review programs institutionalized; best practice tracked; processes and procedures updated; returns measured against market expectations.

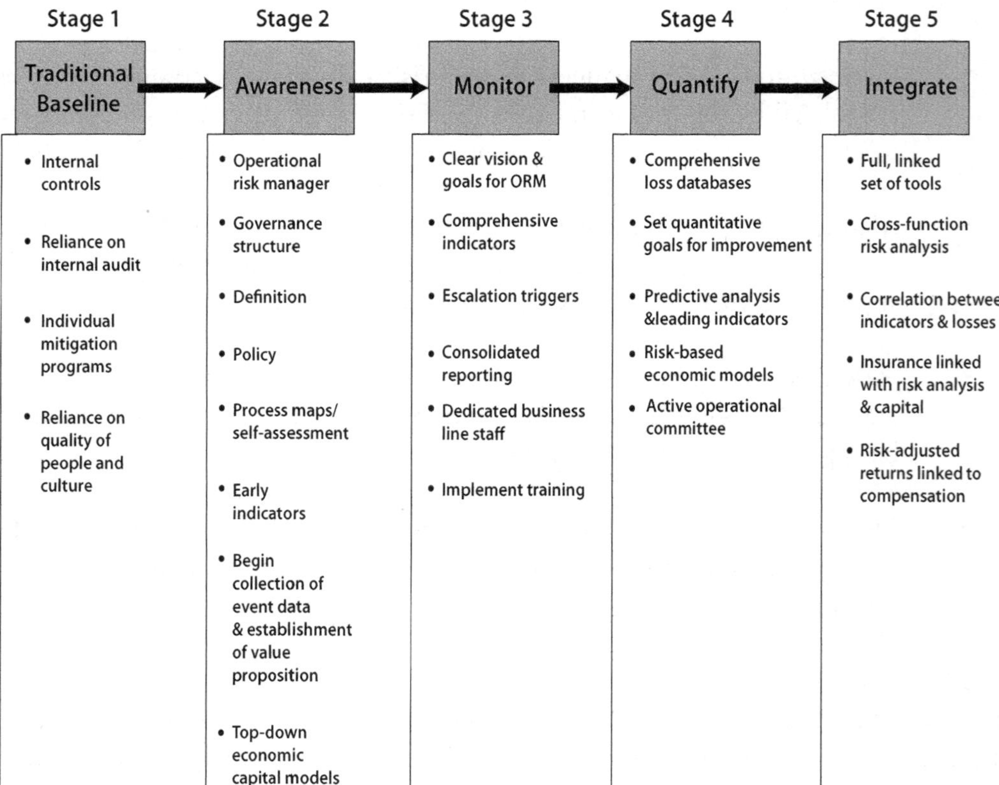

Fig. 7.7 Operational Risk Stages

Risk management generally helps people reach a consensus and make better informed decisions leading to quantifiable results. Worldwide legislative changes and newer regulations for businesses such as the Sarbanes Oxley Act 2002 have made companies more focused upon risk management.

Further, enterprise risk management (ERM), which provides a framework for analyzing and confronting risks, is a practice now widely accepted by business managers. In the present environment, board members and senior managers view risk management as an increasingly important priority, with the need to respond to corporate governance requirements driving this, along with understanding strategic and operating risks.

Where enterprise risk management is not present, reasons for this being the case have been the cost and time required, along with competing priorities within organizations. Additionally, it has also been proposed that the true reason is that the benefits of ERM are not universally accepted and such a lack of consensus is the true reason for a lack of adoption.[48]

Companies tend to commence risk management programs by measuring operating risks, before they contemplate strategic risks. The reason for this approach is that financial risks are quantifiable. Strategic risks, by comparison, provide *'what if'* scenarios giving directional guidelines or indicators as to a risk's likelihood, its potential impact and how critical it is to a company.

In addition to this, the strategic risk management process assists in the communication of risk, ensuring that managers understand the same risk is often identified differently throughout a company. Senior managers' perspectives are heavily influenced by their own unit's work and often disagree when trying to determine the key risks. However, an ERM program gives them the opportunity to define risks along the same parameters and this can then be used in the prioritization process.

Operational Risk

Taking risk management as a discipline that derives competitive advantage for all businesses, and operational risk management as a sub-set, it is logical that the strategic management now has operational risk management as a distinct internal function with its own process, structure, tools and measures.

---

[48] Obuchowski, J. (2006). The Strategic Benefits of Managing Risk. *MIT Sloane Management Review,* Spring Vol.47 No.3. 6-7.

The creation of operational risk management programs has been driven by a combination of management commitment, need for an understanding of enterprise-wide risks, a perceived increase in exposure to operational risk and risk events, and regulatory interest. To lead this operational risk management initiative a new organization model has emerged over the past few years, with the Head of Operational Risk, reporting to the Chief Risk Officer. The role is to develop and implement the operational risk framework and consult to the lines of business.

A framework for operational risk management has also emerged, consisting of a set of integrated processes, tools, and mitigation strategies. While each company may have evolved in its own manner, a five-stage of development of an operational risk management framework has been developed by the banking sector as a whole, for example, which has in turn been driven by the regulatory frameworks within which they must operate. Similarly, exogenous factors specific to other sectors/geographies may lead to a general acceptance of an operational risk framework; the nuclear sector being one such example.

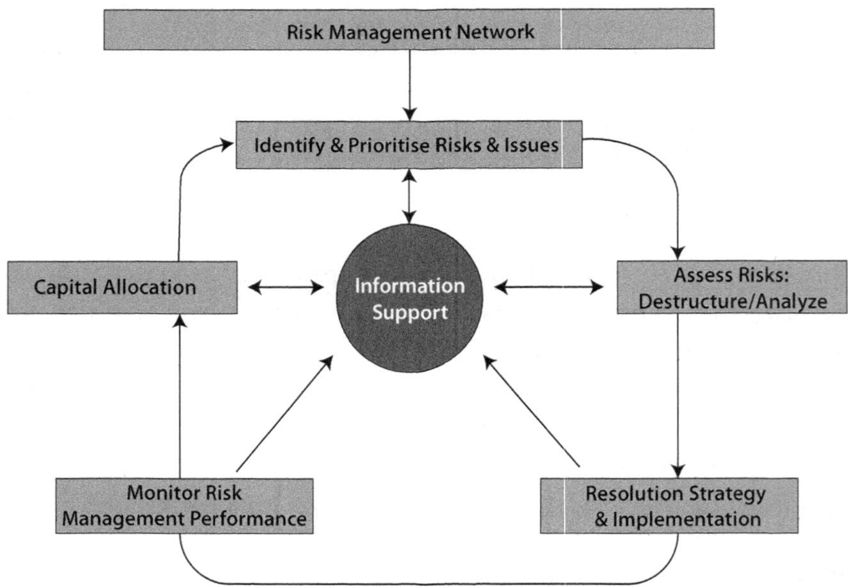

Fig. 7.8 Typical Operational Risk Cycle

It can be seen from the above diagram that the elements and requisite information support that underpin the frameworks previously proposed are the same. For the banking sector, there is an additional step of capital allocated to operational risks, (although this can also be the case for all sectors reviewing their capital allocation policies).

For most organizations, it is still the business units that are primarily responsible for taking and managing operational risk on a day-to-day basis. While the trend for specific risks is towards increasing centralization, such as market risk and credit risk in the case of the banking sector for example, operational risk by its nature is decentralized.

It is claimed that there are three generic organization models for operational risk management.[49] The selection of any one of these three models is determined by the culture of the organization rather than the type of institution. One model has a Head Office operational risk function, the second has a dedicated but decentralized support, and the third has Internal Audit playing a lead role in operational risk management. The Head Office operational risk approach is the trend that continues to gain the global widest acceptance

The Head of Operational risk reports to the Chief Risk Officer. There is also a typically small unit (less than five members of Head Office staff) complemented by staff dedicated to supporting individual business units, as part of either the business units or the corporate function, but in either case, operating under a common framework.

Other aspects of the model are additional organizational units that play important roles: the Board of Directors is taking a more active interest in reviewing operational risk policies and major issues. Operational Risk Committees are being established to heighten awareness and prioritize resources. Other Risk Related functions (e.g., Information Technology, Legal, Compliance, Human Resources) have responsibility for specific operational risk issues.

The Head Office operational risk function is responsible for development of firm-wide operational risk policies, framework and methodologies, and advising the business units. In this emerging model, the most common responsibilities for this new function are:

- Determine operational risk policies and definition
- Develop and deploy common tools
- Establish indicators
- Assess benefits of programs
- Analyze linkages to credit and market risk
- Consolidate cross-enterprise information

In addition, they focus on cross-enterprise operational risk management initiatives such as developing economic capital methodologies and building loss databases. They

[49] PriceWaterhouseCoopers, UK. Growing Basel Data. 2001 Publication.

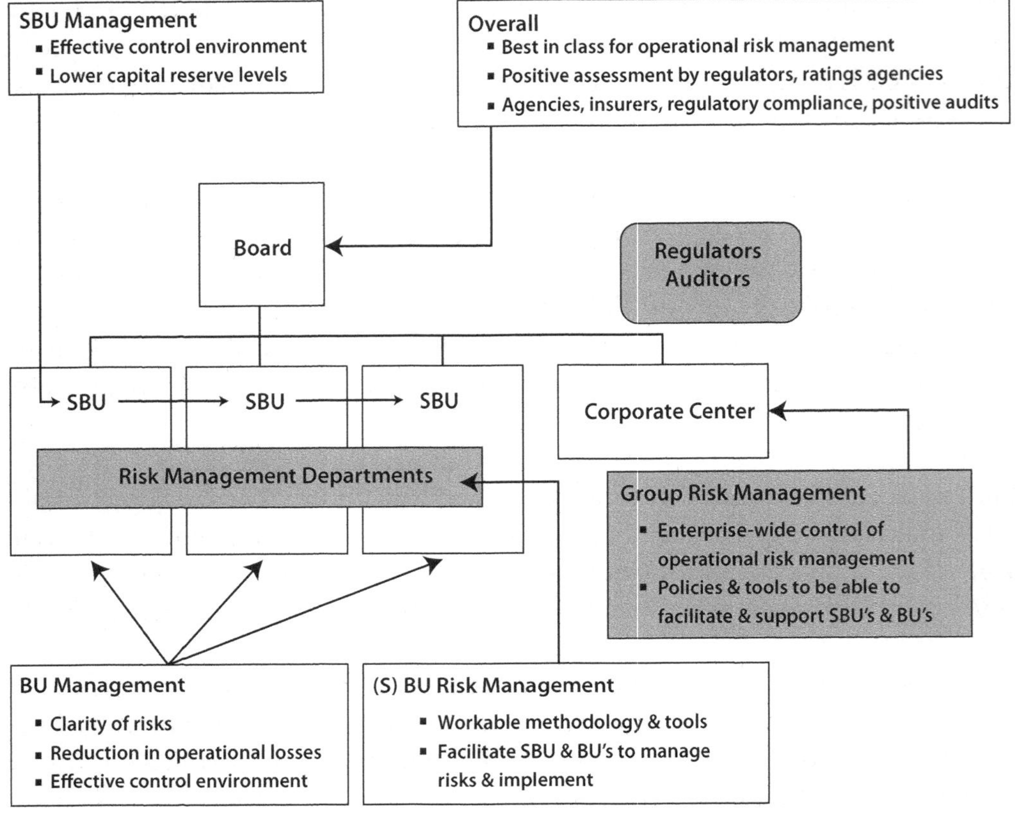

Fig. 7.9 Operational Risk Program Organizational Structure

are also charged in some instances with the management of the firm's portfolio of operational risks.

Depending on the relationship with the business units, they may consult or participate in operational risk management projects with business units. There are a variety of standalone tools that companies are using to manage operational risk. Operational risk management units develop sets of tools for the identification and assessment of operational risk. Individual firms use a wide variety of techniques, but most primarily use five principal tools: risk and self-assessment, risk mapping, risk indicators, escalation triggers and loss event database. However the gap between what most firms want to achieve and what they are able to achieve remains significant. As a consequence, operational risk measurements are not generally used to drive economic decision-making.

As a result of this, a diversity of approaches may be applied along a continuum between top-down and more risk based bottom-up approaches. These methodologies often rely on actual data, can quantify the level of exposure to each type of risk at the business line level, and react to changes in the control environment and actual operational risk results. Since no single approach is satisfactory most firms currently use multiple methodologies to provide a result.

The Emergence of an Operational Risk Framework

Consolidating information from a number of sources, the following summarizes the framework for operational risk that has emerged, consisting of a set of integrated processes, tools, and mitigation strategies. There are six areas to be addressed within the discipline:

1. *Strategy.* Risk management starts with the overall strategies and objectives of the institution and the subsequent goals for individual business units, products, or managers. This is followed by identification of the associated inherent risks in the strategy and objectives. Both hazards – negative events (e.g., a major loss that would have a significant impact on earnings), and opportunities (e.g., new products that depend on taking operational risk) are considered. As a result, a firm can set a risk appetite – specifically, what risks the company understands, will take, and will manage versus those that should be transferred to others or eliminated. It is the basis for decision-making and a reference point for the organization.

2. *Risk Policies.* Risk strategy is complemented by operational risk management policies, which are a formal communication to the organization as a whole on the approach to, and importance of, operational risk management. Policies will typically include a definition of operational risk, the organization approach and related roles and responsibilities, key principles for management, and a high-level discussion of information and related technology.

3. *Risk Management Process.* This sets out the overall procedures for operational risk management:

    - Controls – Definition of internal controls, or selection of alternate mitigation strategy, such as insurance, for identified risks.
    - Assessment – Programs to ensure that controls and policies are being followed and determine the level of severity. These may include process flows, self-assessment programs, and audit programs.
    - Measurement – A combination of financial and non-financial measures,

risk indicators, escalation triggers, and economic capital to determine current risk levels and progress toward goals.

- Reporting – Information for management to increase awareness and prioritize resources.

4. *Risk Mitigation.* These are specific controls or programs designed to reduce the exposure, frequency or severity of an event or the impact of an event or eliminate (or transfer) an element of operational risk. Examples include business continuity planning, IT security, compliance reviews, project management, and merger integration and insurance.

5. *Operations Management.* This refers to the day-to-day processes, such as front- and back-office functions, technology, performance improvement, management reporting, and people management. Every process has a component of operational risk management embedded in it.

6. *Culture.* There is nearly always a balance between formal policies and culture, or the values of the people in the organization. In operational risk, cultural aspects such as communication, the "tone at the top", clear ownership of each objective, training, performance measurement, and knowledge sharing all help set the expectations for sound decision making. In addition, the integration with market and credit risk in an enterprise-wide risk management framework is noted, as well as alignment with the needs of the stakeholders.

Enterprise Resilience and I.T. Risk Management

Drivers of earnings, definitions of risk, underlying risk interdependencies and ways of managing them have changed for many organizations. Enterprises have previously regarded risk as the downside hazard to their financial portfolios and have concentrated their efforts on managing this. However, managing operational risks can create competitive advantage, since it ensures an organization-wide understanding of the risks posed to the business and, in so doing, develop a level of enterprise resilience.[50]

The need for developing enterprise resilience arises from the expansion of the boundaries of organizations and thus the level of vulnerabilities to which it is exposed, together with enhanced opportunities for gaining competitive advantage. It is especially relevant in the current environment where the need for greater security, a global

[50] Delurey, M., Newfrock, J., and Starr, R, (2003). *Strategy and Business* Spring.

economic slowdown, increased dependence upon global financial, operational and trading infrastructure have resulted in previously unfamiliar risk exposures.

Earnings consistency and reliable earnings growth are the key factors for the ongoing operations and developments of listed commercial organizations. With high levels of earnings volatility come reduced valuations on stock, with consistency premiums being set against poor performers in this respect. The ongoing impact of this is an increase in the cost of capital for that particular enterprise, allied to diminished access to it.

Traditionally, risks have not been perceived in the context of key earnings drivers, but rather in broad categories, each of which was managed in a functionally isolated manner. Rather than process owners being responsible, the risk categorization reflected the board structure, with financial risks falling to the CFO, the operational risks to the , the technology risks to the , without a linking of the parts to create a whole in order for this to support an organization's strategic objectives.

Networks have been one of the major advances in business during the last half century, with the previous vertically integrated organization giving way to the networked enterprise. However, whilst the economic and organizational impact of networks is known, little is understood or researched into their vulnerabilities. With an increasingly fast and agile enterprise being facilitated by networks, so the well-timed methods of operations create a greater risk of discontinuity impact from a network failure.

Within the list of possible impacts arising from such disruption of operations fall items are reputational risk, impact on customer habits, legal and credit standing, earnings performance and, consequently, shareholder value. This linking of areas of impact from a single event can be viewed as the consequence of unanticipated risk exposure across an extended enterprise that is beyond the organization's direct control.

This interdependence risk has a scale and impact that is a function of the degree of importance of the dislocated entity and the degree of its integration into an extended enterprise. Where a dislocation spills over from a single affected enterprise to others within the same or related sectors, then there can be said to be a lack of systemic resilience.

Risk management models have not kept pace with the shift from centralized to networked organizations, with most enterprise risk management programs relying upon "point solutions" which attempt to moderate risks by "hardening" potentially vulnerable spots against attacks. However, an organization cannot simultaneously harden all the nodes within its network; threats will migrate from a hardened node to a more vulnerable one.

In the early 1990s, the U.S. Department of Defense recognized that its fighting doctrine of *"information superiority"* increased its dependence on networked communications systems and it transitioned from the traditional risk management technique of hardening every node, to a *"defense in depth"* model which uses a layered approach to security. However, in the commercial field, where the same threats exist to systems that provide business continuity, there has been no real shift to the same model.

A conventional enterprise risk management program provides a partial framework and facilitates a focus for executives to enable identification of potentially weak points from low probability catastrophic risks. However, they do not prepare the organization for discontinuities that can threaten or destroy earnings drivers, since they do not take into account interdependencies across vertical and horizontal corporate operations and thus tend to underestimate the range and severity of risks. Network discontinuities can accumulate exponentially and result in loss of control and levels of loss without precedent.[51]

By contrast, enterprise resilience planning seeks to prepare the organization to protect the entire entity against new, avoidable risks that are the by-product of interdependencies. Eight fundamental questions have been proposed by academics as a means of creating the thought processes to think of all possibilities:

1. Are the complexity of the extended enterprise and major earnings drivers across it transparent?
2. Are the interdependencies understood and interdependence risks identified?
3. What programs are in place to ensure the viability of earnings drivers?
4. Are these programs fully aligned with corporate strategy and objectives, and is there an understanding of the trade-offs within these programs?
5. Does the organization know what is spent on resilience?
6. How good is the organization's situational awareness (i.e. is there sufficient business intelligence, internal and external, and is it directed to the appropriate parties?)
7. Is such intelligence distilled in a timely enough fashion to react to it?

[51] Hamilton, S., (1999). The Barings Collapse (A): *Breakdowns in Organization Culture and Management.* International Institute for Management Development, Lausanne, Switzerland, 21.06.99.

8. Who is accountable for resilience and how are decisions and progress measured?

Enterprise risk planning commences with the identification of the greatest risks across the enterprise, including interdependencies, and then generates a targeted program, integrated with overall corporate strategy for mitigating these risks and is part of an ongoing process, based upon strategic priorities of the organization. By understanding the risks, their relative correlations and interdependencies and where they impact on the organization, management is able to then make educated trade-off decisions when they develop their risk mitigation strategies, including traditional measurements of return of investment of specific actions as mitigants.

Three stages of an enterprise resilience program

There are three generic steps for an enterprise to commence a resilience program:[52]

- *Diagnose enterprise-wide risk and interdependencies:* an organization must first define its extended enterprise and determine the earnings drivers. Once this is achieved, a transparent and consolidated view of risks across the extended enterprise can be developed and a baseline view of risk mitigation plans and spending can also be developed. Risk mitigation strategies, prioritization and gap analysis will follow, allowing identification of quick-hit opportunities associated with critical risks that management must address in the short-term.

- *Adapt the corporate strategy and operating model:* the enterprise should use a cost benefit analysis that links cross-functional risk mitigation planning to corporate strategy. Equally important, the and board must adopt a common risk management and resiliency vocabulary that is comprehensible and intuitive to all, enabling executives and directors to understand a company's risk exposure and o make trade-off decisions in implementing risk mitigation strategies whilst pursuing strategic objectives.

- *Endure increased risk and complexity:* this step involves developing an organizational structure that oversees and integrates business intelligence and risk monitoring for the extended enterprise; has the analytical tools and support capabilities to improve decision making and responses to risk as it changes; can measure risk mitigation with clearly defined benchmarks; can

[52] Shrader, R. W., and McConnell, M. (2002). Security and Strategy in the Age of Discontinuity: A Management Framework for the post-9/11 World. *Strategy and Business*, First Quarter 2002.

monitor the organization's risk profile; and can implement best practice risk mitigation solutions.

As an initial step to building enterprise resilience, a comprehensive *three-phase audit* can be applied to an organization:

1. Enterprise Topology and Earnings Driver Classification

The organization should identify its key earnings drivers and their associated risks by mapping the extended enterprise and drawing a consolidated and transparent picture of how the company organizes its systems, processes and relationships internally and externally to generate revenues. It must distinguish the earnings drivers themselves, the business processes, capabilities and technologies that support them, and their vulnerabilities.

This phase pre-supposes that organizations have their business processes fully documented and mapped. Where this is not the case, it may be that this omission precludes organizations from achieving enterprise resilience and a program of process analysis is required as a pre-requisite. Most organizations will have undertaken some form of mapping as part of their business continuity planning.

Resilience Profiling and Baselining

The organization should use modeling tools and best practices in enterprise design to produce initial snapshots of the "resilience profile" for each essential aspect of the organization: financial operations, technology, personnel and security. The existing profile should be compared with an optimal level of resilience in each of the operations.

Such activities lend support to the view that environmental scanning is a key activity to acquiring information external to the firm in the transfer and use of existing knowledge. There still remain, however, issues relating to the availability of relevant sector data to enable benchmarking and baselining of all business operations by organizations.

The organization's current risk mitigation plans, procedures and costs, including business continuity planning, are examined during this phase. The intent is to determine how the current programs and the spending on them align with the earnings drivers identified in Phase 1. Both implicit and explicit costs should be included, such as those for marketing for damage limitation should a failure occur.

A critical part of this phase is the development of an interdependency map to identify such risks across the entire organization, for example changes to regulations may affect earnings drivers, as would changes in supplier relationships and other externalities. The Baselining exercise seeks to understand how corporate strategies will influence earnings drivers in the future. From the exercise, gaps between existing risk mitigation programs and identifiable needs are revealed, allowing management to visualize weaknesses and strengths in the organization's current risk exposure and resilience posture and its fit to the enterprise's risk appetite set by executive management.

Resilience Strategy

The last phase of the audit aims to develop a new resilience program based upon the analyses of the organization's earnings-related risk mitigation requirements. The most critical gaps between existing risk management programs and the optimal profile are isolated. After the financial commitment to close the gaps is determined, a cost-benefit analysis will facilitate the rationalization of investment needs.

The cost assessment examines business resilience from three perspectives: people, operations (process and technology) and interdependencies. After setting the gap-closing priorities and developing the full risk mitigation strategy, the executive team should agree on a migration path and gain the board's agreement on the timetable for the institution of near-term and longer-term resilience goals. Business intelligence and information sharing will assist in the development of greater situational awareness, thereby requiring the organization to undertake environmental scanning and possibly to enter into its' competitive environment and influence where relevant.

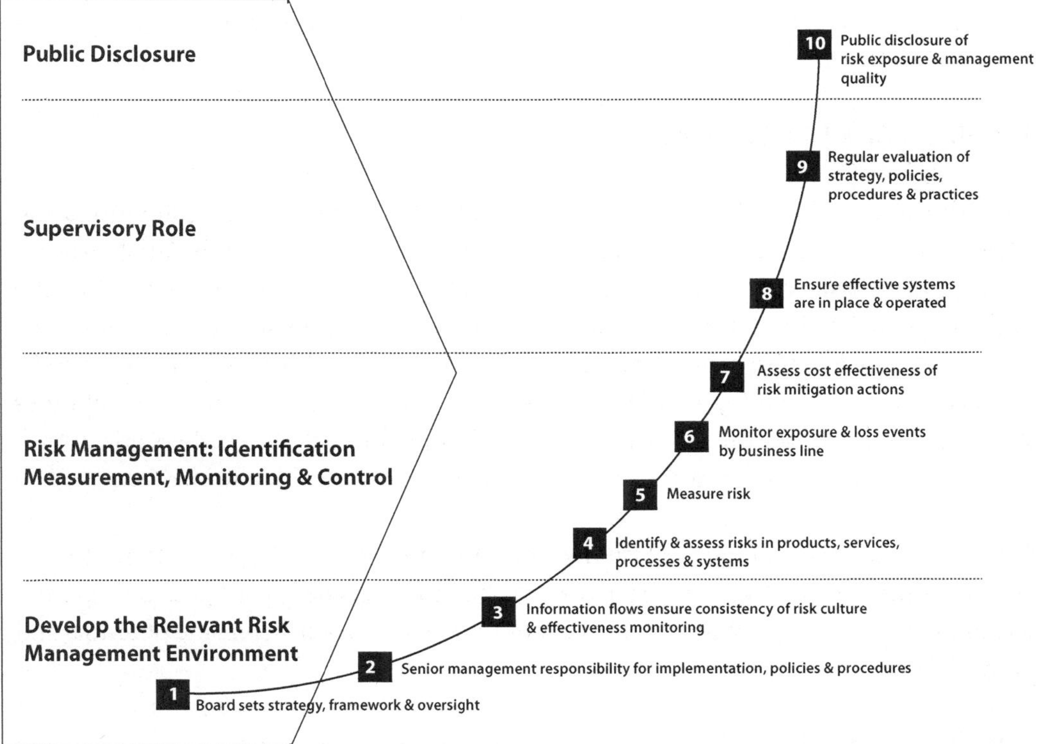

Fig. 7.10 Enterprise Risk and Resilience Phasing

Through adopting a more integrated approach to risk management – one that links strategy to enterprise resilience and business continuity planning, using diagnostic tools and decision support capabilities – organizations are more able to establish a more effective, continuous and consistent methodology for protecting the enterprise from internal and external risks. Through this method, a steady stream of information to the senior management about the organization's vulnerability of earnings drivers can lead to enhanced corporate governance and decision making.

Risk Management Measurement Methods

Many methods of measuring an enterprise's operational and business risk have emerged:

- proxy, analogue or surrogate method
- earnings volatility method
- loss modeling method
- direct estimation or scenario method

The first three consistently run into data problems that reduce either their effectiveness or certainly their freedom from the influence of subjective judgment.

Individual Risk Distributions

At whatever chosen level of detail, a range of individual risks need to be identified and quantified by the relevant line managers with facilitation by independent risk experts. Each of these risks represents a range of possible outcomes. For instance, a broadly defined risk of "computer system failure" would include the possibilities of mainframe computer centre failure caused by, for example, both fire and hardware malfunctions, and also the risk of failure, or even of a local PC crashing. Each of these possibilities has a different impact on the organization – hence for each risk a theoretical "risk distribution" showing the various impacts and their envisaged likelihood.

For operational risk, a range of risk distributions are observed for the different types of risk. Some competitive business risks have potential upside (profit possibilities) and a roughly normal shape, whereas most event risks hand have little upside potential and show a form of exponential distribution.

The individual risk distributions can be seen as either the simple range of future outcome possibilities or as a combination of two underlying distributions: one reflecting the likelihood of a loss event, the other reflecting the severity of loss when one does occur.

A narrowly defined event risk such as a mainframe or data centre failure might be considered to be best modeled by a *credit risk* style approach, while a business risk or broadly defined event risk would seem to be best modeled by a *market risk* approach, given that there is always some outcome.

In order to gain an operational risk quantification that can be combined with credit and market risk measures, to facilitate an overall risk management program to be undertaken, a consistent timeframe for assessing impact without assuming effective remedial management action is required, with this generally a one-year period.

The Loss Modeling Method

This method collects actual loss data and uses it to derive empirical distributions for its risks. These empirical risk distributions are then used to calculate an unexpected loss amount needing to be protected by a capital buffer. The unexpected loss can be theoretically calculated to any desired target confidence level.

This is typically thought of as a "bottom-up" method, but can be done at any level of detail with the loss types able to be defined narrowly or broadly. This method is seen as attractive as it endeavors to anchor itself in objective loss data. However it faces a number of critical problems, particularly if an entity has a goal of a broad measure of risk:

1. The need to collect sufficient data to cover the range of experience that a risk capital reserve buffer would be expected to cover.

2. The assumption that the past is a good predictor of the future.

3. The need to capture full economic losses (including opportunity losses) if the company wishes to pursue a holistic broad loss measure.

4. The need to collect loss data on a consistent basis.

5. The need to have a consistent and clear demarcation between different risk types to ensure that losses are appropriately grouped and avoiding double counting.

6. The difficulty in using this method to project the capital requirements for a

future product, technology structure or business strategy where loss data may not exist.

7. The delay between impact on the risk capital reserves measure and the actual risk management activities in the entity.

A method to overcome the insufficiency of loss data is to collect industry loss data, with scaling to the size of the entity. As in the case for many sectors however, with global competition being the norm, many industries seek to retain as much proprietary information as possible and as such, sectoral loss information tends to be extremely scarce. Additionally, although it is clearly beneficial to learn from the experience of others, this supplementary method has additional problems:

- The need to ensure that a consistent treatment and grouping of losses occurs despite their different sources.

- The need to analyze the losses sufficiently to nominate the appropriate scaling factors to be used to make them relevant to other entities.

- The problem that even total industry experience for a period does not ensure that the data covers the range of experience that a risk capital reserve buffer would be expected to cover.

- The judgment layer required to deal with these problems overshadows the apparent objective nature of this method.

The Direct Estimation Method

The direct estimation method relies on collaborative line manager judgments to estimate a risk distribution for the risks they run. It explicitly incorporates a layer of subjective judgment based on available loss data and other relevant factors, but these subjective judgments are generally at a lower level of significance than the judgments involved in the other measurement methods. It also provides a forward-looking quantification of risk, with the effects of changes in business mix or strategy or structure, readily included in the direct estimation judgment process.

The direct estimation method involves the selection of a risk distribution shape that is appropriate for the risk (generally allocated by default to the risk category) and then anchoring this risk distribution shape with a quantification of the impact of one or more scenarios (which can include actual risk incidents or near misses). This estimated risk distribution can be refined based on subsequent experience (or as appropriate loss data becomes available).

The detail at which risks are estimated (or losses grouped in the loss modeling method) is at the organization's discretion – the level of detail required depends on the level of detail sought in the subsequent risk/return numbers.

Some granularity or level of detail has to be chosen and at any level some bundling of risk types is inevitable. For example, the granularity might be the risk of flood to a state's branch network or it might be the risk of all natural disasters to the organization as a whole – either way the risk encompasses a range of possible risk events. The decision needs to be made on the level of discrimination sought for the results.

Direct estimation does not require everyone to duplicate estimates of the same risks. The appropriate experts who can also define which of the available indicators would be the best proxies of the risk's incidence may be able to estimate common risks. Staff numbers may be suitable for some risks, a number of certain types of transactions for others, etc.

Estimating Individual Risks

The direct estimation method integrates the definition of the risk and the agreed timeframe and confidence level with the judgments of risk assessors and relevant line managers.

The business line managers explore with risk assessors some known or hypothetical extreme loss scenarios in order to quantify their full economic impact and their likelihood of occurrence. Their combined experience is also used to choose or confirm an appropriate shape for the risk distribution. This allows the risk's quantification to be extrapolated beyond the individual scenarios considered to the other confidence levels.

This estimation method is both an interactive and iterative process. The first estimated risk distribution might not stand close consideration, leading to revised scenario quantification or a different underlying distribution shape being chosen.

Underlying loss data is critical to support this confirmation process, but is not often available, at least at first. Moreover, economic loss is much broader than accounting loss, and "extreme loss" incidents may have occurred in other similar organizations. The use of documented external risk incidents is important in validating the "extreme loss" impacts estimated.

Given the reputational damage that occurs when an extreme loss event impacts on an organization, this validating of an estimated loss distribution shape remains problematic for just about every sector.

Controls and Insurance Mitigation

Controls and insurance play a significant part in reducing the likelihood of a risk event, or the amount of loss should one occur. They also have a material cost. One of the drivers of measuring risk is to support a more rational analysis of the costs and benefits of controls and insurance.

At the outset, clarity of the *extreme loss* scenario and its economic impact and likelihood being estimated before or after the effects of controls should be present. In most cases the scenario will be based on experience or loss data that occurred with some level of control in place. In such cases it is important to avoid double counting by reducing the assessed impact further. But when there are new well-defined controls in place that have not been assumed, it is equally important to ensure that the advantages of these controls are also captured as an offset to the assessed risk.

The mathematics of the mitigation offered by controls is not straightforward. A distinction needs to be made between those controls that reduce the likelihood of occurrence and those that minimize the impact should the event occur. These need to be adjusted for separately. The precise mathematics varies with the underlying risk distributions.

Insurance is also a mitigant. Judgment is required to assess how much of the risk's economic impact is in fact covered under the insurance policy. Loss of future business through brand damage is increasingly insurable, allied to a trend towards niche products covering some aspects of reputational risk. One of the forms of such cover is that of risk financing, as opposed to a pure insurance contract.

Group and Segment Risk Distributions

The individual risk residual distributions are the foundations for building a risk distribution for a segment of the organization's business. This segment could be for a product group, a customer segment, a department, and a subsidiary or for an organization as a whole.

A target segment of the organization might have several risks attached to it, with some of these clearly belonging to the target segment only. Others may attach to part of the entity that affects the target segment, for example, a risk that attaches to the organization's data centre operations would impact on all the organization's segments that rely on legal processes. The proportion of this overhead risk that should attach to the target segment can be estimated directly or can be calculated by reference to some relevant statistic, for instance in this case the share of total data centre operation time used.

Risk distribution curves are derived for groupings of risks from a segment risk distribution based upon the underlying individual operational risk distributions. The segment *Expected Loss* might be simply achieved by adding the expected losses of all the underlying distributions (weighted by the appropriate share where a risk covers more than the business in question). But the process is more complicated when it comes to estimating segment *Unexpected Losses* to high confidence levels.

For example if a segment has two underlying risks, A and B, and A and B's unexpected loss to a 1 in 100 year or 99% confidence level were $10m and $20m respectively, this does not mean that the 1 in 100 year confidence level unexpected loss for the segment is $30m. The likelihood of both extreme 1 in 100 year events occurring in the same year is generally much less likely than 1 in 100.

On the other hand, the organization's unexpected loss is more than $20m; the unexpected loss of the larger underlying risk. A means of aggregating the effects of individual risk distributions into a risk distribution segment that represents some part of the organization that management wish to analyze is required and a Monte Carlo simulation is frequently used to answer this need.

Monte Carlo Simulations

Monte Carlo simulations are used extensively in market risk analyses, generally with historical rates data. As extensive data is available the simulation technique allows correlations between different data series to be taken into account.

In operational risk measurement, Monte Carlo simulations are used differently. They are used to construct empirical risk distributions for segments based on the estimated individual risk distributions for each of the risks associated with that segment.

The main problem with this approach is the unrealistic assumption that each of the underlying individual risks is independent of each other. That is, that the randomly generated result of one risk has no influence, positive or negative, on the results of other risks.

However, in assessing cyber threats and their frequency/probability/ALE, a Monte Carlo model can be of use when combined with other measurements and assessment techniques and models. An example of this is in creating either a capital reserve to cover potential cyber threat losses, or in the pricing of a cyber risk insurance contract. The use of specific models in assessing cyber threats is given in *Chapter 9 – Managing Cyber Threats*.

Operational Risk Correlations

Many operational risks are correlated, and there are large sectors of operational risk that are correlated. This is particularly the case with the adoption of a broad definition of operational risk. In practice most correlations are partial, and many risks might be correlated together, but to different extents. A flexible correlation factor model allows for a hierarchy of correlation factors and for a risk being affected by more than one factor. The principle is that risks that are highly correlated will tend to show the same incident tendencies – extreme loss iteration in one risk will tend to be reflected in similar extreme iterations in highly correlated risks. This automatically feeds into the operational risk measurements at the relevant segment and organization levels.

In operational risk most correlations are initially estimated, either intuitively or based on econometric analysis of the relationships between factors. The subsequent pair wise correlations generated between the risks can be calculated and used as a confirmation of reasonableness.

The difference that correlations make can be substantial, but most would be positive correlations which would tend to increase risk capital reserve calculations. There is less chance of negative correlation assumptions. The equivalent danger in operational risk is to fail to recognize the underlying technological factors that underpin many diverse types of operational and business risk.

Distributing Diversification Benefits

At each level of aggregation within a business, diversification benefits accrue, representing the capacity to leverage the risk capital reserve against a larger range of non-perfectly correlated risks. The residual risk capital reserve attributed to each business segment is critical in determining its shareholder value creation and thus its strategic worth to the enterprise. Error at this point can lead to discouraging better value, creating segments and can encouraging ones that dissipate shareholder value.

Problems start immediately in trying to quantify operational risk, since operational losses are difficult to measure, difficult to assess and difficult to identify the causes because:

- High frequency, low impact losses are not adequately accounted for.
- Low frequency, high impact losses occur so infrequently that an adequate sample is difficult to gather.
- There is no framework available that measures operational risk and aligns risk measures with performance measures, alongside a methodology that measures the diverse sources of operational risk, working in conjunction with a modeling capability that allows management both to predict the level of risk and take actions for those that are controllable.

Measurement methodologies for operational risk must be able to measure two sources of operational risk (variations in the process activities and rare events) and traditional measurement methods do not work well for both. Random, frequent fluctuations are an intrinsic part of operations and add value to the firm. Rare events having large fluctuations occur due to a combination of (possibly extreme) factors.

Causal and Predictive Models

Given that there is an imperative to manage risk in order to increase competitiveness, but that there are weaknesses in quantification techniques, organizations have to utilize existing models for measurement. Current methodologies are used for two distinct purposes:

Causal models for operational risk are used to link fluctuations in performance to their causes. A causal understanding is essential in order to take appropriate action to control and manage risk, because causality is a basis for both action and prediction. Knowing what causes what, gives an ability to intervene and change the environment in order to achieve a state of control.

In the case of network operational risk however, since the main issue is a lack of historical data upon which to develop models of causal understanding, the degree to which organizations are able to intervene may be limited.

Predictive models (such as loss models) often use correlation as a basis for prediction, but actions based upon associations are tentative at best. Causation is different from correlation or constant conjunction, in which two things are associated because they change in unison or are found together. Simple cause and effect relations are known from experience, but more complex situations, such as those embedded within the process of business operations, may not be intuitively obvious from the information at hand.

Loss models for operational risk are predictive, with their function being to measure the effects of losses and provide measures for risk to operations that are not linked to causes. They are needed to account for unexplained losses and to predict them over sustained periods.

Risks in operations together with causality and loss, may be divided into those risks that have assignable causes that can be influenced (controllable risks), and those risks that do not have causal factors that can be explained (uncontrollable risks). Their impact is determined through loss models that analyze extreme values (losses), and use classification instead of causes.

However, uncontrollable does not mean that there are no mitigation strategies that can be implemented to reduce the effects of loss. Additionally, an uncontrollable risk may become controllable if an assignable cause can be found and corrective action is possible. Alongside measurement methods sit the methods organizations use in *mapping* and *profiling* operational risks. These can be labeled as being either top-down or bottom up.

Top-down

Top-down risk profiling or mapping looks at an organization from a corporate perspective, seeking to identify and analyze the risks that exist in each part of the company, extrapolating their impact on each other and the organization as a whole and comprises five primary categories:

Risk identification – looking at the company as a whole, with publicly available information assisting in this area, first identifies risks. This information is then used in brainstorming sessions with key individuals, designed to identify the risks within an organization and produce raw information for the portfolio analysis.

Risk assessment – the results of the risk identification process are then analyzed in terms of probability and severity. Information is often displayed on different matrices or axes representing different levels of frequency and severity for each risk. This attempts to give the results meaning and depth.

Risk profiling – these results are then translated into a risk profile, arranging important risks into "risk families", ranging from high-probability, negligible outcomes, to low-probability disasters. This profile can then be used to set risk mitigation strategy priorities.

Risk quantification – risk families considered suitable for subsequent modeling can be fully assessed in a follow-up process, when actual losses and probabilities are estimated and distributions or confidence limits are added to these estimates. The estimates are typically based on the opinions of several experts combined with any valid loss data available.

Risk consolidation – risks analyzed at divisional or subsidiary level need to be aggregated to the corporate level. This can be a subjective risk-profiling analysis performed by a qualified team or, if sufficient quantification is possible, a mathematical process.

Where relevant data and/or expertise do not exist within the organization, best practice theory specifies that organizations should make reference to such information and knowledge external to the firm. However, best practice highlights that drawing solely upon either a qualitative or quantitative approach is weaker than a combination of the two. It would therefore be expected that organizations would employ both methods. The picture that emerges from such simulations is used to develop strategies to protect the company from loss, or to redesign the corporation around a more appropriate risk profile.

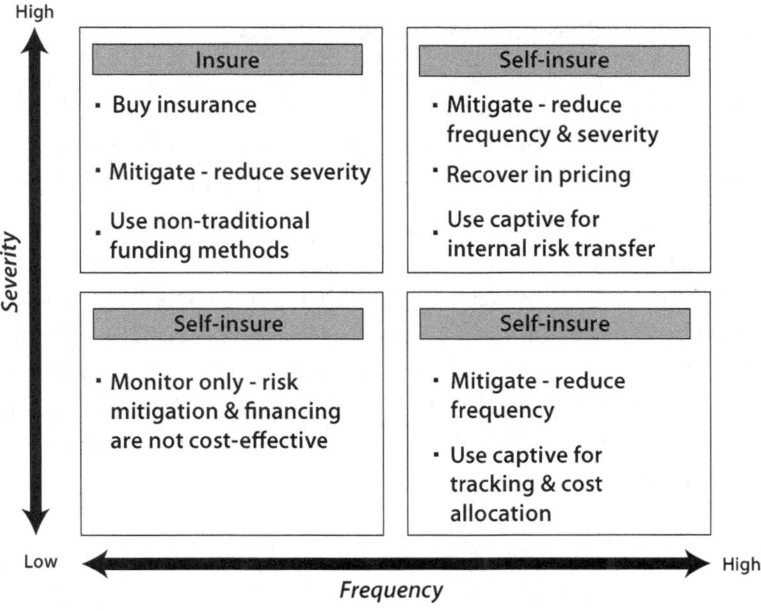

Fig. 7.11 Classical Risk Map

Bottom-up

A bottom-up approach to risk mapping uses an intensive series of shop-floor focus groups to identify, discuss and analyze risks. Selected employees from the participating business units, targeting specific objectives, use the control frameworks to review the controls in place. This data is summarized to produce a board level picture, from which decisions about managing the risk portfolio can be made.

Weaknesses Common to Both Methods

The principal problem with the models described above, is that the quality of the conclusions rests entirely on the quality of the risk data and the ability of the assessment team to interpret it. For loss data and event data, both internal and that available external to the organization, the quality and accuracy is, more often than not, low and therefore introduces a bias into the calculation of the true value at risk within an organization.

Enterprises are generally wary of making data available in any abundance and with limited detailing of losses. The effect of this policy is that companies are unable to use external data sources to validate what are, in effect, primarily qualitative identification, quantification, evaluation and valuation and risk within an organization. Additional problems are generated by reporting formats varying from country to country.

Weaknesses Specifically Related to Cyber Threats

Aside from the known measurement problems afflicting operational risk in general, there are a large number of network-risk specific reasons why existing models and approaches are not suited to network operational risk management. A brief overview of these can be summarized as follows:

- *The list of events* – The list of events that can cause a loss on a single system cannot be listed exhaustively, since there are a potentially infinite number of different attacks. The result is that organizations have a tendency to revert to listing known types of attack and ignoring the remainder, with the consequence that there is then a high probability that attackers will use types within the list.

- *The probability of events* – Research demonstrates that human attackers do not attack in a mode that fits traditional probability distribution functions and as such, most methods are inappropriate for analyzing network attacks.

- *Event Independence* – Multiple simultaneous attacks upon networks are more the norm than not, with multiple attack techniques being employed, as opposed to a single type, resulting in extreme complexity in seeking to model joint probabilities of events related in an unknown manner.

- *Expected loss* – Particularly in the case of insurance loss assessment, there is frequently disagreement as to the actual loss associated with an attack post-event.

- *Mitigation techniques* – As per the number and type of attacks that could be targeted at an organization, so the number and type of mitigation techniques available and relevant to an organization as similarly not quantifiable and listed exhaustively.

- *Reduction in expected loss* – In order to assess the cost effectiveness of each mitigation technique, a figure for reduction in expected loss is required and appropriate models/methodologies that have widespread acceptance as a standard have not as yet emerged.

- *Sensitivity* – Risk analysis is sensitive to details, with a small change in probability or expected loss affecting the choice of one analysis technique over another. Once that technique is selected, it may have cascading effects on subsequent decisions due to the way it changes the mitigation effects of other techniques.

- *Exponentiation for networks* – All of the above issues in risk assessment apply to individual systems, but in the case of networks, there is far great complexity, since each computer within a network may contain or process different information with different value. Further, each could be subjected to different attacks, and each may have different security solutions. These result in combinatory calculations that are complex in the extreme, since each cannot be regarded as independent or combined, but rather each option must be modeled. Further, networking introduces new classes of attack and varying effects upon an organization, leading to different types of losses, and may also substantially alter the expected loss reduction associated with various mitigation options.

In Chapter 9, the various forms of risk identification, analysis, assessment and quantification are addressed. However, regardless of the models used for cyber risk assessment, there is continual evolution of the forms of valuation of such threats as historical data is produced year-on-year. This can be seen as more forms of cyber insurance coverage is offered in various territories as risk carriers feel more confident in their assessment of the portfolios covered. Despite this, the parallel shifts in computing, infrastructure and its' use (such as smartphone, social networking and cloud computing), will require an ongoing effort to best model and value cyber risks for all organizations and regulatory bodies.

Chapter Eight

BUSINESS PROCESS MAPPING, ANALYSIS AND THEIR PROBLEMS

Introduction

This section avoids specific methods for undertaking business process analysis and focuses instead on the analytical skills required for it. The intent is to underline some of the main issues surrounding business process analysis and then to relate them to the specific issues surrounding process analysis.

A number of authors and research institutions on the subject of business process analysis highlight that there is a high degree of subjectivity and that it is an activity that continues to develop in its format, accuracy and methodology.[53] They indicate the following issues relating to the activity as they stand at this time:

- It is not realistic to describe an enterprise by a small number of key business processes: it is more likely that hundreds or thousands are needed, especially in respect of sectors such as telecommunications, banking and financial services.

---

[53] Darnton, G., and Darnton M. (1997). *Business Process Analysis*. International Thompson Business Press. London.

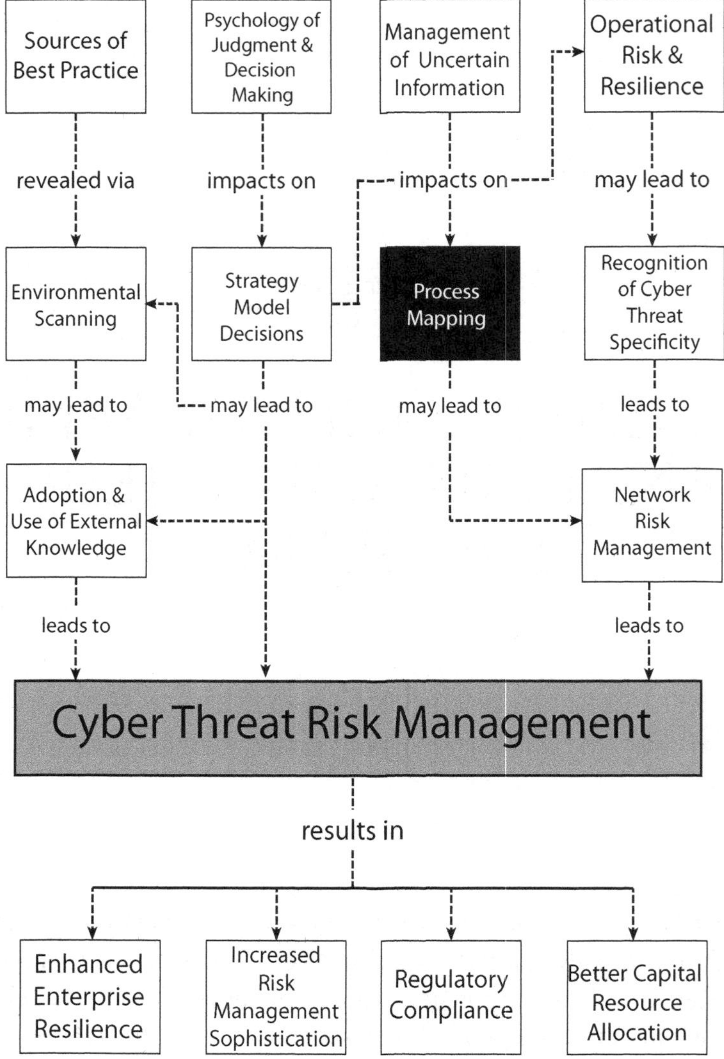

Fig. 8.1 Focus of Chapter 8

- Information technology is not the key enabler of radical business process change, but rather, it is along a much longer line of technical innovation. Radical business process change has accompanied all major technological innovation, not just information technology.

- Despite long-term statements of the priority that should be given to redefine organizations by key business processes, this has still not been truly reflected in the boardroom, where functional and departmental heads rather than process managers are the usual members, that is, there is s till a functional silo mentality prevailing.

- Despite the popularity of graphical methods of analysis and presentation, they are not scalable to manage the complexity of enterprise wide business process description or redesign.

- With ever-increasing volumes of data there is an increasingly strong bias in implemented management information systems towards information attenuation rather than information amplification.

- There remains a mainly monolithic approach to business process analysis, with a bias on information systems, cost, operations or organization; whereas the belief is that the business process analyst needs a broad multi-disciplinary literacy, plus specialist skills in one or more relevant disciplines.

- A major failing in business process analysts has been found in the description process of the analysis. Whilst practitioners may possess skills in some or all of the requisite areas, the reality is that only a small number have the ability to produce high level business process descriptions.

As a result of the above factors, recommendations have been found to lack a sound analysis in support, with a subsequent tendency towards vagueness, with high degrees of intuition embedded within the analysis reports. The belief in the importance of process innovation in management processes is therefore said to be based more on faith and intuition than on empirical evidence.

In the case of many sectors employing integrated networks and automation, due to the degree of complexity and extent of embeddedness of systems, there is a high degree of overlap, interconnection and interdependence of systems that requires a far greater range of skills and techniques from business process analysts than has been the case for earlier generations.

The initiation of business process analysis is frequently driven by a shift in strategy formulation or a high-level review of processes in order to achieve a strategic objective and is viewed as part of the enterprise vision. A more recent trend driving this activity has been the rise in importance of business continuity planning, followed by a greater focus upon overall enhancement of enterprise resilience.

A number of different approaches exist for undertaking process analysis, with most carrying the underlying object property relationship model that has been the mainstay of the function since being formally identified as a core business activity for enterprises, technology developers and consultants.

Definition

It is important to identify what it is that an analyst is supposed to analyze in terms of an operational definition. The term is comprised of two words, and the most common view is that a business process is where a series of steps is required in order to achieve a set goal.

Increasing the degree of granularity in the definition of the term process is widely defined as having the characteristics of time, movement, continuity, regularity or continuation.

The principal deliverable from business process analysis work is usually some form of process specifications. The analyst generally needs to know what to put into a process definition or description. However, there are no standardized forms of recognized good business process specification; although a good software specification has been addressed by several authors. Eight principles of a good specification are been proposed as:

- separate functionality from implementation;
- a process-oriented systems specification language is required;
- a specification must encompass the system of which the component is a part;
- a specification must encompass the environment in which the system operates, similarly, the environment in which the system operates and with which it interacts must be specified;
- a system specification must be a cognitive model (that is, describe a system as perceived by its user community);
- a specification must be operational;
- the system specification must be tolerant of incompleteness and augmentable;
- a specification must be localized and loosely coupled.

The analyst has to be able to represent the results of analysis in terms of what may be termed good cognitive models. This means the resulting output should convey a good and accurate impression of the target system and how it will appear to the users of the system.

In continuing to define a process, the business process analysis literature uses similar terms, but there is a narrowing of the concept and a hardening of the results of process.

Business processes has been defined as a set of logically related tasks performed to achieve a defined business outcome. Similarly, the logical organization of people, materials, energy, equipment and procedures into work activities may be used in the design of a specified work product. This latter implies that there is the inclusion of human related issues. In each case, it is the *how* that is focused upon and not the *what*, the latter being a product rather than a process focus.[54]

However, since there is no product or service without a process, and no process without a product or a service, a process may be defined as any activity or group of activities that takes an input, adds value to it, and provides an output to a client (internal or external to the firm). In addition, there is a difference between a *production* process and a *business* process: a production process is any process that comes into physical contact with the hardware or software that will be delivered to an external client, up to the point the product is packaged, whereas a business process consists of a group of logically related tasks that uses resources in the provision of defined results that support the objectives of the enterprise.

Taking this into account, the case may be made that almost everything done within an organization is a process and states that there are literally hundreds or even thousands of processes. Those critical to the business usually have process owners within the organization. A core business process is a set of linked activities that both crosses functional boundaries and when carried out in concert, addresses the needs and expectations of the marketplace and drives the organization's capabilities. A core business process combines both physical activity and information flows, and addresses market demands. Researchers have claimed that in any one organization that there will be a number of core processes, usually limited to an average of six (five to eight).[55]

A key characteristic of a process is that it can be broken down into less complicated processes. This enables identification of core and support processes. Three types of process have been claimed to exist within all organizations: core, support and management. Core processes concentrate on satisfying external clients, support processes concentrate on satisfying internal clients, and management processes concentrate on managing the core processes or the support processes, or with planning at the business level.

In essence, there is no agreement upon a common definition of what a business process

[54] Davenport T.H. (1993) *Process Innovation : Re-engineering Work Through Information Technology,* Harvard Business School Press, Boston, M.A.

[55] Darnton G., and Giacoletto, S. (1992) *Information in the Enterprise*, Digital Press.

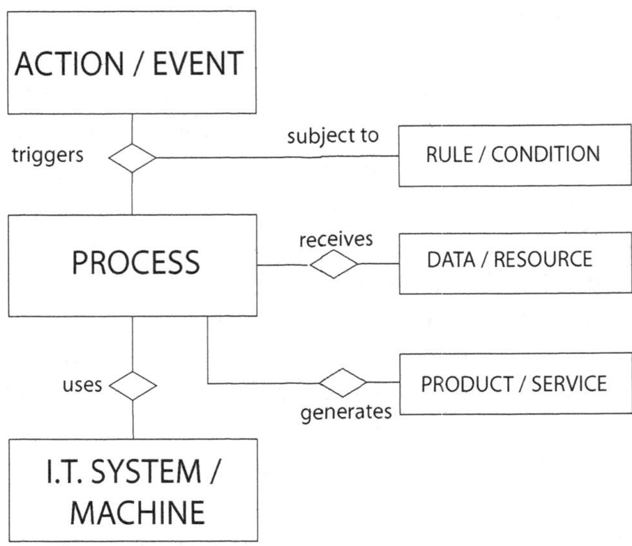

Fig. 8.2 Basic Process Map

is. Much is within the literature, but with different audiences the target of the work and as such there is a substantial difference between the literature aimed at the practitioner and that aimed at senior management. In the case of the latter, there is a requirement for a very high degree of attenuation of process detail and therefore simple, high level abstractions are more general than detailed analysis.

In many cases, the literature indicates that a top-down approach is particularly good at establishing an overall view that encompasses many key aspects of the enterprise. However, their most serious disadvantage seems to be in their failure to represent the hard-learned detail of the day to day operations of the organization. A bottom-up approach is very good at capturing the detailed experiences, but they often lack on overall perspective and there is therefore a need for high-level, simple, abstract approaches.

Given the number of variances in the literature in terms of the definition and scope of business processes, as well as their constructs and quantities within organizations, it is necessary to create a definition for the purpose of this book by identifying a process in the same manner that a bank business process analyst would, for example.

Initial identification of a candidate process is usually arbitrary, with a general statement such as "clearing and settlement is a bank core process". Although this provides a starting point, but problems can arise when an initial and arbitrary identification of candidate processes are not revisited to check them for compliance against some completeness or consistency criteria. The main problem is to be able to decompose high-level processes into smaller components that do something precise with inputs and outputs. However, then the high-level processes are abstractions because the way in which the lower level components are linked together depends upon circumstance.

The identification of core business processes poses additional problems. The concept indicates fundamental importance. Some authors emphasize core processes as chains of lower level processes which provide complete links between enterprise inputs and outputs, and some emphasize core processes as those that support handling enterprise critical success factors. Others still, relate core processes to core competencies, yielding an identification of those activities that the organization should perform itself (the core competencies) and those that could be considered for outsourcing.

A simple input-output model defines an enterprise in terms of the transformations required to convert the various inputs to the various outputs.

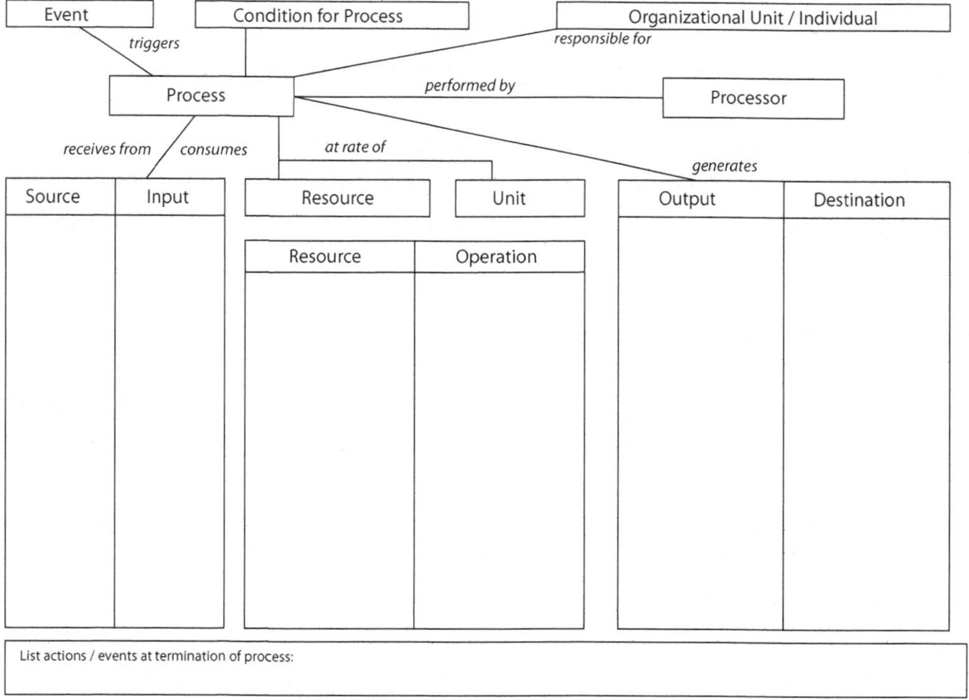

Fig. 8.3 Process Map Model 2

The outputs indicate both objectives and processes and behaviorally, although some person may produce incorrect outputs, the actual outputs can be utilized as evidence of processes. However, not all outputs indicate *core* processes and thus there remain serious classification problems in the identification of which are to be labeled as core business processes and which not.

Additional problems arise in the case of network process mapping due to the manner in which interactions occur. Rather than being identifiable as inputs with a specific event trigger, network interactions occur as a result of processes that may be manually controlled or automatic; the latter being dependent upon variables that may be unlimited. An example within the banking sector is the development of automated trading systems, coupled to straight through processing, which are based upon algorithms and pattern analysis. In mapping such a system, although an input may be mapped as a single entry, for example 'analytics engine output', the description and entry fails to take account of the individual processes feeding the analytics engine, which may or may not be critical processes in themselves.

Business Process Themes

There are several important themes that are related to business processes, with the centre of most process definitions being the idea of input – process – output. This is described and set against a paradox of core competency, and directly related to this is the concept of process flow, which is used by many writers to depict processes. Here a very different view is taken of both the number of processes and the time at which lower level processes are chained together in response to an action/event, labeled as binding.

Two points of importance to the analyst are:

a) Processes may cut across several business divisions/departments, therefore the analyst must understand the relationships between process and function

b) If a process is defined as a collection of activities, the decomposition of them is implied and there is structure in terms of sequence, i.e. one activity precedes/follows/concurrent.

In calculating how many processes exist within a typical large-scale organization, if only the highest level objects in a hierarchical structure are called processes, then few will be labeled as processes. If everything at a lower level is called an activity or task, then the question becomes that of how many activities or tasks may be logically anticipated, and there has been no development as to how to answer this.

To give an example of the number of processes identified within a bank or financial services organization, this has been estimated to be upwards of 20 000 processes, with this being calculated by taking the number of high-level processes and calculating how many levels of decomposition were required to reach elemental processes that could not be broken down meaningfully any further. Some of the high-level activities had already been broken down to that level, but others had not (as part of the audit of an incomplete process model).[56]

Cross-checks can be executed in order to verify the number, which give the number of procedures within the enterprise, these being elemental processes that are triggered in response to some event, with a procedure identifying what is actions follow when an event occurs.

An estimation of process volume can be made by calculating the numbers of elemental processes are required per procedure and multiplying the two figures to give an estimated total number for the organization. In determining the appropriate level of analysis, there is a set of contextual factors that affects the use of formal analysis. It is worth noting, however, that this number was derived at a time of low network utilization and with little or no automated trading and straight through processing or trading and settlement execution.

That business process analysis is concerned with core business processes implies there are activities that are non-core. The two important properties in identifying core business processes from the rest is that they are fundamental and essential to the organization and, also that the business possesses core competencies, that is, when benchmarked against others within the same line of business activity, the organization fares well in assessment.

Where it is accepted that core competencies exist, there are serious implications for the simplistic depictions of business processes. If a process can be represented primarily as the transformation of inputs into outputs, then it would not explain why one organization is more efficient than another since it could simply emulate the better enterprise.

In this sense, a business process is more than a transformation of factor inputs and the risk is therefore in mapping business processes through such means as flow charts. A reductionist approach, illustrating flows of information and sequences of activities, will lose the whole essence of the organizational learning experience. The literature indicates that there are no effective examples of process mapping that reflect the

[56] Davenport T.H. and Short, J.E. (1990) The new Industrial Engineering: information technology and business process redesign, *Sloan Management Review,* Summer.

accumulation of experience and the ability of an organization to exploit deep knowledge and competency.[57] From an analytical perspective, when handling the subject of core competencies, rather than seeing business processes in simple, deterministic ways, systemic approaches are more appropriate to model the depth of the phenomena involved.

The fact that core business processes are essential to the survival of the business results in their influence within the organization reaching across traditional departmental boundaries, as well as functional boundaries. In the case of a bank, for example, an order fulfillment may cut across selling, marketing, administration, legal, purchasing, accounting and information technology departments. Therefore, an analysis of a business process requires an understanding of business functions and how they relate to each other.

Further complexity arises when considering the different actions that comprise a process and their decomposition, since some organizations would regard an activity as being within one functional unit, whilst another within the same sector would see it as being within another, dependent upon organizational structure and governance in terms of responsibility. Therefore at one level a process is orthogonal to the business function in that there may be several degrees of freedom available over the allocation of processes to functions.

Within the decomposition of processes, a differentiation can also be made between core processes and common processes. An example of this would be in the difference between order fulfillment and call handling, the former being critical to all organizations. By contrast, call handling is necessary within an organization for a number of different circumstances, such as inbound inquiries from clients, service requests from maintenance teams, part of an order fulfillment process from one team member to another and so on. In all these cases the common call handling process can be identified, in answering the call, acknowledging the call, logging the call, routing the calls correctly, escalating specific calls and closing the call. Since it takes place at a number of points within an organization, it can be labeled as a common business process. Correct identification of both core and common business processes is claimed to be extremely critical in analysis.

In the case of networks, additional complexity in assigning a label to it is caused by its' level of embeddedness within organizations to differing degrees. In some instances, it may be labeled as a facilitator (with mostly manual inputs) of a common process where the daily batch processing i.e. very high data flows, between one unit/company and

[57] Hammer, M. and Stanton, S.A. (1995) *The Reengineering Revolution,* Harper Collins.

another takes place. This factor has increased in recent years, with subcontracted work to lower salary countries, such as India for data processing or Mexico for manufacturing. How the impact of cloud computing will affecting process mapping has not yet been determined to any extent. Defining infrastructure, for example, where there is use of a third party cloud but used by multiple parties, will create increasing complexity where there is a lack of transparency as to the cloud's operational aspects.

Frequently, in the use of simplified diagrams and charts, there is recourse to predetermined process flowcharts and procedures that represent ideal cases of how these processes should be linked together. That is, the binding between processes is decided at the time of drawing the charts or defining the processes.

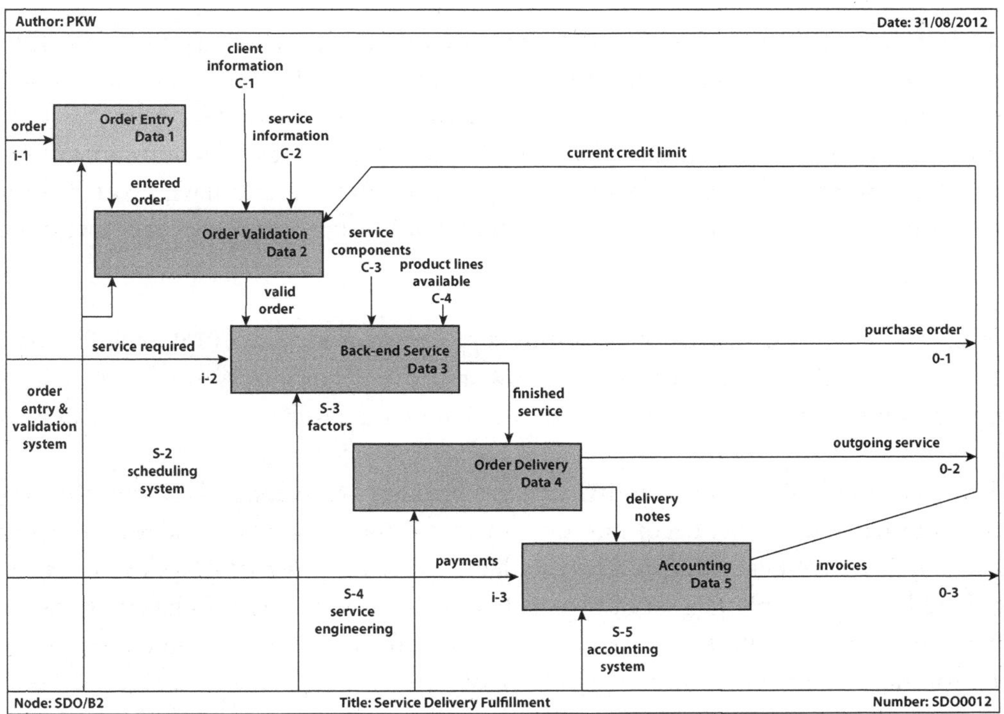

Fig. 8.4 Process Map of Service Delivery

In reality, events are not linked together until an actual event takes place, when personnel managing the process and the context at the time are known, that is, they are linked, not at design time, but in real-time. Some process chains cannot be broken, either because there are absolute reasons or because there are very strict rules in place. Event handling occurs as they play out to those in the real working environment, where they are assessed, discussed and addressed.

Frequently, there are major problems in finding a means of specifying requirements for information systems to analyzing the results of enterprise strategy definition workshops. A popular technique for this is the use of object property relationship modeling (OPR). Other alternatives that have not yet been widely proven are those using artificial intelligence and in the use of business objects.

Systems development is usually accomplished by an organizational unit, and each time the process is executed it results in a new product: the new system. There may be many attempts to improve the process and the product. One such approach is based upon the observation that the development of information processing systems is itself an information processing activity that can be aided by a computerized information processing system.

Further, it may be the case that although a particular process can never be fully automated, it may be possible for it to be computer aided. Development of mapping tools utilizing analysts workbenches, comprised of databases of data items has been more increasingly used within technology led sectors, such as telecommunications, where a wholesale change of operational practices and services have proffered the opportunity to completely redesign and document business processes and operations bottom-up.

In many cases, commentators view business process workflow as employing the main techniques of the analysis of process flow and the decomposition of higher level processes into lower level objects, such as activities and tasks.

However, if a highly complex entity such as a banking organization is greater than the sum of its parts, then after decomposition into parts, there must be some residual value that will not have been captured by the decomposition process. A system has been defined by many as being a set of objects (elements or parts), with relations between them and their attributes (properties, or qualities) and it is embedded in an environment containing other inter-related objects.

From a systems perspective, there are a number of elements that comprise the activity of business process analysis in this area. These include cybernetics, information theory, game theory, decision theory, topology, factor analysis, and general system theory in the narrow sense.

It is, therefore, not only the individual component parts that derive a system, but rather the relationship between them and in addition, the interaction between the components, the relationships and the environment within which they are embedded.

Commentators have also indicated that where process descriptions have been produced primarily by manual means (including text and diagram processors), there are frequently serious deficiencies and inconsistencies in the descriptions.[58]

Incompleteness and inconsistency are additionally the two most important problems relating to information theory and also to business process analysis (see also Chapter 5: Managing Uncertain Information). Statements about processes may be incomplete and a range of possible meanings may lead to potential or actual inconsistency. The latter arises when different descriptions of the same process depict it in different ways.

Ambiguity and equivocation occur frequently in text sources, and the former may be described as being either patent or latent. Ambiguity may lead to incompleteness but it is not the same as incompleteness. In cases of latent ambiguity the sense may seem perfectly clear on initial review of a document, and it is not until further facts are disclosed that ambiguity then appears.

Where there is a lack of a prescribed manner by which enterprises should map their business processes, the opportunities for inconsistencies throughout most sectors remain high, this despite the need for accurate mapping for business continuity planning, and more recently, in understanding risk exposures arising from data leakages.

Analyzing Organizations

Academic literature speaks of "learning organizations" and "knowledge-based enterprises", which seek to harness the intellectual activity of employees. However, when it comes to hard analysis of organizations, techniques are difficult to find that facilitate validation of such claims.

Additionally, there have been many organizational models proposed this century, including hierarchical, matrix, webs, etc. and in analyzing organizations, it is necessary to:

- be able to recognize many of the possible forms of organizational structure and dynamics;
- be aware of the key issues related to the different organizational possibilities;
- be able to identify appropriate organizational structures for the various business processes;

[58] Oakland, J.S. (1989) *Total Quality Management*, Butterworth Heinemann, Oxford.

- be able to model the behavior of different organizational forms

Due to the complexity of organizations, it is not generally possible for analysts to portray a complete view and many critiques of traditional hierarchical views of organizations are based on real flows of information and materials do not follow the lines of authority on organization charts. Real-world work involves many informal structures in addition to the formal. In the case of large organizations, these need to be broken into smaller units because of diseconomies of scale arising from the excessive bureaucracy needed for very large hierarchical structures implied by the hierarchical management of large enterprises.

By contrast, more agile and responsive enterprises require smaller, quasi-autonomous units. This is particularly the case with technology start-up organizations, from which small numbers of personnel working in boutique-type enterprises emerge as large-scale employers with autonomy given down to individual level in order to drive innovation of processes, products and services. Nowhere more has this been evident than within the social media sector in recent times, followed by web services integration with social media and cloud computing.

The organization has also been described as a system of flows, comprising five parts:[59]

1. Operating core,
2. Strategic apex,
3. Middle line,
4. Technostructure, and
5. Support staff.

These parts are joined together by different flows: authority, work material, information, and decision processes, with work flowing from one grouping to another. With a continuous adoption and development of information technology, the key benefits may not arise primarily from the automation of tasks performed previously by other means. Rather, they can arise from a redefinition of fundamental processes and the ways in which they are performed.

In traditional management hierarchies, control no longer works, with top-down, central planning systems not being effective because of the increasing complexity and size of the information processing task. In respect of the synergy interaction between information technology and the organization, top managers have a third choice from the traditional centralized structure, or a decentralized structure in that there is the

[59] Gehani N., and McGettrick A. (1986). *Software Specification Techniques,* Addison-Wesley, Reading, M.A.

possibility of a hybrid structure. Again, recent developments in managerial hierarchies stem from tech start-ups where the leaders form part of a flat organizational structure, as opposed to the physical relocation to individual offices and a command and control style of management.

A further aspect to the impact of information technology upon the organization is in the shift of focus from headcount, budget or other traditional factors for the acquisition of authority, towards a manager's ability to set the direction for a team of professionals or individuals who are given scope within the normal work pattern to experiment with processes and/or products.

Traditionally, many middle managers have been performing the roles of information attenuation, information amplification, and a variety of attenuation tasks that information technology often performs very well or better. As such, a piece of added value that was provided through information gathering and distribution has been eliminated and layers of management have been omitted for both communication and decision making. Since knowledge now forms the basis of wealth creation, just as owners historically became dependent upon professional managers for knowledge, so now managers are becoming increasingly dependent upon their employees for knowledge.

Organization and Practical Analysis

The analyst may have recourse to modeling the organization, not as an organizational structure, but to model the organization itself as a process. Reasons for doing this stem from the emergence of a contingency approach to organization design, in response to the recognition of different kinds of organization that may be appropriate for different forms of task. As such, there should be some indication of the relationship between process linkages and the degree of co-ordination needed.

With regard to the relationship between information and decision theory, where the business process analyst is working in the context of an enterprise that is seeking competitive advantage, a grounding in both is required, Game theory, for example, is in essence based upon an arrangement of players and/or coalitions of players each of whom has the objective of developing a strategy for achieving the objective of winning.

Further problems are posed in analyzing an enterprise's environment and context. A good example of this is where a terminal decision is required and the decision maker is about to make such a decision, when they are then presented with the opportunity to obtain additional information prior to the decision. The question then arises of what and how much additional information should be obtained and at what point should information gathering cease and the terminal decision made. This again becomes linked to environmental scanning practices executed within individual organizations and forms part of the general operation and culture within organizations. It has particular bearing when allied to the forming of a risk appetite for an enterprise and is intertwined with the psychological impact upon judgment and decision making.

Information Technology and Business Processes

With the increase in volumes, flows and velocity of information/data throughout society, there has been an increasing in the perceived value of information as an asset. This implies added value from the ownership of information, and future streams of revenue from the exploitation of those information assets, with the link between information assets and technology arising from the volume of information to be managed as well as the extensive processing required. Information technology is the principal enabling technology for business processes and has become a fundamental enabler in the creation and maintenance of business networks. Information technology has also facilitated organizational forms, with these being proposed as being internal structure; team-based work groups; disintegrated (but interconnected) organizations, and systems integration.

Similarly, it has been proposed that there are five levels of information technology induced reconfiguration: localized exploitation; internal integration; business process redesign; business network redesign, and business scope redefinition. Each of these levels is positioned with increasing values of range of potential benefits and degree of business transformation. Although information can be regarded as assets, IT infrastructure can and has been viewed as a strategic resource, categorized as independent, reactive or interdependent with respect to the enterprise's strategic context.

However, if technology/network deployment is only superimposed upon pre-existing organizational conditions then its' deployment may only deliver marginal benefits to an enterprise. This is to say, that without changing the organizations' underlying strategies, structures, processes and culture, there is a depletion of the maximum gains that could be obtained from technology/network deployment. Interdependency may be created between information technology and business processes where there is some form of inseparable combination of properties of information technology and business processes i.e. the two cannot be disassembled in their analysis.

Information as an Asset

Difficulties frequently arise when organizing an enterprise by function rather than by process. Where the emphasis is placed upon function, processes that cross functional boundaries are more difficult to organize for smooth performance; where emphasis is placed upon process, it is more difficult to organize for functional excellence.

Further, with regard to infrastructure and business units, whilst the infrastructure provides an opportunity to realize economies of scale and commonality across a wide range of functions and processes, business units have a deep understanding of their business responsibilities and may require pressure to contribute to infrastructure.

The tensions between organization by function or process and those between infrastructure and business units often become clearer with respect to the management of information, with information systems' planning requiring identification and deployment of those information systems needed to support the strategy and operations of the enterprise. Responsibility for infrastructure is usually assigned to an enterprise's management information systems, information technology or information systems departments.[60]

Information, as an intangible asset, is more problematic from an accounting view than physical assets, since an asset is something that has either intrinsic value in its own right, or can contribute to future cashflows for the enterprise. Business processes are focused upon the utilization of assets in order to provide the maximum added value. Although exploitation of physical assets is well understood, the management of information assets is less so; it requires identification, valuation, protection and exploitation, with the responsibility to exploit information assets resting with business units.

The area of asset classification and valuation has also changed in recent times, with changes to accounting practices on a piecemeal basis and with greater disparity within national accounting standards. As information/data has increased on both an operational and transactional cross-border basis, so different regimes have increased the complexity of how valuations of information/data are handled.

Thus, the decisions within organizations to recognize, leverage and exploit information assets to their maximum have a profound impact on information systems planning, with planning moving away from being management information systems focused, to

---

[60] Horngren C.T., and Sundem, G.L. (1987) *Introduction to Management Accounting,* 7th edn, Prentice-Hall, Englewood Cliffs, NJ.

being more business process centric. The objective in so doing is the optimization of activities within available time, which will contribute to the future cashflows of the organization.

Assets have been defined as economic resources that are expected to benefit future activities and the distinction has been made between tangible and intangible, with the former be capable of being physically observed. By contrast, intangible assets are a class of long-lived assets that are not physical in nature and are rights to expected future benefits derived from their acquisition and continued ownership. Therefore, the key to intangible assets is their likely contribution to future cash flow, but they remain difficult to measure/treat from an accounting perspective. In some territories, for example, it may be permissible to separate total cost into current expenditure to be written-off immediately, from that which is a true asset that can be valued and reported as such.

With the trend of enterprises separating their service activities from their manufacturing activities, it has been proposed by many authors that there has been a shift since the 1990's, from a manufacturing economy, to an information economy. This is certainly true of certain sectors, including banking, finance, insurance and securities, telecoms, aviation and logistics which have all experienced a vast increase in the use of information.

In viewing an information structure as being far broader than an information technology infrastructure, enterprises must recognize that it is the information and not the hardware and software that are the major resource available to it.

However, valuing information is complex and differentiated by context. For example, the market value of a company reflects both tangible and intangible assets. Methods of valuation have been proposed by many authors.[61] One such is based upon finding a calculated intangible value as the net present value of the amount by which the after-tax earnings exceed average returns on investment. This is to say, returns on tangible assets for companies in the same industrial sector. The benefits of such an approach extend to facilitating benchmarking by private companies with publicly owned ones, as can divisions or business units. A concise concluding definition of information as an asset is proposed as being that information is an intangible asset, represented strictly by the difference in value of an enterprise with it and without it and by contribution to future cashflows arising from its exploitation.

Given the lack of generally agreed accounting practices for the treatment and valuation

[61] Strassman, P.A. (1990) *The Business Value of Computers,* Information Economics Press.

of intangible assets, together with common treatments of intangibles by the tax authorities, the business process analyst faces a number of issues. The most common approach taken is to first define standard accounting procedures along with alternative accounting procedures to give management information to value information assets and assess the extent to which they are being exploited (or not).

An example of this would be in the case of data warehouses where it may be necessary to retain a high level of granularity of transactional information so that the formal balance sheet and income and expenditure statements are seen only as particular views of those transactions, with alternative views that can be generated to evaluate intangibles, or to support simulation of alternative business scenarios or cost classifications.

The analyst's role when handling data warehouses and in the valuation of information is to decouple underlying information models from current views and implementations of those models, that is, analyzing the requirements for specific functions or processes, but retaining the multidimensional details and ensuring no loss of the fine granularity.

In the context of cyber threat management, therefore, it is critical that an organization has mapped its' business processes, operations and infrastructure. Without this requisite, valuation and assessment is not possible to the degree of granularity necessary to quantify and value security breaches resulting from a successful attack.

The absence of process mapping prima facie results in a lack of interdependency mapping and a lack of available data from which to model risks and/or business continuity. Since continuity planning has increased in perceived importance in recent years, backed by standards issuance and the creation of professional bodies, it may be concluded that many organizations have, at the very least, some form of mapping from which to at least base initial risk assessments upon.

Chapter Nine

MANAGING CYBER THREATS

Methodology Overview

To commence with, there should be clarity as to what/how/why components of a cyber/network risk management program are included or excluded. This will vary according to need per enterprise and include in the process the risk appetite of the organization and/or resources available.

The overall scheme may vary similarly, according the requirements, capital and knowledge of the organization. However, there is a common theme for cyber/network threat management which comprises the following elements that in themselves are comprised of multiple components:

Table 9.1 Methodology Overview

Data Modeling	Data Required	Program Components
• Acquisition of data • Analysis of data acquired • Assessment of the data • Quantification of the data • Valuation of the data	• Network threat data • Business process mapping • Business strategy • Risk appetite • Existing risk management programs • Existing continuity plans • Business case financial acceptable thresholds	• Organizational structure • Environmental scanning • External information • Internal survey analysis • Recognition of cyber threat specificity • Risk strategy formulation • Data flows • Regulatory compliance

The preceding chapters have sought to provide a basis for organizations to develop their proprietary cyber threat/network risk programs, whilst by no means claiming to have provided all the answers. One area not touched upon is the recent emergence of regulatory and legal pressures being placed upon enterprises, primarily driven in the U.S. but currently spreading to Europe and beyond.

This regulatory and legal compliance regime will continue being developed. However, it is worth recognizing that the creation of policies, procedures and penalties, with an absence of global acceptance of them and the means by which to enforce them, results in their value remaining questionable at best.

Until very recently, governments have left the technology industry self-regulate on privacy, possibly due to a lack of awareness of potential for privacy breaches or simply due to the slow pace of legislation and implementation of laws. However, several major organizations have been viewed as overstepping the mark through altering settings on mobile devices and/or web browsers, ignoring copyright (in particular in respect of written works, music and video). Social media sites have also come under attack for their laissez faire attitude to privacy settings set as default on their websites. The threshold of what was previously viewed as acceptable practice has been exploited through technology providers altering the mode of operation a related application running on a device to trick users into changing their privacy settings from a higher level of security to lower ones, whereby personal data and user behaviors can be monitored and of course then monetized (through selling more targeted advertising).

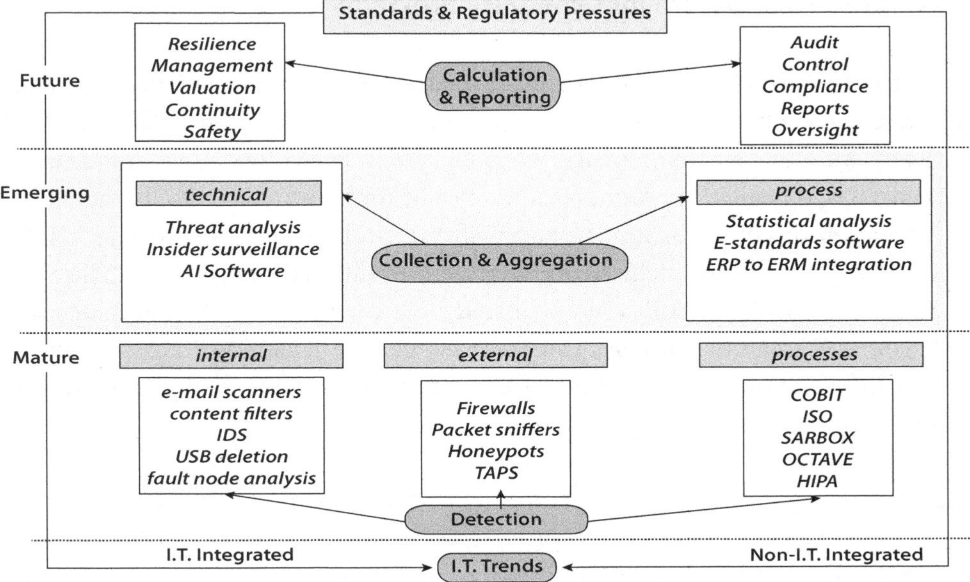

Fig. 9.1 Trends Environment

The most recent changes in the laws are those relating to the storage and provision of data by organizations to national regulatory/legal departments, such as the Cyber Intelligence Sharing and Protection Act (CISPA) which was passed in April 2012 in the United States and which provides for the sharing of internet traffic information between the U.S. government and certain technology and manufacturing companies. It has been proposed that the Act is a simple and effective means of sharing important cyber threat information with the government, whereas the many opponents to it (including the standing US President) claim that CISPA contains too few limits on how and when the government may monitor private individual's internet browsing information and the new powers could be used in surveillance activities targeting the general public rather than to pursue malicious hackers.

At the time of writing, there is a clear divide between major corporations as to support or rejection of compliance with the new Act. For this reason, although a legal and regulatory compliance stance is required within any cyber/network threat management program, the lack of clarity precludes the means by which the mandated compliance terms will have to be met.

Overall, the structure for the management of cyber threats can be summarized as having multiple components and players, as opposed to it being viewed purely as an I.T. security issue and the intention of this book is to reinforce the view that the specificity of the risk type requires a broad as well as a deep approach.

Organizational Structure for Cyber Risk Programs

As stated in earlier chapters, organizational structures that are aligned with the objectives of a cyber risk management program are critical if the pitfalls common to vertically and horizontally reaching programs are to be avoided. The politicization of a cyber risk and resilience program should not be underestimated due to the scope and authorization required for it to be successful. Examples here are where the CIO/IT departments feel disenfranchised and that their traditional silo power is being eroded by the handover of control to senior management without any IT/computer science background. Circles of influence thus bear a large part in gaining access, acquiring the correct information required and in forming credibility for cyber risk management teams.

Since such programs are so far reaching, a large cross-section of the organization will be involved at some stage of the process and also compose the risk management committee that oversees the entire program. Below this level is the chief risk officer and associated department personnel, with size dependent upon the size and type of organization. Frequently, this role is assumed by person/persons who have a full-time role in another capacity and this tends to be the case for small to medium sized businesses and in local public authority departments, where typically the person also fulfils the role of business continuity officer.

Reporting to the chief risk office are the various departments that comprise the main departments affected intrinsically by the risk program and typically comprise those listed in the diagram below.

Fig. 9.2 Organizational Composition for Cyber Risk Program

The objective of this group is to determine and set the risk appetite for the organization through a two-way dialogue with the risk management committee, who take full responsibility for the level set with a senior Board member sitting on it, in much the same way any other major project has as a sponsor of the program. This will enable much of the internal politicking to be resolved swiftly, with communication top-down from the committee being a de facto mandate to act in the best interest of the programs development, execution and ongoing working.

It is then the responsibility of each department to undertake analysis utilizing whatever tools and methodologies that have been deemed to be the most appropriate for this to form part of the initial analysis. The data and other information pertinent to the risk analysis is passed to the program project management team, who in turn pass this to the chief risk officer, who then reports to the risk management committee. This flow of data is unidirectional and it is for the risk management committee to utilize the data, determine which will be utilized within the risk program, how and when.

Fig. 9.3 Input Composition from Analysis and Methodologies

Of importance in all projects and programs is of course the ability to fund their development, implementation and any ongoing operational activities, as in the case of cyber risk management in particular. Many early attempts within organizations to roll out so-called e-enablement failed in the face of the absence of a solid business case, where traditional measurement metrics were assigned to assess the viability and cost-benefit of such projects.

As has been the case subsequently, more rational financial assessment models have been designed to take account of the nature of such projects, whereby some of the benefits of undertaking them cannot be measured by traditional models. In the case of IT security, this has also had problems when a business case is required to meet strict internally set financial criteria and traditionally has been viewed as a cost, rather than adding value.

As organizations have changed fundamentally in recent years, with technology and subsequently internet traffic becoming intrinsic to operations in general, and for competitive advantage in particular, so the measurement models for assessing viability of e-projects have similarly developed. Consequently, there are several modes of validating the cost-benefit of a cyber risk management program where the benefits can be viewed as soft or delayed in their delivery, or as an opportunity cost measure, whereby the contrary path would lead to substantial losses to other difficult to measure attributes, such as brand or reputational damage. The risk program Board is involved during the development of the business case and they co-ordinate and communicate in a bidirectional manner with the project program management team and the chief risk officer.

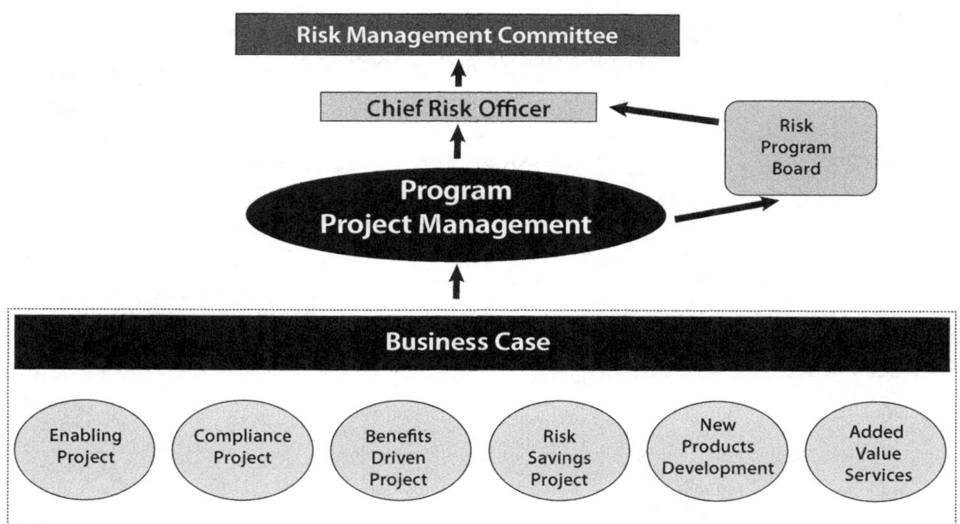

Fig. 9.4 Examples of Types of Business Case Benefits

With a clear mandate and financial commitment from the risk management committee, an organization can then begin to construct the cyber risk program main components and identify whether the tools and expertise lie within the organization or external to it. This activity can, in effect, be split into individual items and analyzed within the context of skills and tools available and whether the organization will require external assistance. An example here would be where the ability to capture internet traffic, analyze it, assess it for threats and quantify the risks arising from them. This will in all probability require different tools, methodologies and skill sets than those required for business process analysis. Therefore, the components required for both, essentially the tools and methodologies required are the same components, but the details remain different. Mapping the requirements and sources enables the project program management team to assess how the program will need to be resourced, the costs involved and the authority required (along with the budget) to acquire and run the overall project.

Once the risk appetite, the tools, methodologies, business case and the risk program organizational structure have been established, then the program can commence its analysis of the organizations current risk exposure, with inputs from each of the relevant departments/divisions. At this stage, the project may still be at a coarse rather than granular stage, with a drill-down occurring as the program develops. This is frequently the case, with senior management seeking the existing financial impact of a successful cyber attack and the cost-benefit of each risk reduction/mitigation measure available to the enterprise. In effect, the program project management team sits between the departments who calculate their risk exposures and the chief risk officer. The latter reports to the risk management committee and provides it with a breakdown

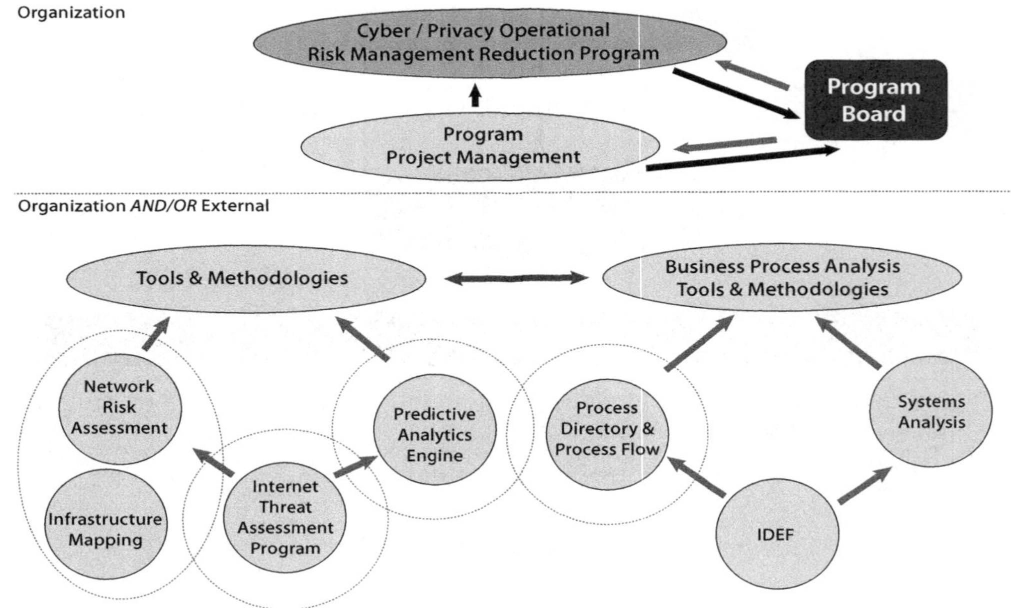

Fig. 9.5 Mapping Internal and External Resources, Tools and Methodologies Required

of the current exposure, a reiteration of the target exposure (to ensure at this stage there is no miscommunication of the objectives) and the costs per mitigation action versus the impact on the total risk level. With a cost-benefit analysis of each reduction action provided, the risk management committee is able to better allocate resources (capital and personnel) to the management of cyber risks posed to the organization.

Again, of note is that the available data at this stage is insufficient for a through and in-depth quantification of the cost-benefit of each mitigation action. For example, developing either an insurance or risk financing product to cover a large-scale organizations risk exposure will take a great deal of time and risk assessment by the risk carrier. The exercise however, should provide an early project critical path and an indication of the risk appetite that is acceptable to the organization that can be clearly communicated to the departmental heads who can then more easily identify through gap analysis whether the burden will fall to them or another division and the likely financial requirements that will require budgeting for in the succeeding reporting period.

Taking this organization structure and developing the risk assessment and analysis will bring the enterprise to the point where the gap between desired and existing exposure needs to be managed strategically in order to maintain competitiveness through efficient capital allocation to the management of enterprise and cyber risks.

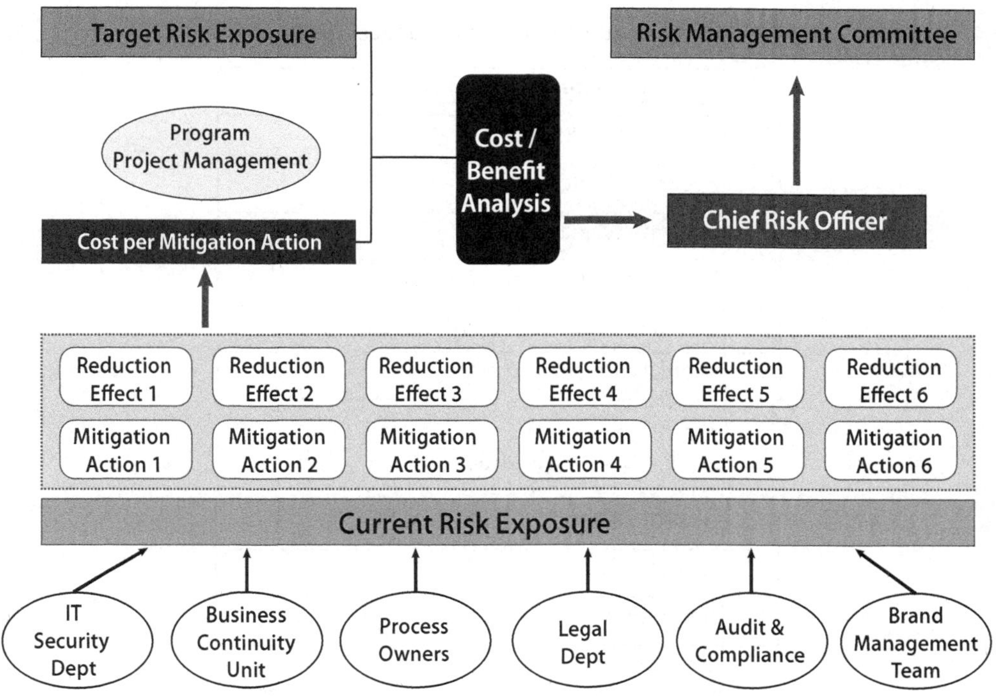

Fig. 9.6 Gap Analysis and Cost-benefit for Managing Cyber Risks

Strategy of Risk Management

The overall strategy of risk management relating to information and network security impacting on corporate risk cannot be viewed on a piecemeal basis, or as the sole responsibility of a specific department/division but rather, only through a holistic approach to the problem.

It can be viewed as a multi-layer issue, with each layer within the organization peeling away to reveal a further set of issues. In simplistic terms, the three main legs of the approach can be viewed as the foundational practice areas; the security practice areas and the overall context-sensitive risk management process (Tables 9.1, 9.2 and 9.3).

Network & Cyber Risk Assessment

As the technology base increases in size and complexity, so networks expand, with applications migrating from centralized systems to decentralized ones. Cloud computing has added a further layer of decentralization of applications, access capabilities and connectivity. The cloud computing model now utilized extensively by

Table 9.1 Foundational Practice Areas

	Organization
1	Institutional knowledge
2	Security Strategy
3	Security Management
4	Security Policies and Regulations
5	Collaborative Security Management
6	Security Practice Areas

Table 9.2 Security Practice Areas

	Technology
1	General Staff Practices
2	Security Architecture and Design
3	Encryption
4	Authentication and Authorization
5	System and Network Management
6	Monitoring and Auditing
7	Incident Management
8	Contingency Planning/Disaster Recovery
9	Physical Security

Table 9.3 Risk Management Process

Identify *(Self-directed Assessment)*			Critical Assets
	Mitigation Plans		Organizational Issues
		Vulnerabilities	Technical Issues
Mitigate			Technology
			Practices
	Prioritized Risks		Organization Improvements
Analyze & Prioritize			Mission & Asset Value Data
			Threat Data

the major providers globally means that companies do not have to install and maintain their software themselves. Instead, cloud providers run the software in their data centers and users connect via the internet. This cuts software costs up to half of traditional back-end software programs. Business-to-business network integration has similarly expanded at an exponential rate, with administration of them increasingly difficult to manage and maintain. Thresholds of expertise to maintain integrity and continuity have risen, without a commensurate increase in the number of skilled personnel to undertake the tasks.

Allied to this has been the vast growth rate in the integration of operational data centrally with the ability to control access to that data. This flies in the face of the capability of networks in adding more nodes on a network to facilitate modes of work requiring remote access to the centralized operational data.

Thus the enterprise is increasingly comprised of a network or series of networks, interconnecting a multitude of computers and devices (increasingly this applies to various mobile devices and tablets) for communications and data sharing. With the design of networks often being comprised of dissimilar components as they develop on a piecemeal basis and with the need to facilitate emerging technologies, interoperability becomes paramount. Appropriate data transport and exchange technologies are being implemented, coupled to sets of rules and procedures.

The outcome of the evolution of modern networks has led to series of complex systems consisting of increasingly independent components interacting with each other, creating a large number of possible factors in which the actions of these independent, individual components can achieve has risen inexorably.

Typically, network designs now incorporate an outside network, intermediary network (the demilitarized zone: DMZ) and the internal network. These networks then have a number of mission-critical components such as mail servers, domain name servers, file transfer protocol servers, virtual private networks, and internet access. Securing them are routers, managed switches and firewalls, intrusion prevention/detection systems and other security hardware and software.

This range of systems, components and applications results in a variety of topological designs within cross-functional, cross-sector business environments. Such an amalgamation of I.T. assets and their interconnectedness creates extreme issues in process mapping, valuation and in risk assessment.

Before appropriate security tools can be identified, valued and assessed, an organization must undertake a comprehensive review of the assets comprising the enterprise network. Nowadays it is generally expected that the vast majority of organizations have documented current and anticipated I.T. assets, enabling a risk assessment to be conducted on I.T. infrastructure, critical information system control mechanisms and a review of I.T. security practices, continuity planning and any mitigation and compliance programs.

Over a long period of time, several risk management approaches have been introduced for I.T. and network risk management. Some organizations, for example national defense, have developed their own risk management approaches. However, most organizations do not manage their cyber threats explicitly, but rather it is based upon experience, the values imbued in the enterprise by senior management, and it remains part of overall enterprise risk management and resilience programs.

The factors attributed to creating this situation are unclear and the concept of network risk management is vague with teams frequently feeling there are insufficient tools available for them to effectively execute such a risk management program. Further, the quantification of network risks is difficult and models are felt too inadequate/inappropriate to provide sufficiently accurate estimates for probability and loss for the analysis of results to be reliable. Other methods are viewed as lacking the granularity for them to be of any use in the prioritization of risks.

Organizational issues also play a role, in that risks have differing potential impacts on an enterprise and thus are viewed through different lenses by the various stakeholders within an organization and expectations vary accordingly.

These issues can be addressed by evolving differing strategies that create on overall strategic vision of what an enterprise resilience program should be, who it affects, and how. There should be a clear definition of objectives, constraints and other program drivers that may influence the program (both positively and negatively). Conversion of various levels of expectation into goals can give a program the direction and political buy-in required for advancement to completion, removing obstacles that can otherwise easily derail a program.

Where goals cannot be clearly defined at the outset, they should, at the very least, be documented as far as possible, with the limitations of the scope and definition also being listed. Similarly, the various types of risks require defining, without any possible ambiguity being attached. Risk may mean the possibility of loss, actual loss that result from a risk occurring as an event, a factor or any element that may be linked to a threat, or even down to a person whose acts/omissions may pose a risk to the organization. The scope for defining risk is broad and may be comprised of dictionary definitions, the way the word is used in everyday use within an organization, and so forth. The potential inadequacy in the definition must be removed in order to secure the program and to ensure the goals set are aligned with the definition of risk.

It is widely accepted that both qualitative and quantitative modeling of risks should be utilized within organizations due to the differences between the two methods filling gaps that can otherwise occur. An example of this is the ability of qualitative measurement to deliver a conceptual and graphical representation of the measurement to users that is easier to understand that raw statistical output. Further, using this modeling methodology early in the project can lead to a more relevant deployment of quantitative modeling further into the program. By enabling a fuller cross-organizational understanding of risk and the management of it, there is a better basis for understanding and communicating risk.

When developing a methodology for risk assessment and quantification, it is important to understand the role that scaling has within the process. Much academic work has been undertaken on the subject and how ratio and ordinal scaling impacts on how questions are perceived and answered. In the case of a cyber threat management program, incorrect scaling can lead to an underestimation of risks. Ratio scaling can lead to incorrect prioritization of risk management actions and at the outset there should be recognition of this important but often overlooked component. It may be more appropriate at the commencement of a program to simply begin by identifying the greatest risks and impacts and how they may be controlled or the losses mitigated. The probability of expected losses and their values may be more relevant further into a program, when more meaningful data is available for analysis.

There are frequently occasions where a cyber threat management program forms part of an existing risk and resilience program. A real risk that may arise from this is the risk assessment method used by the main program creating an inappropriate impact on the latter, in that frequently, risk management programs utilize risk ranking methods. These are based upon the loss caused to certain components within an organization. These may have certain attributes attached to them, such as cost, time delays, loss of quality and a single metric is then attached in order to rank the loss associated with each risk. Further, recognition of the specificity of cyber threats by a risk management group can often result in the desire to include a cyber threat management program, but they are often launched in the face of the lack of a clear business case to support them.

Frequently, such programs commence as enabling projects, whereby there is no clear cost-benefit in undertaking them in the short-term, but have a greater than proportionate impact in secondary areas. Where a single metric is attached to in the cyber threat assessment phase, these secondary benefits may be overridden by the focus upon a single, primary goal.

Additionally, the quantification of losses can be skewed through utilizing a single metric such as loss. Decisions are made based upon the changes in the expected utility of alternatives and since the utility functions of stakeholders are likely to be non-linear, the use of single, direct-loss estimates can lead to incorrect measurement and/or ranking of risks. It is therefore important to utilize a selection of metrics, measures and then compare/rank risks according to the utility loss attached by stakeholders.

There is general consensus among information security professionals that a 100% infallible security solution is not attainable or cost-effective. Programs such as business continuity with a 100% failsafe are similarly unrealistic due to their cost and scope i.e. the cost of establishing either of the above would cost more than the asset values being protected.

The emphasis therefore moves from cyber risk avoidance to cyber risk management, which comprises cyber risk analysis together with cyber risk management. The former is generally defined as the identification and assessment of the levels of cyber risks calculated from the known values of assets and the levels of threats to, and vulnerabilities of those assets. The latter involves the identification, selection and adoption of countermeasures (which may include mitigation actions) and the reduction of said risks to a level acceptable, according to the risk appetite of the organization.

Once assessment and quantification have been undertaken, the options for managing cyber threats are:

- reduce the risk levels through mitigation actions/deploying countermeasures;
- accept the level of risk (where the value of the assets is less than the cost of risk reduction for example), or accept the residual risk after applying mitigation actions/countermeasures;
- seek the means to transfer the risk (such as insurance: see below).

During the process of assessment and quantification, both qualitative and quantitative measurement methodologies are utilized in arriving at an annual loss expectancy (ALE). In the case of the latter, this is usually driven by experience and opinion and often has a tables–based approach to it such as that given below by way of example:

Table 9.4 Example of Qualitative Assessment

	Severity of Threat	Probability of Threat Taking Place	Potential Financial Loss	Effectiveness of Perimeter Security	Effectiveness of Intrusion Detection	Effectiveness of Insider Threat Identification System
CIO	4	2	4	4	3	2
SysAdmin	2	3	3	4	2	1
IT Security	2	3	3	4	2	1
Db Manager	3	4	3	4	2	1
Process Owner	5	4	4	4	4	2
Results	3.6	3.4	3.6	3.8	3	1.4

The arguments for using both quantitative and qualitative are that in the case of quantitative analysis this is essential in delivering a ranking of options in cases of risk mitigation, since in its absence it would not be possible to assess the cost-effectiveness of each mitigation action. In the case of qualitative analysis, descriptions rather than calculations are utilized, it does not, unlike the former, provide a solid probability percentage when determining the likelihood of cyber threats and risks.

In the latter case, it is based more upon estimated potential losses, with no probability data being used. As mentioned earlier, this methodology is fairy broadly used at the commencement of cyber threat management programs, which is later supplemented by quantitative analysis as threat and risk data becomes available in increasing volumes, permitting meaningful data analysis.

The classic quantitative calculation underpinning risk assessment is:

(Asset Value x Exposure Factor = Single Loss Expectancy) x Annualized Rate of Occurrence = Annualized Loss Expectancy

The pros and cons of both quantitative and qualitative methods can be summarized as:

Table 9.5 Quantitative Analysis Pros and Cons

Quantitative Analysis – Advantages	*Quantitative Analysis – Disadvantages*
• Assessment and output are based upon objective methods and metrics, enabling statistical analysis • Information assets are valued, with a quantifiable monetary worth attached, enabling truer expected loss calculations • Risk mitigation actions are valued and cost-benefit analysis of each is undertaken for better resource allocation • The performance of the organizations' risk management program is facilitated for enhanced overall enterprise resilience • A financial assessment and analysis creates a risk culture based upon well understood managerial metrics i.e. financial terminology	• Complexity of analysis and calculation, with difficulty in communicating the methodology deriving the output (or requires opacity and a "black box" approach in order to avoid politicization of the calculation methodology) • Requires substantial and a broad base of data in order to execute a risk assessment program • Threat type and frequency (especially in the case of cyber threats) can change dramatically, reducing the effectiveness of the models used in assessment and quantification • Decoupling processes and the IT infrastructure is difficult in the extreme in determining values at risk for operational losses

Table 9.6 Qualitative Analysis Pros and Cons

Qualitative Analysis – Advantages	*Qualitative Analysis – Disadvantages*
• Calculations are simple (if used) and are understandable and have an ease of execution • Valuation of information assets is not required • Threat frequency and/or impact data is not required • Risk mitigation actions do not require valuation and/or cost-benefit analysis • Provides a generalized overview of risks and their priority ranking for managing/mitigating	• Subjective risk assessment for both method and metrics • The perceived value at risk may be misaligned with actuality due to a lack of valuation of information assets • Lack of cost-benefit analysis can lead to misallocation of resources to a subjectively determined risk • Lack of effective measurement of the risk management performance within the organization

One area of major complexity for many organizations is where the requirements and activities change over time, allied to changes to information assets and infrastructure. This can lead to a miss-alignment and inconsistency between the policies and procedures relied upon for information security and the types of threat faced by the organization as this will similarly change over time.

It is therefore essential that reviews and updates of such policies, personnel roles, IT infrastructure, information assets and their repositories/structures/relationships are updated and the procedure triggering such updating is itself reviewed and assessed over a moving period of time. In the absence of this, risk management programs have a tendency to be based upon a single point in time, akin to a still photograph, leading to autopsy-type risk management (analysis and reporting on causes of failures), as opposed to proactive risk management.

Modern day complex business environments have created difficulties for conducting risk assessments due to the interplay between people, processes and technology that cannot be easily overcome even with current automated tools. Interdependencies within networked environments, coupled with assets values operate in upstream and downstream dimensions, creating variances in valuation of those information assets i.e. the level at which an asset is utilized within the organization may affect its importance and thus value at any given level.

Valuation of information assets is also complex, in particular in cases of mission-critical infrastructure. For quantitative analysis and valuation, additional issues are posed by data availability. In many cases, organizations do not have accounting practices that facilitate information asset valuation. In the absence of this, calculations for expected losses, either for single events or annualized figures, can become worthless, rendering any cost-benefit assessment for risk mitigation/management actions questionable at best. In the case of cyber threats and networks, further complications are added due to a lack of accounting practices for personnel as well as support infrastructures for networked environments.

Over the past decade, various formulas and modeling methods for IT/network infrastructure valuation have evolved, which attempt to take account of interdependency and the overall risks posed to IT infrastructure. Many of such models utilize some form of multiplier rather than relying upon a single value for a single loss expectancy. One such is the cascading threat multiplier, but this is one model among many and is mentioned here simply as an example. The formula is expressed as:

Cascading Threat Multiplier (CTM) = 1 + (UEA x EFS) / AV

UEA = Underlying exposed assets $ EFS = Secondary Exposure factor

AV = Asset value

failure of a particular asset. The *asset value* (AV) comprises the hardware, software, proprietary software of the organization plus the data. The *secondary exposure factor* (EFS) comprises a percentage loss on the UEA and is present to factor in the importance of an assets' logical location on a network. If the asset is not directly linked to other parts of a corporate network, if this asset was compromised, then the secondary exposure factor would be low, since there would not be a subsequent compromise/impact, and vice versa.

Taking the cascading threat multiplier for the purposes of cyber threat management cost assessment, the following table of variables and formulas/expressions can be adapted to suit in order to determine cost-benefits accruing from mitigation actions.

Table 9.7 Return on Investment and Risk Equation Examples

Variable	Formula/Expressions
AV (Asset Value)	AV = hardware + software + proprietary organization software + data
EF (Exposure Factor)	EF = % estimation of exposure of the initial compromised asset
UEA (Underlying Exposed Assets)	UEA = estimation of $ value of assets behind the initial compromised asset
EFS (Secondary Exposure Factor)	EFS = % estimation of the exposure of UEA
SLE (Single Loss Expectancy)	SLE = EF x AV x CTM
ARO (Annual Rate of Occurrence)	ARO = estimated number based upon industry statistics or organizational experience
ALE (Annual Expected Loss)	ALE
ALE1 (Annual Expected Loss With Mitigant 1)	ALE1 = SLE x ARO
ALE2 (Annual Expected Loss With Mitigant 2: Assumed Anticipated 50% Reduction in ARO)	ALE2 = SLE x ARO / 2
T (Annual Security Technology Cost)	T
R (Annual Recovery Cost from Cyber Attacks)	R = ALE
E (Annual Financial Gain From Deploying Cyber Attack Countermeasures)	E = ALE – (ALE1)
ROSI (Return on Security Investment)	ROSI = R – ALE where ALE = (R – E) + T
ROSI2 (Return on Security Investment)	ROSI = ALE2 – (ALE2 – (ALE1 – ALE2)) + T)

By using such formulas and adapting them to suit an organization, the cyber risk management process takes on a broader scope and introduces new factors into the analytical discussion. The accuracy or otherwise of such models/formulas may be for further discussion, however, the fact that an awareness is created of the specificity of cyber threats, as opposed to other risks, is in itself of inherent value.

Countermeasures

Threat Modeling is the activity of attempting to think about the vulnerabilities of an organization of being linked to the internet and involves trying to identify all of the parameters relating to systems and infrastructure generally. Attacks generally follow the path of:

- Identification of the target
- Collect as much information about the target as possible
- Analyze the information to identify potential weaknesses
- Use the weaknesses to gain access
- Attack the target
- Exit without leaving traces where possible

This is the same pattern followed in almost any systems attack, whether online or offline. A good example here would be in a bank robbery: both the physical world and digital one would have the same incentives and follow the same attack pattern.

The weaknesses in threat modeling are usually through not being able to create the correct context for an attack, that is to say, the rationale, target and means of acquisition are not fully comprehended by those creating the model. Examples of this happen in all organizations, NGO's, military, commercial, are many, all with the same lack of understanding or lack of acceptance of the real risk.

Threat modeling should be viewed as a continuous process, rather than a one-off or annual process, with external validation being used to verify that the vulnerability context modeled is the correct one with no omissions.

Technical Solutions

The currently available and ongoing growth in the offerings of physical and software systems, devices and technologies that seek to assist in reducing or eliminating cyber threats is such that even specialist publications have difficulty in keeping abreast of them all. This section therefore simply seeks to inform at a high level of the basic systems in order to inform the reader of their modes of operation, as opposed to providing an in-depth and detailed technical analysis of all within this sector.

Intrusion Detection Systems

Just as a sophisticated home security system might comprise cameras and sensors and monitoring equipment to watch for suspicious activity within a house – i.e., an unauthorized intruder, so an intrusion detection system alerts IT system administrators to potential security breaches within a corporate network environment. Like other traditional security technologies that have been assimilated into the broader scope of IT security planning, intrusion detection systems have emerged over the years as a growing requisite to the security paradigm.

However, even with the most well-planned and strategic implementation of these systems, either alone or in conjunction with other technologies, an ongoing variety of security attacks have shown repeatedly that such technologies are not doing the complete job of securing enterprise networks. These technologies are also accompanied by an increasingly complex and substantial administrative burden that further compounds the problem. The following outline serves to illustrate the different types of intrusion detection systems in use today, as well as their weaknesses.

Intrusion detection technologies fall into two categories: *host-based* and *network-based*. Products are both software and hardware designed to monitor a device or network for malicious activity. Intrusion detection software is designed to compare network/resource activity to a list of signatures known to represent malicious activity. It forms part of the overall security strategy or an organization.

As organizations rely more and more heavily on internet connectivity as a means of undertaking day-to-day business, the burden placed on traditional security technologies becomes stronger and the associated stress points are more clearly defined.

Network Intrusion Detection Systems (NIDS) are dedicated software systems that "sit" on a network wire and analyze network packets. The data encapsulated in these packets is compared to a database of known attack signatures. If the data passing along the network does not match a known attack listed in the database, then that traffic continues without suspicion. However if the packet data matches a known attack, then some sort of response may be generated. Such a response might come in the form of an alert that is sent to a log file or perhaps even a page to a network administrator.

Host-based Intrusion Detection Systems (HIDS) have emerged as a result of historically monitoring audit log files. With traditional systems, administrators search through log files at the end of the day to detect any suspicious activity that had occurred during a defined time period. The negative aspects of this analysis became obvious in that the work itself is not only tedious, but also untimely.

Current forms of HIDS offer a local agent performing the same scanning activity as an event occurs. As the event is logged to a log file, the local software agent installed on the resource checks to see whether that event matches any of those listed in its attack database. Some HIDS also have the ability to monitor application log files for evidence of additional attacks. HIDS also have the ability to monitor local files for any changes or modifications. When an event indeed matches an attack profile, the HIDS will send an alert and generate any one of a series of potential actions in hopes of deterring damage caused by malicious activity.

All IDS technologies share the same critical flaw as other traditional information security technologies: they are passive and reactive. Because these solutions are predicated on signature detection, even when they are efficiently installed and administered, a variety of attacks will still cause damage to network resources and files on individual machines. There are several weaknesses endemic to both network and host-based intrusion detection systems.

Signature-based security products have to have a signature for each threat signature in order to protect against attacks. This increasingly requires an ever increasing number of new signatures on a daily, or even hourly, basis to be incorporated into such systems. Signature-based security is therefore struggling to keep up with the growth trend, requiring users to update their security solutions on a more frequent basis. A good example of this is the case of home PC users with a large number of domestic software products that result in a seemingly daily routine of updating to one or more of them. The exponential increase in reported vulnerabilities suggests that the likelihood of a successful attack that is signature based is increasing as the rate of updating increases, that is to say, there is a strong possibility that a security hole will not be patched sufficiently quickly to eliminate successful attacks being executed on a broad basis. Further, attacks are increasingly targeting data-rich environments such as web-based e-mail and social media accounts.

A major issue for pattern and signature matching technologies is the degree to which they become prone to high numbers of false positives and false negatives. This is the state whereby the signatures that they deploy generate false alarms that indicate possible malicious activity when in fact appropriate host and network behavior is taking place. False positives crowd administrative consoles, reducing the effectiveness of the product and administrator, forcing administrators to respond to unwarranted security alerts.

Of greater dangers are false negatives i.e. there is no response to a threat when there should be. This can occur where filtering becomes coarser due to the high number of false positives being generated by security systems, rendering everyday operations impossible. This can be seen in the physical environment too, at airport arrival halls for example, where checking every passenger scrupulously would inhibit the functioning of an airport. The issue therefore becomes one of determining the level at which an organization is willing to operate its security thresholds.

Algorithmic Modeling of Cyber Threats

It is impossible to design algorithms that will be both practical to use and also optimal in every possible circumstance.

Weighted linear regression is a mathematical technique for extrapolating from past data to make predictions about the future. It is well documented, understood and widely accepted and this makes it appropriate to use in modeling of cyber threats. The use of weights allows the user to give more credibility to recent data.

The downside of using weightings is that an element of judgment is introduced into the process, as there is no right or wrong answer as to what the weights should be and this aspect can be influenced by the psychological effects upon judgment and decision making. To overcome this, initial calculations should be carried out using two standard types of weighting: equal weights and exponentially decaying, with a default decay rate (so that more weight is given to more recent data). Weighted regression results should also always be compared with un-weighted regression results. Upon review, it may be necessary for the user to specify their own weights by resetting the decay rate away from the default or by inputting an array of their own weights.

Further, it should be possible within the model used to overwrite the results from any of the regressions/calculations where they believe that another value is more appropriate (for example where the user believes that the past is no longer representative of the future). However, where this is made possible, some important decisions as to the model/calculations are made and the danger lies in the incorrect selection of model/calculation/weighting/decay rate. As such, it is important that any changes are indelibly recorded in some manner and that such logs are capable of audit (either internally for improving the cyber risk management process, or externally for underwriting and/or regulatory compliance).

The overall number of viruses/attacks and the proportion of such viruses/attacks that are successful should be modeled separately and is superior to modeling the number of successful viruses/attacks directly as it allows for two different trends to be modeled.

However, the restriction of extrapolating in a linear manner over time may be inappropriate. For example, it may be that the number of viruses worldwide grows exponentially over time, rather than in a linear rate of growth. If a linear model is used, there is a danger that it could significantly underestimate the future number of viruses. There are two approaches to correcting this that are worth exploring. The first is to extend the regression to include an exponential term. The second is to still calculate the original linear regression where the natural logarithm of the data is regressed against the predictors. Which prediction is ultimately used could be determined by which is the better fit to the data, as measured by having a smaller sum of squared residuals.

In some models, there is a prediction only into the next time period, so that if the data is annual, for example, the model will only predict the next year, if monthly, it will predict the next month, etc. However, the models should extend to model a flexible number of time steps into the future. This is straightforward to do; it requires using the same regressions used previously to extrapolate further into the future. However, as with all extrapolations, it is worth remembering that the further the data is extrapolated, the less confidence can there be in the results (and in particular, where there is exponential growth in the growth rates of viruses/attacks). This does not mean that such extrapolations are not useful, since a prediction based upon monthly data could be used to calculate an annual expected cost and/or the insurance premium required to cover such cyber risks.

Algorithms have to deal with a multitude of permutations as to viruses/attacks, for example, where a single virus may attack two targets. Consider an extreme scenario where there are two viruses each period (a period being defined by the user, e.g. per day/week/month/etc) each of which attacks the two targets. If the algorithm does not handle the scenario correctly, the output could be a projected 50% of viruses attacking each target. Then if the next period is projected, the output would show each target being attacked by one virus rather than two. There is therefore a high degree of complexity required in developing an appropriate algorithmic model to handle, not just the current possible cyber threat combinations, but the constant changes over very short timeframes to consider and handle as well.

Some models may estimate the average or expected cost arising from a virus or hacker attack. Whilst this information is useful, there are many reasons why information from a whole range of possible outcomes is of greater value. The most important of this possible range of outcomes are used in capital modeling; pricing in cyber insurance and in undertaking cost-benefit analyses for improving network security.

IT-related risks form part of the mitigation strategy in the form of insurance and broadly speaking, the capital to be held for a risk is the value of the 1 in 200 year event, although overall capital is significantly reduced by diversification between different risks. Thus an algorithm needs to be able to predict the potential variability in costs so that this cost can be assessed.

In general, insurance is priced at a margin above the expected claims, with the margin being in part related to the extent of the risk. Two risks with the same expected loss may attract very different insurance premiums if they exhibit very different characteristics in terms of the variability of claims. Once again, the algorithm which predicts this variability will be far more useful in setting the premium than one that does not. For an organization seeking to offset some of its' cyber risk through insurance, the development of such an algorithm is therefore important in terms of understanding the possible costs of not establishing an insurance contract to cover, but in maintaining such cover over a sustained period of time.

Failure to undertake such an exercise can lead to a laissez faire attitude to cyber threat management in that the group responsible may assume that the cost of the insurance premium will be maintainable and alternative options ignore. In the event of a series of claims however, the risk premium required by the risk carrier may make insurance cover unviable or the risk carrier may decline to offer cover, rendering the risk management team under short-term pressure to implement alternative solutions at a reasonable cost and having the desired effect in terms of reducing the risk exposure to align with the risk appetite of the organization. By continually assessing both the ongoing cyber threats posed to the organization and the cost-benefit of various mitigation actions, the effectiveness of remedies can be monitored and altered to fit over time to the organizations needs and changes that occur to operations, products and service during the life of the enterprise.

An example of this ongoing assessment of mitigation options would be where a cost-benefit analysis of potential security upgrades is undertaken. This will require the assessment of the impact on worst case scenarios as well as the expected cost. For example, it may cost $10 000 to reduce the expected cost by $7 500. On that basis, the organization would not proceed. However, spending the $10 000 may in fact significantly reduce, or eliminate the risk of a $100 000 cost and thus the improvement in such a scenario would be undertaken.

In modeling the uncertainty prevalent within I.T and in particular cyber threats, it is worth noting that there are three forms of uncertainty that are more important than others. The ultimate cost of a claim depends to a great extent upon numerous assumptions that cannot be known with certainty and this is termed parameter uncertainty. For example, a best estimate of the probability of a claim being successfully defended can be made, but it cannot be ascertained with certainty that this is the true probability.

Even if the true probabilities are known, the reality is still stochastic or probabilistic. This process uncertainty results in the fact that it will never be known with certainty how claims will turn out in advance. As an analogy, assume a coin that *may* have some bias in its form. If it is tossed 10 times and there are 7 heads, it may be deduced that the probability of a head is 0.7. However, it is not certain that the probability is not 0.6 or 0.8 for example. This is parameter uncertainty. If the coin was known to be fair i.e. there is no parameter uncertainty and the coin was tossed 10 times, it would not be a surprising outcome if there were, for example 4 or 6 heads and this is process uncertainty.

It is therefore important that any model developed has the capability to allow for both of these types of uncertainty. However, there is a third important type of uncertainty and that is of model uncertainty, that is, the risk that the model chosen is the incorrect one. For example, the question of whether the number of viruses grows linearly or exponentially is a question of model risk. This can only be dealt with by considering a variety of models.

Using regression techniques for modeling uncertainty is a valid and advantageous methodology. It is possible to extend regression calculations so that rather than simply reporting the best estimate of each parameter, it is possible to obtain a distribution for each parameter, centered as the best estimate. It is also possible to obtain the correlations between the various parameter estimates. The residuals (the differences between the data and the fitted model) from the regression can be observed and this will give an idea as to the extent of the process uncertainty i.e. how uncertain is the actual outcome even when the parameters in the model are known.

It is also necessary to allow for the uncertainty in the costs of each successful virus or attack. The distribution of such costs is difficult to ascertain. However, a sensible and practical approach is to assume that these claims follow a lognormal distribution, where the mean and the standard deviation are specified by the user of the model. The lognormal distribution is a skewed or asymmetric distribution which has greater scope for costs to be higher than expected then lower than expected and is frequently used in modeling insurance claims.

As previously stated, parameter uncertainty must be allowed for i.e. the uncertainty over the true mean and standard deviation, as well as the process uncertainty i.e. that costs are log normally distributed. However, given the approximate nature of this area it is not generally possible to model with a high degree of accuracy and rather, users of the model should use a mean and standard deviation slightly above this best estimate as a proxy for parameter uncertainty.

Events that are accepted as having a low frequency/high impact should be modeled stochastically through specifying probability distributions for the number of events and the impact of each one of those events. For the impact, a Poisson distribution is now generally accepted as the correct model for the number and log normal distribution for the impact, since it is a common choice for modeling the number of rare events. It requires one parameter; the expected number of events/claims.

Again, parameter uncertainty is best allowed for through prudent assumptions specified by the user. For these factors, modeling using a Monte Carlo simulation is perhaps the best option, with the generation of thousands of scenarios of what may happen and then calculating summary statistics from the results.

Each simulation would involve replacing each regression with a two-stage process:

- Simulate the parameters from their assumed distributions
- Simulate the quality of interest using the parameters generated above

Additionally, rather than multiplying the number of successful viruses/attacks by the assumed cost, it would be better to sample from the lognormal distribution the appropriate number of times and sum these values to obtain the total cost in this simulation.

The combined impact of low frequency/high impact events should be modeled similarly by first simulating the number of such events from the specified Poisson distribution and then for each of the events, simulating the impact from the log normal distribution. The process should be repeated at least 10 000 in order to obtain a good idea of the potential variability, especially at the extremes.

Where possible, within the model used, it should be possible to switch off either the parameter and/or process uncertainty. This would involve always using the best estimate value rather than carrying out a simulation. This would allow the organization to understand the relative impact of the two types of uncertainty.

In summary, for modeling cyber threats, the results of the simulations should deliver to the user, at a minimum:

- The mean
- Standard deviations
- A number of percentiles (as defined by the user) of the total cost
- The number of successful viruses/attacks

Drawing from the above modeling process, an organization will be in possession of the information required to populate a typical value at risk type of framework, based upon the balanced scorecard and widely used for a considerable period within the banking sector:

Table 9.8 Example Annualized Expected Loss Calculation Table

Event	Risk Value	Frequency	Annual Risk Rating	VAR ($)	Mitigation Action 1* VAR ($) Reduction	Mitigation Action 2** VAR ($) Reduction	Mitigation Action 3*** VAR ($) Reduction	Residual VAR ($)
Type 5	0	1000	A	1000000	100000	500000	Etc	400000
Type 4	1	1000000	B	10000000	2000000	2000000		6000000
Type 3	2	10000000	C	100000000	40000000	40000000		20000000
Type 2	3	100000000	D	1000000000	400000000	400000000		200000000
Type 1	4	1000000000	E	10000000000				
Etc	Etc	Etc	Etc	Etc	Etc			Etc

The mitigation costs to reduce or manage or eliminate each risk as it is felt appropriate can then be ascertained and mapped against each risk in the traditional manner, until the NPV reaches a point where the mitigation cost is higher than the risk if accepted by the bank.

Cyber Risk Valuation Systems

Throughout this book, the reader has been presented with various concepts, models, strategies and information relating to cyber risks and their management. For the professional IT manager, such threats are probably an everyday focus and not something that requires explanation. For those managers (and others) the question that may seemingly always be unanswered by managerial books on either risk management or IT is that of "well, what are we actually talking about". This section seeks to provide the actuality and how IT managers are required to act to secure an organization 24/7/365 from a plethora of attacks upon the corporate infrastructure.

There are many security systems and associated solutions that seek to assist both risk managers and IT managers in their activities. Bearing in mind the previous section relating to algorithmic modeling of cyber threats, many do not take full account of the specificity of cyber threats and/or of the means by which to value them. In the absence of accurate data, cyber threat risk management and ongoing resilience will be extremely difficult to achieve in the short-term, let along on an ongoing basis.

To illustrate a fraction of the problem, the figure below demonstrates the inflows of traffic towards a corporate security perimeter from the internet.

Table 9.9 Example of Actual Cyber Threat Data

1	ObservedThreats ObservationEnd=”2007-11-12T00:00:00” ObservationStart=”2007-11-05T00:00:00”> -<Threat SeverityScore=”7” **Target=”Unknown”** Category=”Indiscriminate” ID=”DOS MSDTC attempt”> <Observation Count=”50” To=”00:59:59” From=”00:00:00” **Day=”Monday”/> <Observation Count=”1844” To=”01:59:59” From=”01:00:00”** Day=”Monday”/> <Observation Count=”2324” To=”02:59:59” From=”02:00:00” Day=”Monday”/> <Observation Count=”2140”
2	-<Threat SeverityScore=”7” Target=”Unknown” **Category=”Indiscriminate”** ID=”ICMP redirect host”> <Observation Count=”50” To=”00:59:59” From=”00:00:00” Day=”Monday”/> <Observation Count=”1844” To=”01:59:59” From=”01:00:00” Day=”Monday”/> <**Observation Count=”2324”** To=”02:59:59” From=”02:00:00” Day=”Monday”/> <Observation Count=”2140” To=”03:59:59” From=”03:00:00”
3	-<Threat SeverityScore=”1” **Target=”SQLServer”** Category=”Indiscriminate” ID=”MS-SQL version overflow attempt”> <Observation Count=”150” To=”00:59:59” From=”00:00:00” Day=”Monday”/> <**Observation Count**=”5532” To=”01:59:59” From=”01:00:00” Day=”Monday”/> <Observation Count=”6972” To=”02:59:59” From=”02:00:00” Day=”Monday”/> <Observation Count=”6420” To=”03:59:59” From=”03:00:00” Day=”Monday”/> <Observation Count=”7320” To=”04:59:59” From=”04:00:00” Day=”Monday”/> <Observation Count=”5370” To=”05:59:59” From=”05:00:00”
4	Threat Category=**”Directed”** ID=”DirectedID_17” **SeverityScore=”8”** Target=”Target_22”> <Observation Count=”2” Day=”Sunday Monday Tuesday Wednesday Saturday” From=”01:40:00” To=”13:55:00”/> <Observation Count=”7” Day=”Sunday Tuesday Wednesday Saturday” From=”01:58:00” To=”22:04:00”/> **<Observation Count=”1”** Day=”Wednesday Friday” From=”01:42:00” To=”23:21:00”/> <Observation Count=”1” Day=”Sunday Monday Tuesday Thursday Saturday” From=”10:53:00” To=”17:02:00”/> <Observation Count=”3” Day=”Monday Tuesday Wednesday Thursday Friday Saturday” From=”04:07:00” To=”14:10:00
5	**Threat Category=”Directed” ID=”DirectedID_17” SeverityScore=”10” Target=”Target_49”> <Observation Count=”4”** Day=”Sunday Wednesday Thursday Friday” From=”07:45:00” To=”21:10:00”/> <Observation Count=”8” Day=”Sunday Friday” From=”02:29:00” To=”15:01:00”/> <Observation Count=”4” Day=”Sunday Thursday Saturday” From=”06:58:00” To=”14:46:00”/> <Observation Count=”9” Day=”Monday

Within each block of traffic are the same parameters, but the values of these inputs vary. The parameters used can be categorized as:

1. A temporal input, using days of the week and the times of the day, with traffic captured on a 24/7/365 basis for analysis and assessment;
2. A severity score being assigned to each threat identified within the traffic by the threat database;
3. The number of instances a specifc threat has been found within the traffic;
4. A categorization of every threat identified;
5. An identifier attached to each threat found within the captured traffic, assigned by the threat database;
6. The target of the threat found according to the threat database.

A brief explanation of the above is that unlike many systems, this particular one captures traffic by copying all of it and then analyzing all via a threat database that is comprised of both commercially available data, academic and research institutions data, plus the organizations IT security departments' additions to their own database. Many systems use a traffic sampling methodology, which if the temporal profile and the threat volumes per minute together with the type differences are examined here, it is clear that this is a flawed technique.

The severity score assigned to each threat is provided through the threat database. Where a threat is not within this, the system administrator can examine the type and assign a value within the database, thereby adding continually to the organizations' proprietary threat data. Since the enterprise topology and infrastructure, plus the mode of process operations will always vary from company to company, the impact upon each organization from the same threat will differ. As such, the severity score is in organization-specific item that can be assessed in the context of what the security community states but with the context of the enterprise itself being an overarching consideration when allocating a severity score.

Similarly, where there is a target specified, for example, within block 3 the target is specified by the threat database as being to MS SQL Server, one enterprise may rely heavily upon this particular database server software and as such assign a higher severity score than one using a competing product.

The final input of note is that categorization of the threat as being indiscriminate or directed. In the case of the former, these types of threat are generally of the automated kind, such as e-mail worms, whereas the latter are more insidious and are generally hacking attempts directed against a specific organization. When the numbers of threats of the discriminate type are reviewed, the norm is for these to be of a low number, whereas for the indiscriminate types of threat the volumes have a tendency to be high.

Taking the above into account, it is clear that the types of threat vary and even within the categorization there are differences. For example, even if the target of a threat is identified by the threat database, it may still be of an automated type, and as such be categorized as being indiscriminate, or still be indiscriminate with the target unknown. It is therefore the number of variables that, when combined with the multitude of permutations of process/system interdependency that creates the problems associated with effective management of cyber threats.

Taking the threat data from the organizations' traffic (inbound and outbound) is a technical starting point from the IT end of the spectrum. From this comes the requirement to be able to value such threats identified and then utilize mitigation strategies and options in order to manage the exposure level down to the meet the target set that meets the risk appetite of the enterprise. There are many solutions available to achieve this goal and the figures included herein are provided solely as examples of the types of systems available.

Taking the threat data generated by an organizations' back-end capture system, as in the case of the sample given above, this can then be used in several ways. In the first example, the traffic is taken and analyzed statistically by a particular software system that then displays the threats as shown in Figure 9.7.

Figure 9.7 illustrates the volume and dates of attack data for a particular organization. On the left of the screen are the risk hierarchies that enable the user to select various threat types and identify within the plot the level and dates that are applicable to that particular type of attack. The models used can be altered to suit the user/organization in terms of the method of fit, the curve type and the time weighting, which can be varied by day/week/months/quarterly, etc.

Some systems, such as the one used here, allow a simpler representation, together with a warning light system to illustrate the current status, making for an easier reporting solution for non-statistically minded personnel (Figure 9.8).

This simple, but effective representation gives a quick and easy to understand graphical view of where the organization stands at any given time, using historical data to illustrate whether the risk exposure posed is increasing, constant or decreasing and

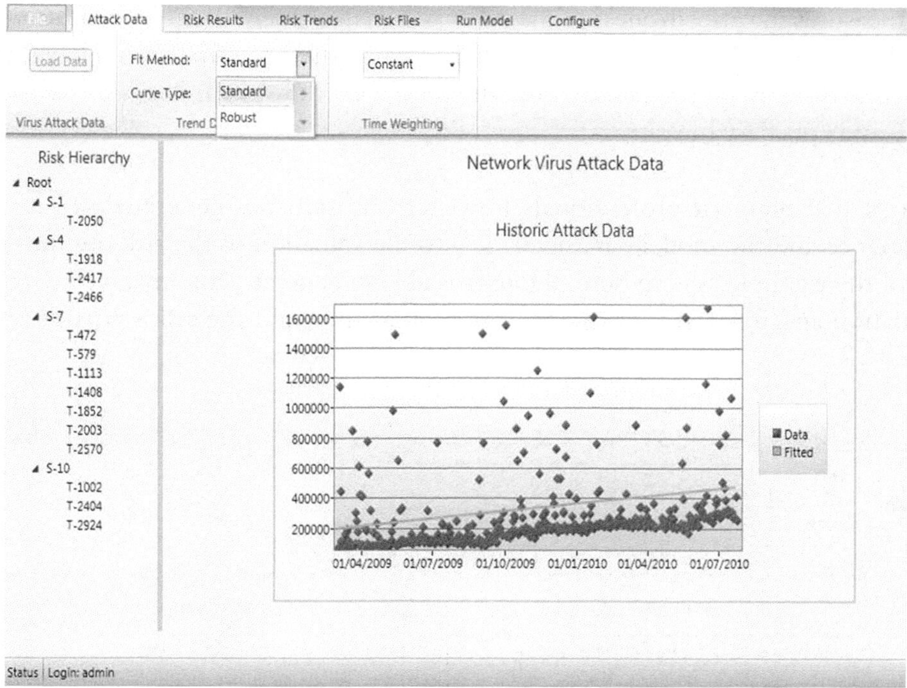

Fig. 9.7 Statistical Output of Virus Attack Data

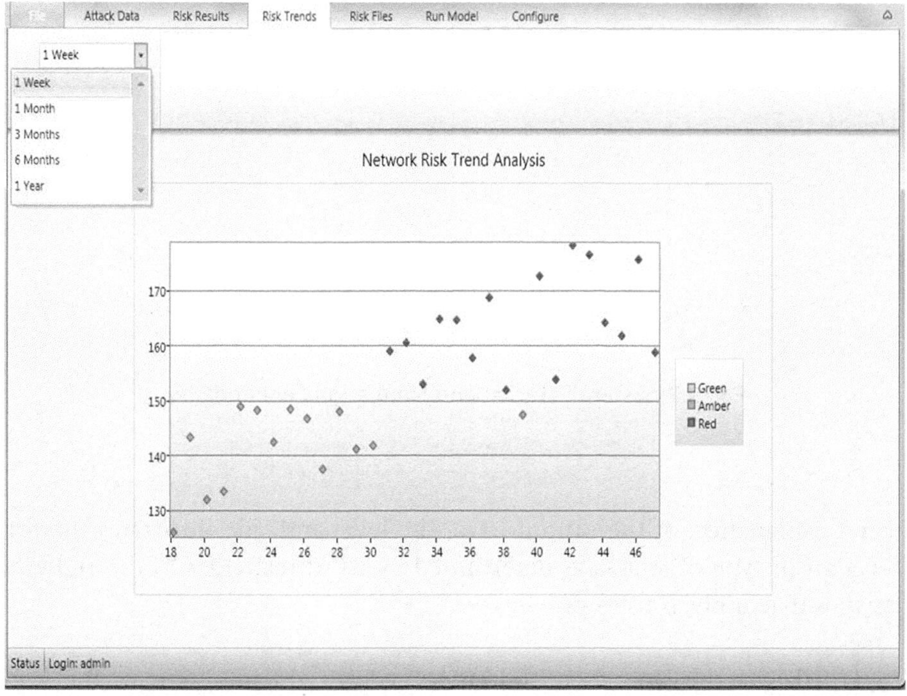

Fig. 9.8 Cyber Threat Trend Representation

thus measures the effectiveness of the cyber risk management of the organization. The Risk Trends have the x-axis as the number of days (since the first stored dataset) and the y-axis is the risk measure, that is, whichever one the system has been configured to use as its primary measure.

For risk management professionals however, the statistics generated are of more importance and the model parameters key to the valuation of the risk output. In the case of the example system here, the user is able to generate, for any given data set, a simulation and forecast for both the cyber attack rate and the risk statistics (Figure 9.9).

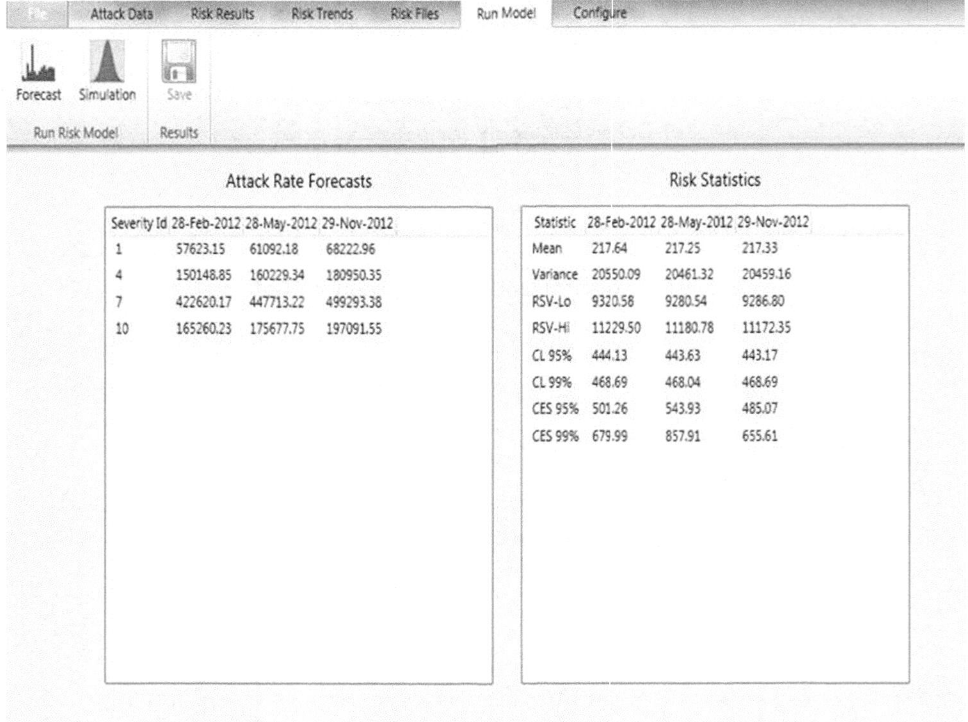

Severity Id	28-Feb-2012	28-May-2012	29-Nov-2012
1	57623.15	61092.18	68222.96
4	150148.85	160229.34	180950.35
7	422620.17	447713.22	499293.38
10	165260.23	175677.75	197091.55

Statistic	28-Feb-2012	28-May-2012	29-Nov-2012
Mean	217.64	217.25	217.33
Variance	20550.09	20461.32	20459.16
RSV-Lo	9320.58	9280.54	9286.80
RSV-Hi	11229.50	11180.78	11172.35
CL 95%	444.13	443.63	443.17
CL 99%	468.69	468.04	468.69
CES 95%	501.26	543.93	485.07
CES 99%	679.99	857.91	655.61

Fig. 9.9 System Forecast and Simulation Functionality

For a brief explanation of the output here, the left hand side illustrates the forecast rates for a given type of attack, as determined by its' threat ID. On the right are the risk statistics that apply as follows:

RSV-Lo/Hi: this is the Root Semi Variance Lo/Hi, which is akin to the standard deviation. However, in this case it is computed separately for the upper and lower part of the loss distribution. The rationale for this is that where there is a skewed distribution which is 'fatter' on the high side than the low side, then the figure for the 'Hi' number will be greater than the Lo number. If these are the same then the distribution will be symmetric.

CL: This is the Confidence Level (for a percentage level X).

CES: This is the Conditional Expected Shortfall, which is to say that this is the expected loss if the loss exceeds the given confidence level of loss. The CES should always be greater than the associated confidence level and the amount by which it is greater reflects how 'fat' the tail of the distribution is and as such this is a better measure of risk than the confidence level.

On the results graph – the x axis is a computed loss measure – the y axis is probability density (or at least proportional to it).

As a final example of the types of statistical output that can be derived from the actual threat data taken from an organization, the probability distribution function can be generated, which is of the type that most personnel will be familiar with:

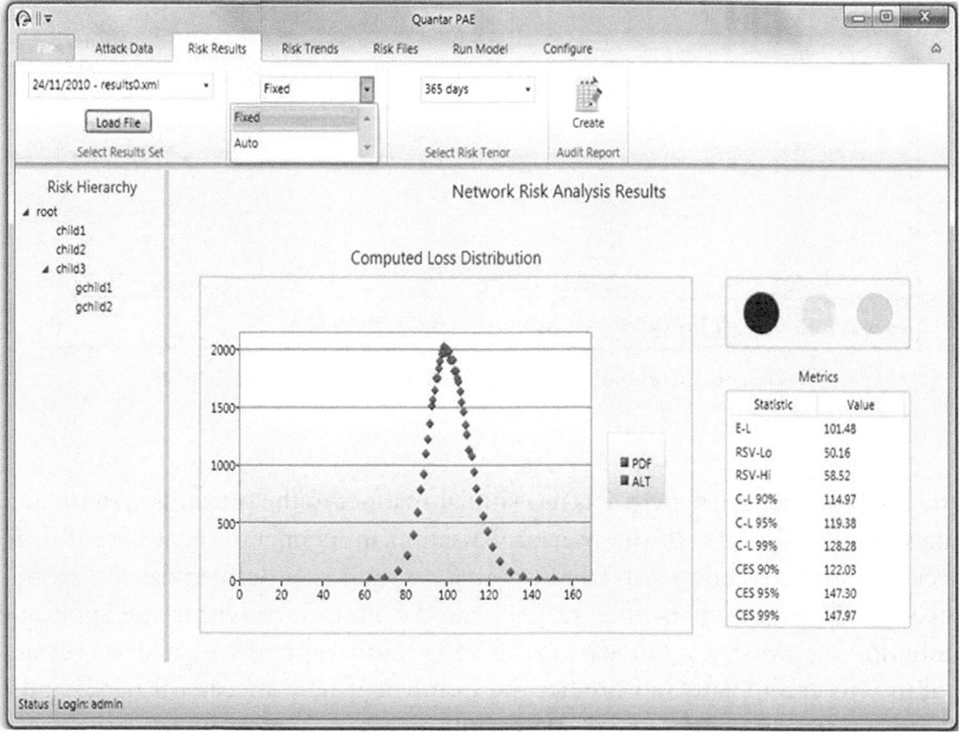

Fig. 9.10 Computed Loss Distribution for a Given Threat Data Set

The PDF stands for the probability distribution function and the ALT for an alternative view illustrating the probability in the tail of the distribution on a log-scale. The general statistics are displayed, along with the red/amber/green warning, together with the ability to change the temporal mode to up to a year. Finally, it is possible with this particular system to generate an audit report; something that is becoming increasingly a regulatory requirement.

By contrast however, the following example is provided to illustrate a completely different means of achieving a value at risk posed by cyber threats to the operation of an organization and uses an approach that may be more familiar to personnel with process management and business continuity planning backgrounds.

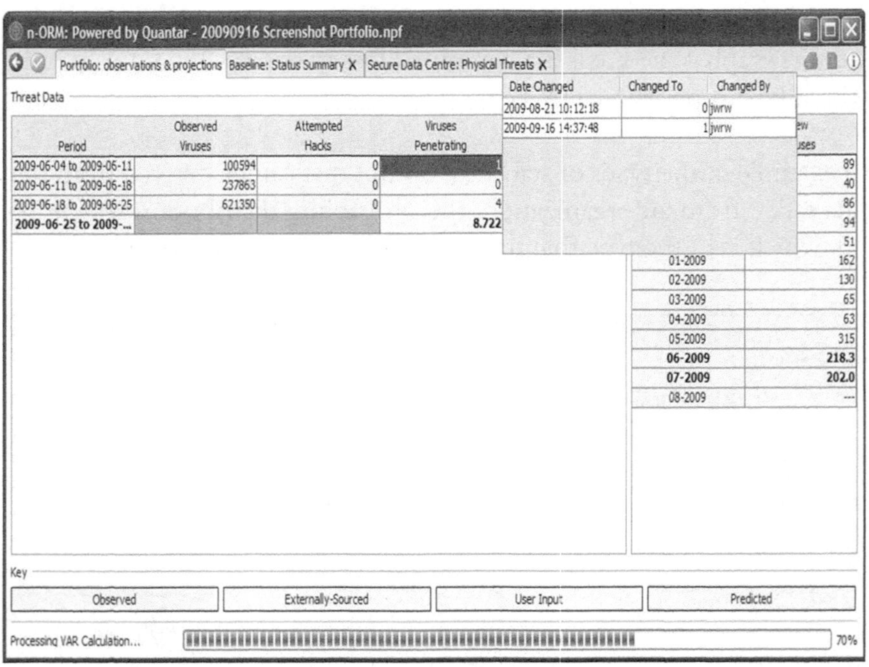

Fig. 9.11 Extrapolation of Data for Future Threats Prediction

In the above figure, the system acts in a similar manner to the previous system, in that it takes the actual traffic of the user organization in its operation. Where it differs, however, is in the means it also takes external data and user defined data i.e. from the company's IT security personnel to populate the algorithms within the application. Combining the three sets of data and 24/7/365 traffic capture and analysis results in the ability to extrapolate and predict the number of new successful hacks and the number of viruses/worms that will successfully penetrate the perimeter security of the organization before (hopefully) being neutralized.

Where this particular cyber threat management system differs from the previous one is in the inclusion of operational data in the calculation of the overall risk exposure and delivering a final network value at risk figure. Here the system provides a drag-and-drop interface to facilitate mapping of interdependencies between processes, systems and categories. The user/s link their processes to whichever systems that particular process relies upon. They also link from the systems to the categories, which in the example given below are geographies, but this could quite easily be departments, business units or down to floors of a building, where applicable.

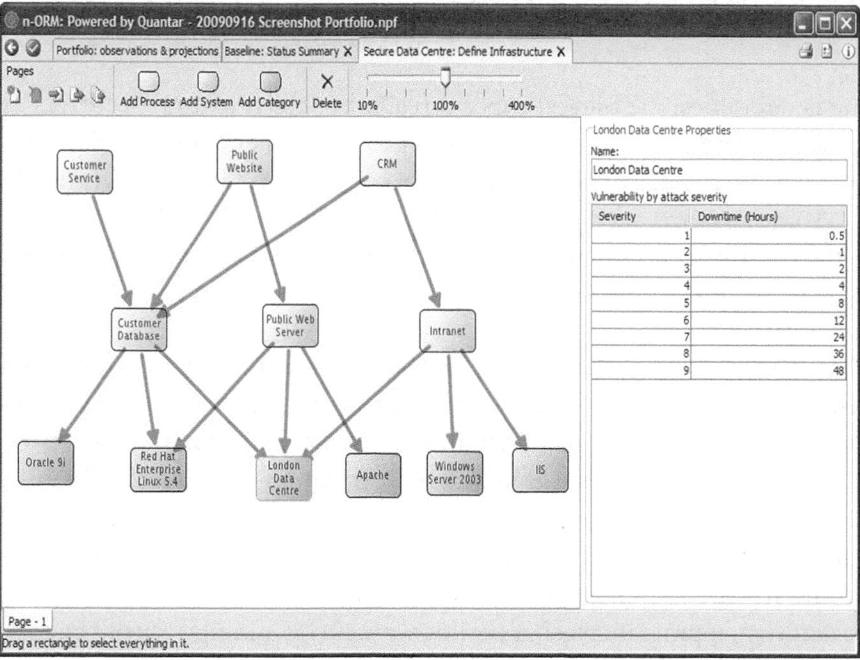

Fig. 9.12 Technology-Process Interdependency Mapping

The users then assign inputs for various parameters, including assigning a value for severity according to the amount of downtime a category experiences as a result of a successful cyber attack, whether a process is outsourced, time-zone of a process and the value of a process. In the case of the latter value imputed, this is where business process mapping as part of an enterprise's overall business continuity planning can play a vital role.

Most large-scale organizations will also have process owners/managers who will be in a position to either validate the figure provided by the business continuity management team or provide it themselves through their department's analysis of their respective process/es. Where there is an absence of a hard figure and/or other parameter inputs, estimates can be utilized and subsequently replaced as more accurate data becomes available.

Of importance to note here is that theoretically, if the back-end system was installed inside the organizations' perimeter defenses and the security was maintained at a 100% effective level, then all the risk values should be zero. Further, cyber threats do not always originate externally, with a large percentage of spreading of viruses and worms arising from insiders who either breach security rules (a typical example here would be in using USB memory sticks at work when they have come from an un-trusted source) or, in many cases, willfully seeking to damage the organization for any number of reasons (passed over for promotion, theft of proprietary data, theft of computer access codes, espionage, infiltration by groups opposed to the organization, etc).

In some geographies, the biggest cyber threat arises from natural occurrences such as earthquakes (Japan, Turkey, Iran, etc), water (The Netherlands, South East Asia, etc) or man-made ones, such as bombing to data centers (Middle East, North Africa, East Africa). Some systems such as that used to illustrate here, include this component within the process/threat calculation, even if in the case of natural disasters the statistics may give a 1 in 100 year probability.

Once the data has been utilized from the back-end i.e. the actual threats posed to the organization together with the user defined information relating to process/system interdependency and downtime, then the systems generally calculate a network value-at-risk. Systems may vary in the graphical representation of the results. In this instance, they are displayed as a bar graph for ease of understanding the existing financial risk exposure for the enterprise. In some systems, such as the one illustrated, there is then a capability for the risk managers to model various scenarios, such as changing the infrastructure mapping, increasing perimeter security, adding security guards, etc and measuring the mitigation impact on the network value at risk. This can be undertaken in stages until the risk exposure meets the target set or the risk appetite of the organization (Figure 9.14).

In this mode, the systems are similar to those used in business continuity planning, albeit operating with different data sets and with different end objectives. The systems may also graph the value at risk per process in a simple table format with the risk values in the axis. This combination of outputs enables risk management teams to rapidly understand where their attention should lie and which areas within the organization financial and other resources should be allocated in order to effectively manage cyber threats. Further, the ability to communicate the output to all levels of the organization in an understandable manner ensures both senior management buy-in and support from IT department heads who, in many cases, finally have the solid data required to validate their IT spend and ongoing budgeting (Figure 9.15).

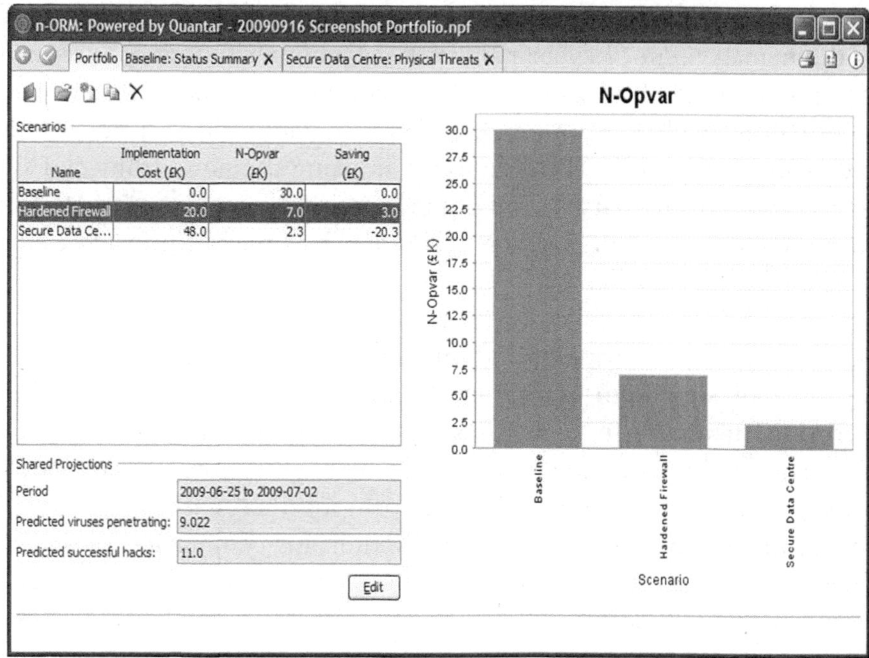

Fig. 9.13 Threat Portfolio Display and Valuation

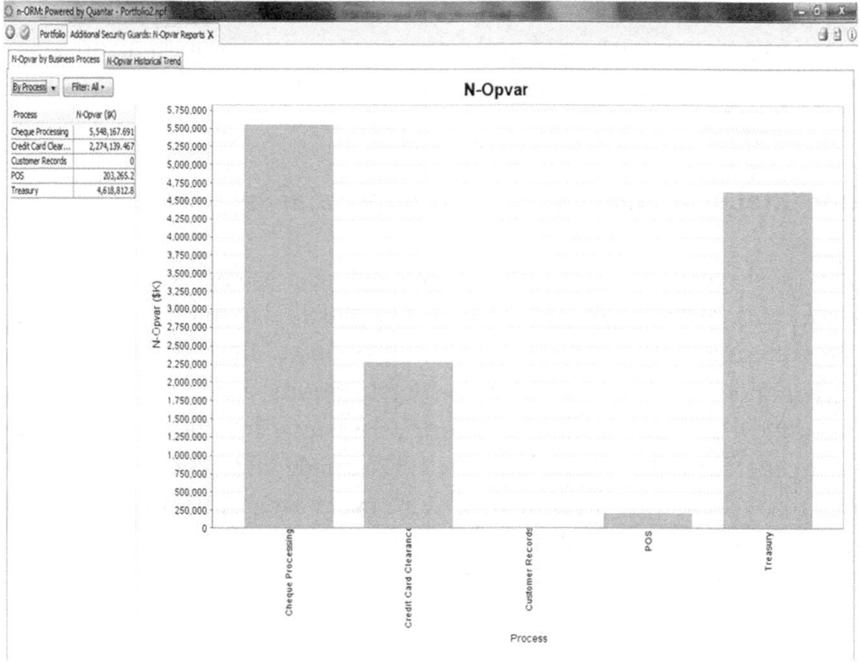

Fig. 9.14 Per Process Risk Exposure Representation

Whilst on the face of it these types of systems provide valuable data and act as excellent tools in the management of cyber risks, they serve other functions increasingly as well. A prime example of this is in regulatory compliance, where it may be possible in some instances to add a second back-end system within the security perimeter to copy and analyze all outbound traffic. By then using the same front-end systems, organizations can ensure that they are not permitting the transmission of viruses, e-mail worms, etc which has in many countries now become a criminal as well as civil liability.

Further, in certain sectors (banking and financial services, nuclear and aviation) there are regulatory requisites for measuring and managing operational risks, including those arising from IT failures. In such cases, systems that provide an ongoing threat assessment and risk exposure identification (by highlighting those process/systems at highest risk, as opposed to a purely financial risk) together with traceability of every change made to the management of cyber risks, audit and compliance rules can be met on an ongoing basis. As more industries become internet enabled, so this aspect of the systems ownership will increase in value to an organization. Supervisory control and data acquisition systems (SCADA used in industrial process controls), for example, are in the main now IP based due to the cost reduction opportunities they offer. Manufacturing, road infrastructure, water distributions systems and so forth therefore have a risk exposure arising from cyber attacks.

In other cases, the systems can be utilized as part of the underwriting, conditions compliance and proof of attack and loss in cases where an organization has transferred part of its cyber risk exposure to a risk carrier, as in the case of insurance and/or risk financing.

Mitigation Strategies and Options – *Insurance and Reinsurance*

One of the most recent trends in the risk products sector has been in the launch on a widespread basis of cyber insurance targeting particular market segments and/or sectors. Initially, only large-scale enterprises were able to find risk carriers who could include cyber and network risks within the organizations' general insurance pool. The risk of having cyber risks combined with I.T. risks and bundled with various other risks into a general pool is that where there is a single large event/claim, the overall coverage within the pool is diminished. With cyber attacks having the capability of multiple occurrences within a short period, there is thus the risk that multiple claims would not be covered due to coverage depletion.

Taking the example of a risk carrier covering every car within a particular geography, with a subsequent motorway/freeway multi-car pileup, the possibility that every car involved in the accident could be covered by a single insurer is present, but the probability is that it will not be the case. Insurance is priced at the margin, with volatility in claims/premium income determining the profitability of an insurance product over a sustained period of time. For the case of a cyber attack, the probability that a single risk carrier could be exposed to a massive volume of claims from a single event is far different than previous claims patterns. For this reason, cyber insurance has been specifically underwritten for major corporations, but with strict provisions, underwriting pre-requisites, limitations and audit requirements.

As part of the underwriting process, a thorough I.T. risk assessment is executed, often utilizing external agents, with claims coverage generally limited in scope and frequency. Substantial premiums increases allied to a reduction in payout have resulted in many cases where the policyholders have failed to provide sufficient evidence of security integrity.

For small to medium sized enterprises, cyber insurance has been of very limited availability, primarily located in the U.S. In Europe and other countries, the lack of products has been addressed in very recent times, with specific coverage offered, with varying degrees of loss values within policies.

The reason for this limited availability of available cyber insurance products has been the lack of data available to underwriters, allied to a lack of a sectoral claims history per country/sector/company size. An example of this is where a risk carrier offers a cyber insurance product in the U.S. but not in the E.U., despite having the U.S. products underwritten in the E.U. (and in London, U.K. in particular). There is a large demand for such products in the U.K., Germany and France from online retailers in particular. However, risk carriers are still unwilling to risk exposure to large-scale claims without sufficient evidence that such a product line would remain profitable in the long-run. In order to understand the role of insurance and of risk carriers, the following sections provide a brief overview of the insurance and reinsurance processes and in no way seeks to provide a detailed explanation of the workings of the insurance market.

Reinsurance

Reinsurance is a contract or program between a primary insurer and one or several reinsurers. Through a reinsurance contract, the organization that buys reinsurance spreads its risk by ceding (transferring) a portion of its liability to one or more reinsurers. Reinsurers themselves may also buy reinsurance to spread the risk even further. It is for this reason that it has often been referred to as the insurance of insurance companies. A ceding company usually enters into a reinsurance contract for a very specific reason. That reason, together with the business strategies of all the companies involved, combines to provide a number of possible combinations of how the risk can be mitigated.

When a primary insurer (this can also be an organization itself, where they have their own in-house insurance company for insuring their own risks, known as a captive) meets its reinsurance needs by entering into multiple contracts with more than one reinsurer, the resulting package is known as a reinsurance program. The advantages of a program rather than a single reinsurance contract with a single reinsurance company are flexibility and control for the ceding company. It retains maximum flexibility to adapt the program as its requirements change over time.

Primary insurers exist to serve the insurance needs of businesses and individuals. The variety of those needs is reflected in the many different types of primary insurance contracts available. By the same token, the reinsurance market exists to serve the insurance needs of insurers, both primary and reinsurance. The needs can also vary widely, hence the many types of reinsurance products available. A company buys reinsurance to satisfy some or all of the following needs:

1. Increase capacity
2. Enhance stability
3. Protect against catastrophes
4. Obtain surplus relief to enable growth
5. Gain access to underwriting expertise
6. Withdraw from territory or line of business

Regulations typically prohibit a primary insurer from risking more than 10 percent of its surplus on any one risk. With reinsurance, a primary insurer can increase its large line capacity, i.e., its ability to provide coverage for large, individual risks. Reinsurance also can be used to increase a primary insurer's premium capacity, which is also usually limited by regulations (and by the opinions of rating organizations) to a 3:1 ratio of written premium to surplus.

It is also often used to smooth out the volatility of a primary insurer's earnings. By reinsuring some of its risk, the primary insurer gains a steady flow of profits, which improves its ability to attract and retain capital. In effect, the primary insurer is giving up some of its potential profit in return for a steady revenue flow.

Some types of insurance are more predictable than others and some hazards are, by their nature, wildly unpredictable. Natural disasters such as earthquakes and storms have the potential to create catastrophic losses, as do events like plane crashes, industrial accidents, and major fires or explosions. Cyber attacks fall into this category, given the risk of widespread losses resulting from a single successful type of attack e.g. a particular e-mail worm that is not detected by a particular security system that has a wide customer base.

Often a reinsurance product is created specifically for catastrophic losses, to limit a primary insurer's maximum potential loss to some fixed and manageable amount. Such a contract will be written to cover multiple losses under multiple policies that are all caused by a single event.

Treaty and Facultative Reinsurance

The two basic categories of reinsurance are treaty and facultative. The difference between them is that a treaty contract covers multiple risks of a certain type, while a facultative contract is for a single risk.

A typical treaty type contract will cover an entire category of risk line of business, sometimes up to a certain limit or for a specified period of time. As long as a new risk that is accepted by the ceding company meets all the specifications for its category, as defined within the reinsurance contract, acceptance of that risk is automatic. Treaty contracts can be written in two ways; obligatory and non-obligatory.

In a non-obligatory treaty, the client can choose what is ceded based upon the prior agreement. For an obligatory treaty, the cedant does not have that option. By contrast, in a facultative contractual relationship between the primary insurer and the reinsurer, the reinsurer retains the faculty (ability) to accept or reject each individual risk offered by the primary insurer.

Primary insurers choose treaty or facultative reinsurance based upon their specific needs, and often the two are combined. For example, facultative reinsurance may be utilized to provide capacity over the limits of a treaty contract, or when the primary insurer is seeking to protect their treaty from a potentially adverse risk.

Cyber risks are one such category that is frequently declined and outside the scope of facultative contracts. For this reason, risk financing products were developed during the 1990's in order to offer the means by which to mitigate cyber risks for large-scale organizations.

Proportional and Non-Proportional Agreements

Regardless of whether the contract form is treaty or facultative, the same loss-sharing methods are available. The contract can be either proportional or non-proportional. In a proportional agreement for reinsurance, the reinsurer agrees to pay for losses in the same proportion as the share of premium it receives. For example, if the primary insurer cedes 55 percent of its liability to a reinsurer, it pays an amount equal to 55 percent of the original premium for the privilege.

Proportional reinsurance is also called pro-rata reinsurance and can be written on either a quota share or a surplus share basis. In a quota share arrangement, the reinsurer assumes a fixed percentage of each risk. In a surplus share arrangement, the ceding company sets a retention limit and the reinsurer takes the balance (the surplus). The alternative to proportional reinsurance is excess of loss.

Table 9.10 Characteristics of Pro Rata and Excess of Loss Reinsurance

Pro Rata (Proportional)	Excess of Loss (Non-proportional)
Liability based upon predetermined percentage	Liability in excess of the cedant's retention
Sharing of risks	No sharing above the retention
Focus is on the size of the risk	Focus is on the size of the loss
Rate is percentage of the original premium less the ceding commission	Separate rate. With or without commission
Settlement of premiums and losses by account (Bordereau)	Settlement of premiums by account. Settlement of losses individually

Table 9.11 Characteristics of Quota Share and Surplus Share Reinsurance

Quota Share	Surplus Share
Property or casualty	Often property only
Fixed percentage sharing	Variable percentage sharing
No individual cessions	Individual cessions
Reinsurers' premium is a percentage of the original premium, less a negotiated ceding premium	Reinsurers' premium is a percentage of the original premium, less a negotiated ceding commission
Settlement of premiums and losses by account	Settlement of premiums and losses by account

Excess of Loss Reinsurance

In an excess of loss agreement, an attachment point is set. In the event of a claim, the reinsurer pays nothing unless the claim amount exceeds that attachment point. For example, if there is a primary insurance policy with a coverage limit of $4 million, the primary insurer takes an excess-of-loss reinsurance contract with an attachment point of $1 500 000. If there is a claim of $3.6 million, the primary insurer is responsible for $1 500 000 and the reinsurer is responsible for the balance. If the claim was for $1 000 000 instead, then the primary insurer is responsible for the full $1 000 000 and the reinsurer pays nothing.

Excess of loss reinsurance can be written per risk, per occurrence, as in the case of a cyber attack and subsequent losses, or as an aggregate or stop loss. In per risk excess of loss reinsurance, the reinsurance limit and retention applies "per risk" (building/location) rather than per occurrence, per event, or in the aggregate. Per occurrence is used to reinsure against catastrophes and is usually written for property exposures. And is generally the form of contract offered for cyber risks and consequential losses such as reputational damage, regulatory breaches, etc. Aggregate excess of loss or stop loss stipulates participation by the reinsurer when the aggregate losses for the primary insurer exceed a certain level, usually stated as a loss ratio. Stop loss can cover the property and casualty books of business or property only and is used for cyber risk coverage for major organizations where full cover would carry too large a premium to be of benefit.

For all types of excess of loss there is no relationship between premium and loss in a non-proportional agreement. The premium is negotiated separately and based on a variety of factors.

Conceptually, proportional reinsurance focuses on the size and nature of the overall risk, whereas non-proportional reinsurance focuses more narrowly on the size of the potential loss to the reinsurer.

Given the lack of historic underwriting data, combined with the potential for large-scale losses arising from a single successful attack, risk carriers have increased their underwriting criteria and transferred much of the onus of maintaining security integrity and records of this to client organizations. This in turn has resulted in data retention and growth in order to fulfill the provisions of the underwriting process and in providing proof that an organization has not been negligent in its security provisions and maintenance. In this respect, costs for maintaining insurance cover for cyber threats has increased, not directly through premium increases, but through the costs associated with data acquisition, storage and retrieval/reporting.

Table 9.12 Characteristics of Non-Proportional (Excess of Loss) Reinsurance

Per Risk	Per Occurrence	Aggregate (Stop Loss)
Negotiated rate exposure basis, usually no commission	Negotiated rate exposure basis, usually no commission	Negotiated rate exposure basis, usually no commission
Premiums are settled by annual adjustment of deposit premium	Premiums are settled by annual adjustment of deposit premium	Premiums are settled by annual adjustment of deposit premium
Usually minimum premium	Usually minimum premium	Usually minimum premium
Losses settled individually	Losses settled by catastrophe or event	Losses settled annually
Retention is for each risk/ location	Retention is usually above a minimum of two full-risk losses	Retention and limit is stated as a loss ratio
Usually has a pre-occurrence limitation	Often has co-insurance provision when the reinsured shares in the loss above the retention	Often has co-insurance provision when the reinsured shares in the loss above the retention

Underwriting Reinsurance

Typically, a reinsurance underwriter evaluates an entire book of business, as well as the stability, practices and pricing of the primary insurance company. In particular, the reinsurance underwriter must evaluate the loss exposures covered by the primary insurance company and the specific terms of that coverage. In the case of facultative reinsurance, the underwriter is evaluating all of this as well as a specific risk. In the event of a loss covered by a reinsurance contract, the reinsurer pays the amount owed to the entity holding the reinsurance contract, typically a primary insurer or another reinsurer.

Part of the expectation of the ceding company is that this payment will be timely, since in many cases its solvency is at stake. The ceding company is therefore obliged to inform the reinsurer(s) about both actual and potential losses. Normally, the ceding company pays the claimant(s) first and is reimbursed by the reinsurer(s). The lapse of time between payment to the claimants and reimbursement by the reinsurer is usually stipulated in the reinsurance contract. However, in cases of cyber risk coverage, a major issue of contention for both the primary carrier and the reinsurer is in the valuation of loss, which in turn impacts upon payout speed. Clearly the impact and consequential losses arising from a single attack varied according to the individual client organization, since the volume of variables is vast. Further, loss types will also vary in terms of the temporal aspect. A good example of this is where a weakness in a webserver that is subsequently exploited has the potential to cause financial loss if the victim organization has online commerce as its primary business activity, versus longer-term damage caused to another enterprise through a defaced website belonging to a global brand.

Traditionally, the key items to be considered by a reinsurer in the underwriting process have been:

- The financial status of the primary insurer
- Loss exposure of the primary insurer
- The extent of coverage provided by the primary insurer
- Risk retained by the primary insurer
- Premium pricing of the primary insurer
- The exact wording of the reinsurance contract

From the above, it is clear that cyber risks do not behave in the same manner as traditional risks in terms of the potential loss exposure, the claims frequency, nor the potential for losses. Further, the process of undertaking a loss adjustment and assessment may take far longer than in cases of traditional loss, with the client having to be examined in detail as to the cause of the failure and whether there was contributory failure on the part of the client through negligence in maintaining cyber security systems and processes. The potential for multiple large-scale losses and a lack of underwriting data/claims history causes underwriters to either formulate policy requirements/limitations in such as manner to be a little use as a risk mitigant, or the value of coverage so low that even if a claim is accepted, the costs of acquiring coverage do not make a good business case for many small and medium sized enterprises.

Alternative Risk Transfer

Alternative risk transfer has its origin in the emergence of the captive insurance market more than thirty years ago, when large corporations, with a strong capital base, created captive insurance companies in tax havens. The main goal was to retain more risk by means of risk management solutions deploying self-financing mechanisms.

In the 1980's, specialized reinsurance companies were established in offshore financial centers and other markets, offering financial reinsurance products with little or no insurance risk transfer. The clear focus was on risk financing features utilizing the favorable accounting and tax environment typically provided by offshore centers.

During the past two decades, an increased demand for financial concepts, including risk transfer, led to the development of second generation, so-called finite risk reinsurance products combining risk financing and risk transfer techniques. Newly issued accounting and regulatory guidelines in some leading financial reinsurance markets have also contributed to this demand.

Encouraged by an objective regulatory environment and the insurance sector's increasing need for finite risk reinsurance, traditional reinsurers have committed a greater degree of know-how, capacity and security to providing sustainable solutions.

Most recently, the convergence of insurance and capital markets has also provided an array of innovative concepts to integrate financial risks into reinsurance cover and to access capital markets for the financing of insurance risks.

An example of this type of development is in the provision of risk financing for cyber risks, albeit limited to large-scale commercial organizations. Further, this type of cover is still generally formed as part of a cluster of policies under one over-arching instrument and usually formed to cover operational risks (and within the banking and financial services sectors in particular).

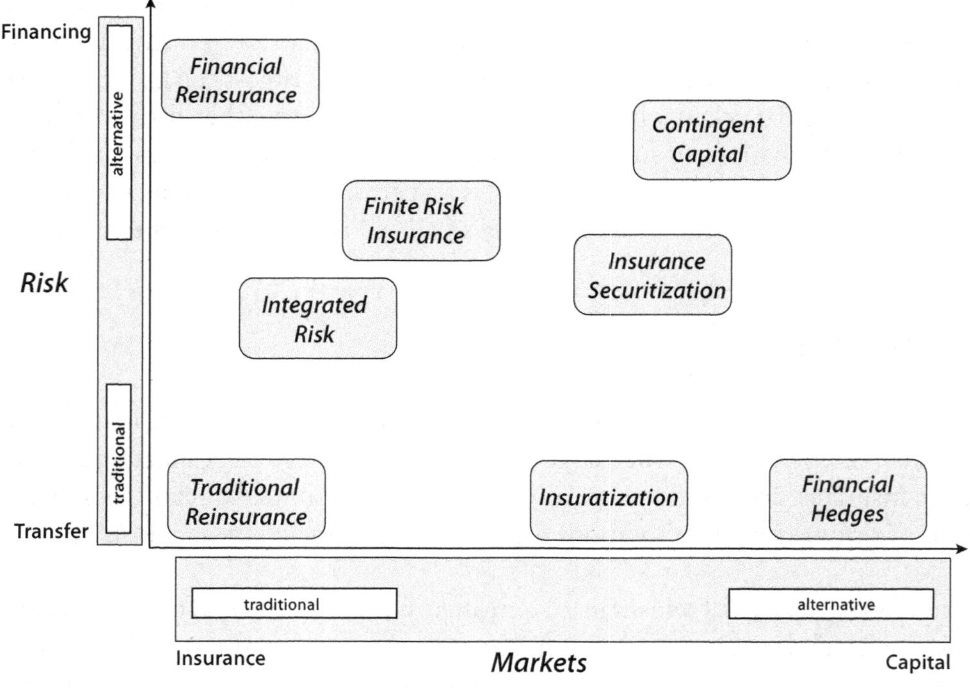

Fig. 9.15 Risk transfer and financing spectrum

Forms and Operation of Alternative Risk Transfer

Natural catastrophes reached new record levels in the last 20 years, both in terms of loss amounts and intensity. This brought to light a discrepancy between economic and insured values, capacity and price fluctuations on international reinsurance markets, as well as doubts regarding the ability of certain catastrophe (re)insurers to pay claims following a major catastrophe made it important to look for alternative methods of risk transfer and to take advantage of the nearly inexhaustible capacity offered by the global capital markets.

A broad spectrum of new financial market instruments such as risk bonds, futures, swaps and options have proved to be suitable instruments for risk transfer to the capital market. The volatility of available reinsurance capacity and reinsurance prices makes capital market solutions appear to be attractive hedging alternatives for insurance risks.

This mode of risk financing has been used by major risk carriers for cyber insurance coverage for major corporations. The risk is therefore not transferred and as such the underwriting methodology and criteria that would be imposed in the traditional manner for such things as natural disaster coverage does not apply.

Capital market instruments that are available today to cover insurance risks can be distinguished from one another as follows:

- Risk financing instruments
- Contingent capital ("contingent liquidity")
- Risk transfer instruments
- Securitization of insurance risks by way of bond issue
- Insurance derivatives

For many years now capital markets have been providing insurance companies with limited capital via so-called contingent capital programs for the event of a natural catastrophe and loss of equity. This process merely involves providing capital, which is repaid, to the creditors or investors after expiry of the contingent capital transaction (no transfer of the insurance risk, simply pure financing). Insurance securitization, i.e. the securitization of insurance risks and the transfer of risks to the capital market via bonds and derivatives have only been widely used as an instrument for covering insurance risks since 1997.

Insurance securitization has given insurers access to the capital market as a new additional source of capacity to supplement traditional reinsurance. As insurance risks do not correlate with other investment classes, insurance risk bonds as well as insurance derivatives and contingent capital programs provide investors with the means for diversifying their investments.

This market has become depleted in the face of the recent global financial crisis. However, as bond yields have remained low following sovereign debt risk and financial bailouts of certain countries, the potential yield on such risk financing may once again become popular. This may also offer the potential for creating specific/specialty risks underwriting capability for certain types of cyber risks in the future for large-scale enterprises with higher operational risk exposures from technology-process interdependency. Where the cost of risk financing is lower than, for example, creating fully redundant processes and/or systems, then the business case should facilitate developments in this particular area.

The most common insurance securitization model via an insurance risk bond, the insurer, acting as the sponsor of the transaction, concludes a reinsurance agreement with the reinsurer, who then cedes the risk to a special purpose reinsurance company (SPC) under a retrocession agreement. This SPC covers any liabilities from the retrocession agreement by issuing a bond.

The proceeds from the bond issue are then invested in top-quality bonds through a collateral trust, with management of the collateral trust being in the hands of a trustee whose task is to ensure the proper administration and use of the trust assets. The assets of the collateral trusts serve as a guarantee for any liabilities on the part of the SPC arising from the retrocession agreement and thus allow top security rating (AAA) of the cover for the insured.

The investment income from the collateral trust is generally based on a reference interest rate, such as the London Interbank Offering Rate (LIBOR). This is made possible by means of an interest rate swap between the trust and a swap counterparty, which swaps the investment income rate from the collateral trust for the LIBOR rate and thus ensures a fixed interest rate for the investors. The reinsurance and retrocession premium rate is passed on to the investors as a spread over LIBOR and offers the investors an incentive to invest in this bond.

Insurance risk bonds can have different structures. In the case of principle-at-risk bonds, the entire nominal value serves as liability. Liability can, however, also be restricted to the interest payment, as is the case with principle-protected bonds. In such a case, the nominal value of the bond is repaid to the investor five to ten years after a loss event. If a loss occurs, only a portion of the bond serves as liability.

The other portion is invested in discounted "zero-coupon" bonds, which are paid back at par after five to ten years, thus securitizing repayment of the bond at nominal value. The basis for cover can be the actual loss sustained by the cedant (insurance portfolio), a loss index or a parametric trigger.

For use in cyber risk financing it is therefore necessary for both the insurer and reinsurer to cap the coverage offered to the numerous client organizations. In this manner, securitization of the insurance cover for a sector or segment is feasible for a reasonable bond yield rate and thus cost to the end-user of the risk coverage.

Bond securitization products seek to model the underlying loss experience on a portfolio of insurance risks within the corporation. For cyber/network risks, they would be based upon a Sectoral need, rather than a single corporation. In essence they would be low-grade bonds, offering investors an uncertain rate of return. These bonds would be attractive for both their high-expected rates of interest and their low systemic (market) risk. The underlying insurance losses would in all probability be random in nature, which can assist in efficient portfolio diversification.

Insurance Derivatives

Insurance derivatives, which transfer insurance risks to the capital market and which, in contrast to insurance risk bonds, do not provide prior liquidity to safeguard the maximum liability; can be structured as swaps or options. The basis for such a transaction may be a market loss index, or a parametric trigger. A market loss index reflects the losses incurred in the insurance industry after a natural catastrophe. A parametric trigger links the trigger of cover to a natural catastrophe, which must comply with precisely defined and transparent criteria in terms of severity (magnitude of earthquakes, wind velocity or air pressure for windstorm).

It is therefore possible that this form of risk financing could be developed for the cyber loss market if there is sufficient data and history for investors to accept acquisition of the risks provide sufficient margin without an accompanying excessive financial loss exposure. A potential model for this has already been created by the Chicago Board of Trade (CBOT) in respect of standardized option contracts trading.

The CBOT has, for many years, been trading in standardized option contracts on the basis of market loss indices for nine regions in the USA with coverage periods of up to one year. Through the option contracts, participants can buy or sell cover against natural catastrophes in the USA (hurricanes, earthquake). The option premium here corresponds to the reinsurance premium. In addition to insurers and reinsurers, other financial institutions such as investment banks or unregulated funds can also be active in this sector.

For the case of cyber risks, a similar model could be employed if there were sufficient take-up of cyber risks coverage by major corporations i.e. capable of having sufficient volume and value to create standardized option contracts and for them to be traded.

As the regulatory environment becomes more punitive in both financial terms and in attributing personal Board level liability, so the risk valuation and desire for fuller coverage for a loss event has increased. In the case of cyber risk coverage, demand and values attached have similarly increased, with regulatory breaches and operational loss reporting becoming the domain of the Board rather than being viewed as an I.T. departmental issue.

Data losses, privacy breaches, changes in the placement of legal obligations and compliance (away from regulators and towards organizations) are all driving forces for risk management divisions to better identify and incorporate network/I.T. value-at-risk within operational risk and resilience programs.

Outside of commodity exchanges, derivatives are negotiated and agreed upon between the parties on a case-by-case basis. These are referred to as over-the-counter (OTC) derivatives. With an OTC insurance swap or an option, the cedant pays the investors a premium and receives indemnification in the event of a loss. From a purely technical point of view, this construction is comparable to a standard (re)insurance contract. The cedant acts as the option buyer, the investor as the option seller. The option seller receives an option premium (fixed-rate payment) in advance from the cedant (option buyer), which is comparable to an insurance premium. The option can be exercised when an agreed market loss index level is exceeded or a parametric trigger occurs.

The option buyer receives the fixed nominal amount as "compensation" or "indemnification" (floating-rate payment). The option buyer does not require proof of an insured interest or the occurrence of a loss event for payment from the derivative. The deciding factor is merely the point at which the agreed market loss index level is exceeded or a parametric trigger comes into effect.

In this manner, the issues surrounding data to underwrite, the lack of claims history, the probability versus possibility as to claims are removed from the equation and may provide a long-term solution to financing cyber risks for large-scale enterprises, either on a per country or per sector basis (and in particular, sectors with high I.T./process utilization rates such as the banking and financial sectors). As cyber/network risks become better understood by the risk carrier and capital market sectors, so the ability to trade a risk financing insurance derivative increases.

The option can also take the form of a second-event cover under which the option buyer receives coverage at a previously fixed price if an agreed market loss index level is exceeded or a parametric trigger comes into play and the option is exercised. Similar risks can be swapped without payment of a floating rate or option premium on the basis of a risk swap. In this way, the over-exposure of one party in a risk class can be ceded or swapped for another risk class that is underrepresented in the insurance portfolio.

This allows a multi-dimensional diversification effect (risk-class, region) and produces a more efficient risk portfolio. For example, it would be possible to swap US cyber risks for E.U. cyber risk or the banking sector cyber risk for the insurance P&C sector cyber risk, assuming that these have the same probability of loss and identical exposure (nominal value).

The transfer of insurance risks to the capital market and the financing of insurance risks through the capital market is still a relatively young field of business when compared with traditional risk underwriting and financing. In the securitized risk classes, there remains a focus on natural catastrophes, whereas in other risk classes such as life, credit, weather or residual value insurances, individual, large-volume transactions still dominate.

Historically, it has essentially been risks with a low probability of occurrence and a high loss potential that have been transferred to the capital market. In the face of a hardening reinsurance market and an increase in capacity shortages, the capital market will have to prove that it can effectively generate additional and alternative capacity in the long run.

Reinsurers generally support their clients in the transfer of insurance risks to the capital market, functioning as a structurer and project manager, drafting and putting capital market solutions into practice (as previously mentioned above in relation to creating cyber risk financing structures). They are able to assume important functions in insurance securitization and insurance derivative transactions that have a decisive effect on whether the transaction is a success or not.

National legislation covering insurance in individual countries specifies the types of insurance or risk transfer products an insurance company can offer. Even within the scope of insurance regulations, there are market limitations however. First, the risk transfer relationship must clearly define the legal trigger of a potential loss at a point in time and ensure the contract itself is enforceable. Second, insurance can only be supplied in a sustainable way if it can be adequately priced; an insurer must have sufficient information to estimate the underlying loss distributions.

At present, this is not the case for cyber and network operational risks which is why they tend to be included in the overall basket of operational or IT/system risks. Where there is cyber/network risk data frequently this is not passed on to the insurance industry for fears of bad publicity and/or signaling to attackers that a company/sector may be vulnerable. This can lead to the problem in the near future of adverse selection, i.e. where the buyer has more information about the probability or severity of loss than the insurance company itself. Where the degree of adverse selection is high, the supply of insurance cover will be curtailed over time.

For cyber/network insurance, where there is a treaty contract, covering typically an entire line of business, then the limits set by the policy will be reached in the cases of catastrophic or high impact events. In cases of shortfall, an organizations' capital reserves could become depleted in covering the losses, which might be spread across the entire enterprise and be extensive. Finding a reinsurer who is willing to carry the risk subsequently may be impossible, resulting in differing methodologies being used over time, with little or no industry standard, creating more problems in defining the risk profile and in creating actuarial models for the future. Covering cyber/network risks with all the attendant issues may therefore lead to increases in the cost of cover for many organizations/sectors, reducing shareholder value and/or operating profit. Where large losses are experienced over a sustained period, the increased cost of premiums will thereby reduce the effectiveness of insurance as part of an organization's total risk management strategy.

Where there is a facultative contract in place covering network risk (within the I.T. general coverage), again the limit will be reached, and although the financial loss is capped by the contract, the damage may be more widespread than that covered under the contract due to the pervasiveness of information technology within organizations. The same arguments as put above relating to covering future risk are applicable in cases of facultative contracts and reinsurers.

Similarly, whether the coverage is determined by either pro-rata or excess of loss contracts, the result will be a diminution of capital reserves and an increase in the cost of covering network operational risk, since the size of the risk for the former type cannot be quantified, nor the size of the loss, in the case of the latter type of contract.

External Information – *Regulations, Standards and Professional Bodies*

In respect of utilizing and leveraging information external to the organization, there are many books written on the subject of best practice transfer and the "not invented here syndrome". However, there has been far greater acceptance in the current post-financial crisis period of the need to regularize standards and practices and this mindset has permeated other sectors globally. Allied with various management practices reaching as far back to the total quality management programs of the 1980's, this has resulted in widespread adoption of ISO certification.

Within the context of cyber risk management, by drawing upon such adoption rates of ISO and other standards produced in various locations around the world, it is possible to create a self-assessment program for each organization, customizing it to fit the needs of the enterprise and the sector/geography/context in which it competes.

The starting point then becomes the question of which standards, practices and/or certification programs are the most appropriate. In the case of cyber/network security, the following may be viewed as the most appropriate:

Table 9.13 Examples of External Information

Title/Number	Type
The Sarbanes-Oxley Act of 2002	Regulation
OCTAVE	Risk Management
COBIT	Risk Management
ISO 31000:2009, Risk management: Principles and guidelines	International Standard
ISO/IEC 27002I Information Security Management	International Standard
AS/NZS 3931:1998 – Risk analysis of technological systems – application guide	National Standard
BS 25777:2008 – Information and communications technology continuity management. Code of practice	National Standard
BS ISO/IEC 17799:2005 Information technology. Security techniques. Code of practice for information security management	International Standard

Sarbanes Oxley

The Sarbanes-Oxley Act of 2002 is a United States federal law, signed into law on July 30, 2002 in response to a number of major corporate accounting scandals. The legislation comprises 11 titles and is wide-ranging, establishing new or enhanced standards for all U.S. public company boards, management, and public accounting firms.

The Act established a new quasi-public agency, the Public Company Accounting Oversight Board (PCAOB), which is charged with overseeing, regulating, inspecting, and disciplining accounting firms in their roles as auditors of public companies. The Act also covers issues such as auditor independence, corporate governance, internal control assessment, and enhanced financial disclosure.

The Act's focus is upon financial reporting and internal controls and sought initially to eradicate the defense of a lack of knowledge utilized by CEO/COO/CFO level management in the aftermath of major corporate failures in the U.S. In respect of cyber risk management, the necessity for understanding risk exposures in operational and thus financial terms means that these aspects, allied to new and emerging regulations which place the burden of compliance upon individuals at Board level, SarBox is a useful source of information.

Sarbanes Oxley Key Provisions

SOX Section 302: Internal Control Certifications

Section 302 of the Act mandates a set of internal procedures designed to ensure accurate financial disclosure. Company officers must certify that they are "responsible for establishing and maintaining internal controls" and "have designed such internal controls to ensure that material information relating to the company and its consolidated subsidiaries is made known to such officers by others within those entities, particularly during the period in which the periodic reports are being prepared." The officers must "have evaluated the effectiveness of the company's internal controls as of a date within 90 days prior to the report" and "have presented in the report their conclusions about the effectiveness of their internal controls based on their evaluation as of that date."

Additionally, under Section 404 of the Act, management is required to produce an "internal control report" as part of each annual Exchange Act report. The report must affirm "the responsibility of management for establishing and maintaining an adequate internal control structure and procedures for financial reporting." The report must also "contain an assessment, as of the end of the most recent fiscal year of the Company, of the effectiveness of the internal control structure and procedures of the issuer for financial reporting."

External auditors are required to issue an opinion on whether effective internal control over financial reporting was maintained in all material respects by management. This is in addition to the financial statement opinion regarding the accuracy of the financial statements.

SOX Section 404: Assessment of Internal Control
Section 404 requires management and the external auditor to report on the adequacy of the company's internal control over financial reporting (ICFR). Both management and the external auditor are responsible for performing their assessment in the context of a top-down risk assessment, which requires management to base both the scope of its assessment and evidence gathered on risk.

SOX 404: Information Technology
The financial reporting processes of many companies depend to some extent on IT systems. Thus, Information technology controls that specifically address financial risks fall within the scope of a SOX 404 assessment. Chief information officers are typically responsible for the IT organization and IT personnel may be directly involved in SOX compliance efforts.

The SOX 404 guidance requires the usage of an internal control framework. The IT Governance Institute's "COBIT: Control Objectives of Information and Related Technology" is used by many companies as a framework supporting IT SOX 404 efforts. However, there are certain aspects of COBIT that are outside the boundaries of Sarbanes-Oxley regulation.

OCTAVE: Operationally Critical Threat and Vulnerability Evaluation

As stated in Chapter 2, this framework identifies and manages information security risks through defining a comprehensive evaluation method enabling organizations to identify the information assets that are critical to the operation of the organization. It also facilitates the identification of threats posed to those assets and any vulnerabilities that may create a risk exposure to provide the basis upon which to found protection and mitigation strategies within the specific context of the individual organization.

By having a framework that is internationally recognized, organizations can use this in its original format, or it can customize it to suit the needs of the company, albeit with the caveat that deviation away from an accepted framework can result in the loss of efficacy of its utilization and even create blindspots that would otherwise have been omitted by following the framework scrupulously.

COBIT: Control Objectives for Information & Related Technology

As with the case of OCTAVE, COBIT is a framework with a business orientation towards business process owners within organizations, as well as providing for the requisites of auditors and other users.

Process owners are charged with the ability of an organization to operate optimally and without interruption, in a competitive manner and have regard to all the interdependencies between systems, processes and personnel. COBIT delivers the ability for those engaged in the process delivery to manage all IT resources involved in execution. As such, the framework enables organizations to develop clear policies for IT control and governance and includes the management of risks and mitigation strategies within it.

ISO 31000:2009 Published November 2009

This international standard seeks to offer generic guidelines as well as fundamental principles for the management of risk. In so doing, it crosses over previously developed frameworks and standards for specific industries or activities in order to provide a single overarching standard that can be adopted by any organization seeking to manage its risks.

A key provision within the standard is that of continuous improvement in the risk management process, which is a fundamental requirement for effective cyber threat management (as opposed to a single assessment and subsequent risk planning).

Further, it entails an organization to place its existing risk management programs within the envelope of ISO 31000 and to remove the traditional silo-based mentality when addressing risk management on an enterprise basis. As such, this standard should be regarded as building upon AS/NZS 4360 and stand as the basic guideline in the formation of a cyber risk management program.

ISO/IEC 27002: Information Security Management

ISO/IEC 27002 is a detailed security standard organized into ten major sections, each covering a different topic or area as follows:

1. *Business Continuity Planning*
   The objectives of this section are to counteract interruptions to business

activities and to critical business processes from the effects of major failures or disasters.

2. *System Access Control*

The objectives of this section are:

- To control access to information;
- To prevent unauthorized access to information systems;
- To ensure the protection of networked services;
- To prevent unauthorized computer access;
- To detect unauthorized activities;
- To ensure information security when using mobile computing and tele-networking facilities.

3. *System Development and Maintenance*

The objectives of this section are:

- To ensure security is built into operational systems;
- To prevent loss, modification or misuse of user data in application systems;
- To protect the confidentiality, authenticity and integrity of information;
- To ensure IT projects and support activities are conducted in a secure manner;
- To maintain the security of application system software and data.

4. *Physical and Environmental Security*

The objectives of this section are:

- To prevent unauthorized access, damage and interference to business premises and information;
- To prevent loss, damage or compromise of assets and interruption to business activities;
- To prevent compromise or theft of information and information processing facilities.

5. *Compliance*

The objectives of this section are:

- To avoid breaches of any criminal or civil law, statutory, regulatory or contractual obligations and of any security requirements;
- To ensure compliance of systems with organizational security policies and standards;
- To maximize the effectiveness of and to minimize interference to/from the system audit process.

6. *Personnel Security*

The objectives of this section are:

- To reduce risks of human error, theft, fraud or misuse of facilities;
- To ensure that users are aware of information security threats and concerns, and are equipped to support the corporate security policy in the course of their normal work;
- To minimize the damage from security incidents and malfunctions and learn from such incidents.

7. *Security Organization*

The objectives of this section are:

- To manage information security within the company;
- To maintain the security of organizational information processing facilities and information assets accessed by third parties;
- To maintain the security of information when the responsibility for information processing has been outsourced to another organization.

8. *Computer & Operations Management*

The objectives of this section are:

- To ensure the correct and secure operation of information processing facilities;
- To minimize the risk of systems failures;
- To protect the integrity of software and information;
- To maintain the integrity and availability of information processing and communication;
- To ensure the safeguarding of information in networks and the protection of the supporting infrastructure;
- To prevent damage to assets and interruptions to business activities;
- To prevent loss, modification or misuse of information exchanged between organizations.

9. *Asset Classification and Control*

The objectives of this section are to maintain appropriate protection of corporate assets and to ensure that information assets receive an appropriate level of protection.

10. *Security Policy*

The objectives of this section are to provide management direction and support for information security.

AS/NZS 3931:1998 – Risk analysis of technological systems – application guide

Whilst some standards provide generic risk management frameworks, others are more targeted at IT systems and processes and that of information security. This is one such standard which, although providing a basic model for risk analysis techniques, does have an IT systems focus of what can go wrong and combines the probability of this occurring together with the consequences of it happening.

It utilizes risk management techniques such as fault modes and effects analysis (FMEA) and preliminary hazard analysis (PHA). Whilst both of these techniques are of value in technological systems risk analysis, a danger lies in the implementation of the methodologies embodied within the standard since there can be ambiguity in the degree of detail used in the FMEA and PHA phases. Since the granularity of the qualitative analysis is not specified, organizations need to be aware that in cases of too high a level of analysis, critical items may be omitted from the analysis. It is therefore a pre-requisite that the methodology fits with the organizations' risk management objectives and risk appetite.

BS ISO/IEC 17799:2005: Information technology. Security techniques. Code of practice for information security management

This standard has increasing importance in terms of both an organizations' internal requirements appertaining to data integrity, but increasingly from a regulatory perspective. As an international standard, it seeks to establish the guidelines and general principles for initiating, implementing, maintaining and improving information security management within an organization.

For the first time ever, the World Economic Forum in January 2009 identified data loss/theft as one of the world's leading global threats. With the assistance of this standard, control objectives are intended to be implemented to meet the requirements of a risk assessment as well as serving as a practical guide as to the development of organizational security standards.

BS 25777:2008 – Information and communications technology continuity management. Code of practice

Increasing interconnectedness and dependence upon information technology infrastructure for business operations has led the drive towards business continuity management and enterprise resilience. Allied to this is the requirement to also manage

ICT continuity and ensure that where service disruptions result, they are managed in an effective manner.

This standards sets out to ensure that compliant organizations understand the threats to and vulnerabilities of information communications technologies as well the impact any disruption may have on the overall organization.

It sets the code of best practice for ICT continuity management within an overall ICT strategy that best meets an organization's risk appetite and ensures cost-effective measures are in place, enhancing confidence in the ability to manage ICT continuity of services, thereby enhancing reputation for prudence and efficiency.

Whilst not a mandated standard, the low cost of retro-fitting an ICT continuity program makes it a desirable objective. This standard assists organizations in the correct implementation of such a program and ensures that the complexities or implementation are addressed through the BSI's recommendations.

BS25999: Business Continuity Management 2006 / *ISO 22301: 2012*

This standard replaced PAS 56, a publicly available business continuity management specification published in 2003. BS25999 is in two parts. The first takes the form of general guidance, with principles, processes and terms established within it. The second specifies requirements for implementing, operating and improving a documented Business Continuity Management System (BCMS). The BS standard was withdrawn in November 2012 and replaced with ISO 22301 which continues the intent of the BS standard. As such, both provide the same information and usage and can be adopted as part of any cyber threat management program as a framework or for certification.

BS 25999 requires an organization to demonstrate to key stakeholders that it practices resilience strategies and recovery objectives that mitigate the impact of day-to-day incidents as well as man-made and natural disasters, thereby preventing irreparable damage, and protecting the organization's reputation and corporate brand.

It is the second part of the standard that acts as the means by which an organization may seek and be certified, since it describes the requirements that can be objectively and independently audited as part of a certification process.

For certification, an organization must subject itself to a multi-part, multi-visit by independent auditors, who, after determining whether an organization should be accredited, shall undertake post-certification checks over a period of time.

Clearly this particular standard has potential wide-spread applicability across and within sectors as well as being well-suited to all size of organizations. Utilizing part one for general contingency planning (BS25999) can obviously include cyber risks and their management/mitigation.

Internal Enterprise Assessment – *Formulating the Enterprise Survey*

Once the selection of external information that is of most relevance to the enterprise has been made, the task becomes one of choosing the scaling of the survey instrument and the design of the questions themselves. It is vital to the accuracy and efficacy of the output that the questions are created based upon the wording of the external information.

A good method for creating the survey instrument is by taking the direct wording of the standard or regulation and reversing the requirements into questions. The personnel allocated to its creation must be clear as to the objectives of the questions and state clearly during its development what the responses will mean and to which standard/regulation the question relates.

A series of examples are given in Table 9.14.

Table 9.14 Examples of Survey Development Using Standards, Regulations and Best Practice

1. The organization's business continuity planning has (11.1.1 ***ISO 17799***):
a. a specified process for its development If YES: The organizations comply with the standard
b. reflects the ongoing changes and developments of the organization and as such has no specified process ***(BIS Sound Practices for the Management and Supervision of Operational Risk No.44)*** If YES: The organizations comply with the standard (11.1.5.2)
c. insurance included as a constituent part If YES: The organizations comply with the standard (11.1.1 c)

2. The organization's business continuity strategy (11.1.1 ***ISO 17799***):

a. is consistent with the business objectives and priorities

If YES: the organizations comply with the standard (11.1.1 d)

---

b. has a focus on minimizing risks to the organization and does not focus on the business objectives and priorities

If YES: The organizations comply with the ***Banking Supervisor's Guidelines (BCBS)*** (11.1.3 e)

---

3. As part of the organization's overall risk management strategy, it has a preference for self-insuring risk. (Risk Management: Identification, Assessment, Monitoring and Mitigation Control BIS Sound Practices for the Management and Supervision of Operational Risk)

If YES: The organizations comply with the ***Sectoral Guidelines***

---

4. The organization's strategy includes using electronic delivery channels to broaden the customer base in existing and new markets. (BIS Management and Supervision of Cross-Border Electronic Banking Activities).

If YES: the organizations have e-banking facilities

---

5. The organization has communication strategies to control reputational risks arising from network attacks on e-banking. (Legal and Reputational Risk Management BIS Risk Management Principles for Electronic Banking)

If YES: The organizations comply with the ***Banking Supervisor's Guidelines (BCBS)***

---

6. The organization forms its' protection strategy for the information systems by focussing on the infrastructure weaknesses. (Section 1 Introduction. The Octave Method)

If YES: The organizations comply with the Risk Management Professional Body's best practice ***(OCTAVE)***

---

7. Through transferring risk to other parties, the risk to the organization is reduced. ***(4.5.1 AS/NZS4360:1999 Risk Management)***

If YES: The organization recognizes the requirement to transfer some operational values-at-risk

Table 9.15 Likert 4 Stage Scaling of Responses

Answer Key: 1 = Agree 2 = Tend to agree 3 = Tend to disagree 4 = Disagree	
Strategy: 1. The organization's business continuity planning has:	
a. a specified process for its development	1 2 3 4
b. reflects the ongoing changes and developments of the organization and as such has no specified process	1 2 3 4
c. insurance included as a constituent part	1 2 3 4
2. The organization's business continuity strategy:	
a. is consistent with the business objectives and priorities	1 2 3 4
b. has a focus on minimizing risks to the organization and does not focus on the business objectives and priorities	1 2 3 4
3. As part of the organization's overall risk management strategy, it has a preference for self-insuring risk	1 2 3 4
4. The organization's strategy includes using electronic delivery channels to broaden the customer base in existing and new markets	1 2 3 4
5. The organization has communication strategies to control reputational risks arising from network attacks on e-banking	1 2 3 4
6. The organization forms its' protection strategy for the information systems by focusing on the infrastructure weaknesses	1 2 3 4
7. Through transferring risk to other parties, the risk to the organization is reduced	1 2 3 4

From the survey base information, the data acquired can then be analyzed to review all points of interest for cyber/network assessment of the organization. It may be that the statements made by management as to cyber/network risk management intent conflicts with the data from the survey and this is not uncommon. By using external information, the basis of initial benchmarking of where the organization stands in relation to its competitors or within the overall sector can be utilized in communicating in a graphical manner to senior management, together with forming the basis of development of a more robust cyber/network risk management program.

When selecting the scaling for the survey instrument, it is important to understand the biases and influences on respondents as well as the impact of the type and number of rankings utilized. For example, for the sample used, there is a four response coding. Giving categories to the respondents (for example, business continuity, strategy, risk management) and having a closed question approach can lead to the acquisition of ordinal data and the continuum for the responses is limited.

By reducing the scaling to, say, a three-category scale this may produce too great a generalization of the responses, with a lack of differentiation that can produce poor results from the resulting analysis. Conversely, using a scaling greater than a four-category one may introduce too great a range of possible responses and can create a greater degree of confusion as to what the categories actually mean to respondents. Further, psychological influences on judgment and decision making can result in respondents answering with a bias towards a non-committal i.e. if a five number/letter scaling is used, respondents may select a 3 or C simply not to be misaligned with what management has communicated as to the organization and cyber/network risk management intent.

Other risks attached to using (as in this example) an "Agree" / "Disagree" approach to closed questions are:

- Agree-disagree questions, in order to be interpretable, can be asked only about extremes of a continuum and this limits the ability to order people in the middle of a continuum.

- Respondents may find it confusing to agree to a negative, such as "I agree that our risk management is poor" or vice-versa;

- Studies have shown that such an approach can result in people both agreeing and disagreeing to the same question when coached in this manner;

- Complex questions with possibly two or more elements can have a response in which it is difficult to define which element of the question the respondent was agreeing or disagreeing with.

In developing the survey, the person/team assigned the task should ensure that the questions have no bias and fulfill the following criteria:

1. Is the language simple? i.e. no use of jargon or technical terms that people will not understand.
2. Can the question be shortened?
3. Is the question double-barreled? i.e. does the question ask more than one question in the same sentence?
4. Is the question leading? i.e. questions that make people feel that they have to answer in a particular way.
5. Is the question negative? i.e. using 'not' in a sentence can be misleading.
6. Does the respondent have the necessary knowledge? i.e. does the question require a filter question in order to ascertain whether they have sufficient knowledge?
7. Will the words have the same meaning for everyone? i.e. can they be interpreted differently by different sub-cultural groups?
8. Is there prestige bias in the question? i.e. is there a possibility that people will answer in a particular way in order to impress?
9. Is the question ambiguous?
10. Is there a degree of sensitivity involved in the question? i.e. is there a possible issue that can be raised by the ethics committee in asking a direct question that has a sensitivity attached to it?
11. Is the frame of reference for the question clear?
12. Does the question artificially create opinions? i.e. where appropriate, is there provision for an answer of 'don't know' or 'prefer not to answer'?
13. Is personal or impersonal wording preferable? i.e. asking how the respondent personally feels about an issue or asking the respondent what they think others feel about the issue.
14. Is the question wording unnecessarily detailed?

Once the data has been acquired from the relevant respondents within the organization, it is then analyzed. The most effective means of undertaking this is to use statistical analysis software, which most marketing departments and/or risk management divisions use as a matter of course. It is important to be clear as to the objectives of undertaking the survey prior to commencement, to ensure that the output actually corresponds to what the survey is seeking to measure. By utilizing categories and standards/regulations, many of the pitfalls involved in creating a sound survey can be avoided and the potential for error/ambiguity and/or bias removed.

Statistical knowledge will be required for analysis and/or explanation of the output from the statistical software. The output can be difficult to communicate to management and there is usually a need to create summary tables and/or graphical representations of the results to ensure that the results and status of cyber/network threat management are clearly comprehended by the target audience.

Examples of the output from statistical software for an investigation into how organizations address the strategic management of computer network risk and whether the organization adopted an organic perspective of strategy are given below:

Dependent Variable: Factors indicating Organic Perspective (RECORGPS)
Independent Variable: Recognize Network Risks (RECNETRISK)

Results from the Logistic Regression:

Table 9.16 Omnibus Tests of Model Coefficients

Chi-square	df	Sig.
.024	1	.878

Table 9.17 Equation variables for "Adopt an Organic Perspective of Strategy"

Variables	B	S.E.	Wald	df	Sig.	Exp(B)
NETRISK	.016	.102	.023	1	.878	1.016
Constant	-.698	1.091	.409	1	.523	.498

In the above example, the model did not have any significance, with the p. value (Sig. = 0.878) being greater than 0.05, and as such there was no relationship between the two variables. To validate this finding, a cross tabulation was created, which confirmed the findings with a p. value of 0.219 being recorded.

Table 9.18 Chi-Square Test for "Adopt an Organic Perspective of Strategy"

	Value	df	Asymp. Sig. (2-sided)
Pearson Chi-Square	1.512	1	.219
N of Valid Cases	68		

Further checks using a scatterplot were made, but this confirmed the finding of no relationship between the two variables (Figure 9.18).

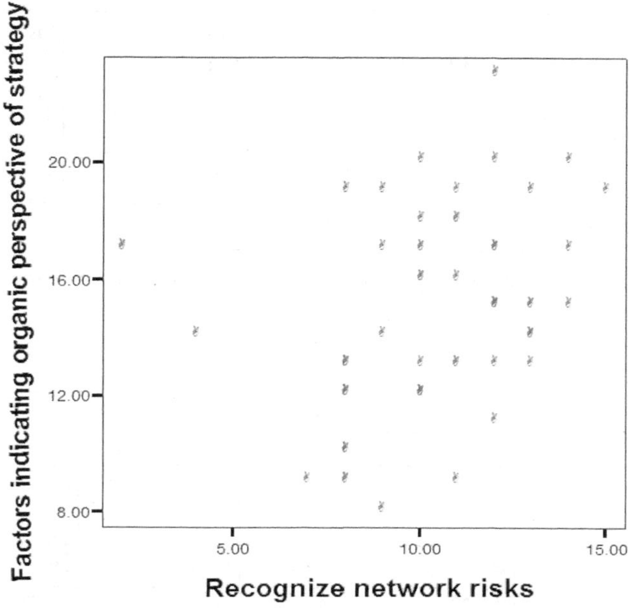

Figure 9.16 Scatterplot Test for "Adopt an Organic Perspective of Strategy"

Using a linear regression, the model found that there was a weak relationship (p. = 0.035).

Table 9.19 Variables Entered/Removed

Model	Variables Entered	Variables Removed	Method
1	Factors indicating organic perspective of strategy(a)	.	Enter

a: All requested variables entered.
b: Dependent Variable: Recognize network risks

Table 9.20 Model Summary

Model	R	R Square	Adjusted R Square	Std. Error of the Estimate
1	.262(a)	.068	.054	2.48281

a: Predictors: (Constant), Factors indicating organic perspective of strategy

Table 9.21 ANOVA(b)

Model		Sum of Squares	df	Mean Square	F	Sig.
1	Regression	28.507	1	28.507	4.625	.035(a)
	Residual	388.354	63	6.164		
	Total	416.862	64			

a: Predictors: (Constant), Factors indicating organic perspective of strategy
b: Dependent Variable: Recognize network risks

Table 9.22 Coefficients(a)

Model		Unstandardized Coefficients		Standardized Coefficients	t	Sig.
		B	Std. Error	Beta	B	Std. Error
1	(Constant)	7.320	1.444		5.070	.000
	Factors indicating organic perspective of strategy	.207	.096	.262	2.150	.035

a: Dependent Variable: Recognize network risks

This level of statistical knowledge may not hold true for small and medium sized organizations, however it should be present in larger sized enterprises. For the latter, there are a large number of external sources of skills that can be employed to analyze statistical data and its interpretation.

Intellectual Property Risk Management

Aside from operational risks leading to direct and consequent financial impairment, other factors need to be accounted for within the assessment of cyber threat/network risks. Prime examples of such items are intellectual property assets. The difficulty in assessing these is the variance in how these may have been treated in terms of their balance sheet values, which in turn may have been determined by the prevailing accounting rules in the respective country in which the accounting is undertaken.

Despite this, there should be clear recognition of the many components within the organization that would be adversely affected by a successful cyber attack/network failure. Items such as the management processes of an enterprise, customer data and other such non permissible balance sheet entries should have some form of assessment, quantification and valuation in much the same way as for the balance of the organization.

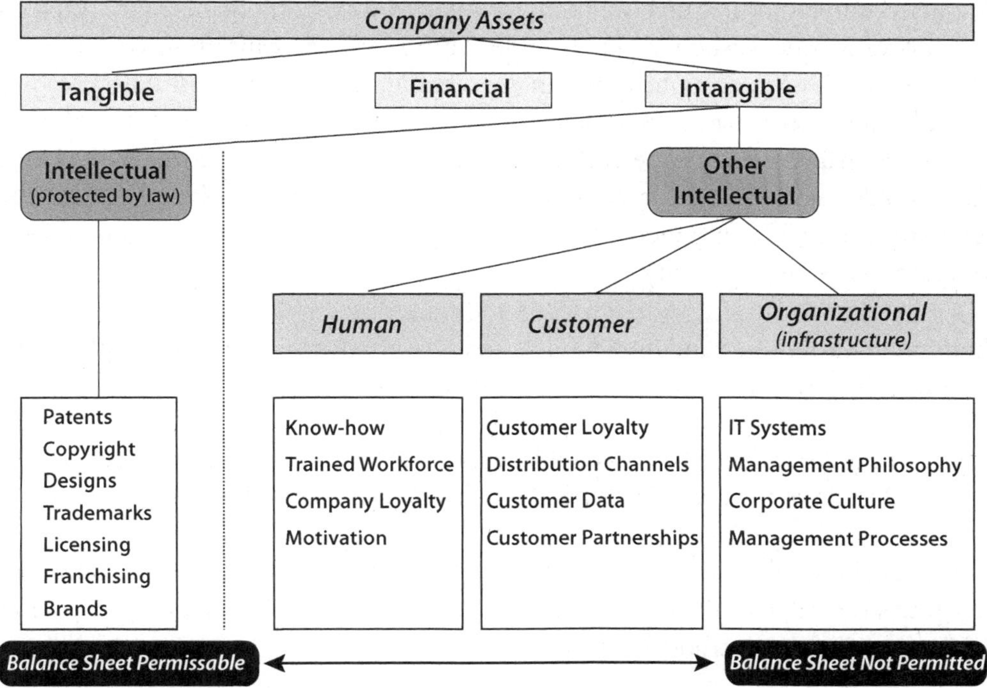

Fig. 9.17 Categories of Intangible Assets and Accounting Treatment

A major intellectual property component of value to organizations is their brand, and within the internet domain, this stands out as a prime target, as mentioned in an earlier chapter, for activists, demonstrators, and paid hackers seeking to damage reputation that may have had substantial marketing and associated costs to build over a considerable period of time. Typical of the type of damage occasioned by attacks is that impacting upon a corporate or product brand.

Brand Risk

A brand is a symbol carrying with it certain associations and images, with functioning brands creating value in a number of ways. They define customer perceptions of value and also reduce the uncertainty of future demand, thereby enabling optimization of manufacturing, logistics and sales channels. Further, brands enhance an organization's ability to raise funds at acceptable cost and protect an organization's freedom to operate by shaping the opinion of regulators and communities. New employees are attracted more efficiently, building commitment and in directing their performance.

Whether positively, or negatively, brand unavoidably drives an organization's capacity to create value and sustain it. Irreparable damage can be caused an organization following a crisis or catastrophe impacting on a brand, such as a successful hack leading to data breaches that may substantially outweigh the immediate and visible costs. A cyber threat management framework without proper insight into the role of the brand is incomplete, and both large-scale and technology companies have experienced breaches resulting in subsequent global adverse publicity and in some notable cases, a reduction in market credibility.

There are a variety of valuation models that are used in various geographies and taxation realms, which are used for two distinct purposes;

- In order to record an intangible asset value within the balance sheet
- As part of the overall valuation for shares over a period of time

For the valuation of a company and for share transfers, a market-based methodology determines the value of the brand by reference to the prices obtained for comparable brands in recent mergers and acquisitions.

For a balance sheet valuation of brand equity, a finance-based model is more generally used, in part due to that variations in global accounting standards and are based upon discounted cash flows models. The approach is also widely used in order to capitalize an imputed royalty stream and is used where co-branding, licensing or endorsement type branding is utilized by the company concerned. The value of royalty fees chargeable within a transfer-pricing model is the standard model base.

A notional royalty rate is applied to an estimated level of future maintainable sales and the resultant after-tax royalty stream is then capitalized at an appropriate rate and this derives the value of the brand. There are other models that are sometimes utilized, such as the NPV of incremental cashflows that are clearly quantifiable as a brand link, or using a valuation according to future potential earnings that can be clearly identified as being attributable to the brand.

In understanding the value at risk to brand damage, and for the brand to be of strategic value, brand equity must be measurable and brand valuation as an exercise essentially produces its tradable value.

Table 9.23 Example Brand Valuation Models

Example DCF Valuation Method:	**Example Market-based Valuation Model:**
Value of the brand = S (t=1 to N) RB / (1+r) t + Residual Value / (1-r) N	Market value of firm = Stock price x Number of shares
RB = revenue expected in year 1 r = discounting rate (based upon the weighted average cost of capital) Residual Value = RBN/(r-g) g = rate of revenue growth	= Replacement cost of tangible assets + Value of non-brand factors (R&D, Patents etc) + Value of industry factors (Regulation, concentration etc) + Value of brand equity (A function of the age of the brand at the time of the transfer, cumulative advertising costs over time x market share percentage)

Brand risk is easier to understand where the three main components are divided, although each interacts with the other: brand equity risk; reputational risk; and structural risk.

Brand equity risk: this is the exposures that can undermine the ability of a brand to maintain its desired differentiation and competitive advantage. These attributes may be defined or measured, and comprise the components of a brand's performance driver and they demonstrably affect the willingness of a customer to pay a premium, transact more frequently, or transact at all. There are many stakeholders within a brand, all with differing but overlapping priorities and perceptions. Where a brand is threatened and pressured, the brand elements weaken over time until a moment of crisis at which point the brand may fail completely and in recent times there have been a number of high profile examples of this phenomenon.

Reputational risk: groups together those exposures that arise from failure to meet basic expectations of performance that apply to any comparable organization operating in the same field. Examples are security/data breaches, unethical conduct, operational outages, or lapses in quality control. Of note however, is that simply complying with norms of performance does not result in competitive advantage, rather they may be viewed as pre-requisites enabling an organization to remain in competition within a sector/segment. This contrasts with bad performance or catastrophe that can quickly destroy the critical bond of trust between the brand and its stakeholders.

Structural risk: describes the exposures that might affect an entire industry and/or market segment. A recent example of this is the global banking crisis where attitudes shifted away from banking/financial products and the new regulatory framework imposed following the failure of a particular organization. The fall from favor of the banking industry amongst potential new employees, directly and indirectly weakened the economic performance of banking brands globally and continues today. These risks are often labeled "demand adjusters" due to their principal potential impact.

Dimensions				External
brand structure	fragmented	associated	coherent	monolithic
public awareness	low	low-medium	medium-high	high
target audience	financial community	business community	public	public
brand attributes	activity	competence	attitude	trust
				Internal
culture	independent	related	integrated	homogenous
leadership style	management by numbers	management by objective	inspiration	dynasty
most valued	financial control	market share	people	reputation
ethos	earning	winning	learning	belonging
	owning	*managing*	*leading*	*being one*
	BUSINESS TYPE			

Fig. 9.18 Example of a Branding League

Taking the banking industry again as an example, reviewing the branding league (see table above) proposed by Barwise[62], it is clear to see that the banking organizations fall within the end column, with a high degree of public visibility being maintained

[62] Barwise, P., Dunham, A. and Ritson, M (2000), Ties That Bind: Brands, Consumers and Businesses In Pavitt, J. (Ed) *Brand New,* V&A Publications, London pp.71-108.

through high spend levels for advertising and marketing. In addition, the brand attribute of "trust" is of some import to the banking community in general and in retail and commercial banking in particular. The recent failure of this brand component resulted in runs on banks in the US and the UK with catastrophic sectoral and economic impact extending far beyond the borders of countries of domicile of the principal actors.

This secondary impact requires risk managers to consider the brand structure/hierarchy of the organization in a similar manner to the process of business mapping. In many instances, corporations create brands that compete with other company owned ones and a failure in one may either carry over to others within the segment or even vertically, damaging more prestigious brands that derive a greater percentage of profits. A good example of this is the car industry, where a small number of platforms serve to create a broad and deep number of brands within a single organization. A failure in a platform upon which a mass volume model is produced (a poor review of handling by the specialist press for example) can result in weakening of sales in the premium brands higher in the branding league of the company product range.

Taking the example of cyber threats, there are a number of possible brand impacts. Examples range from defacing of websites, loss of customer records, to soft attacks such as negative comments being generated and posted automatically and in volume on social networking sites.

It is not therefore the sole domain of technology based (enabled) organizations that stand to suffer financial damage through cyber attacks. Further, the scope, capabilities and ease of undertaking attacks to brand and reputation increase as the technologies underpinning all operational aspects of business multiply and connectivity between organizations and their external environment grow over time.

Concluding Summary

Returning to the initial model of cyber risk management in closing, the model can be used for developing an appropriate proprietary cyber risk management program by most organizations. Some of the concepts and components may, at first appearance, seem ill-fitted to risk management. However it is hoped that by this concluding section their role and function are clearly beneficial to any enterprise resilience program, given that they play a fundamental part in how a program may be organized, what dangers of bias are involved, what the strategic approach should be, as well as matching the risk to the risk appetite of the organization involved, together with those technologies that can assist in the alignment.

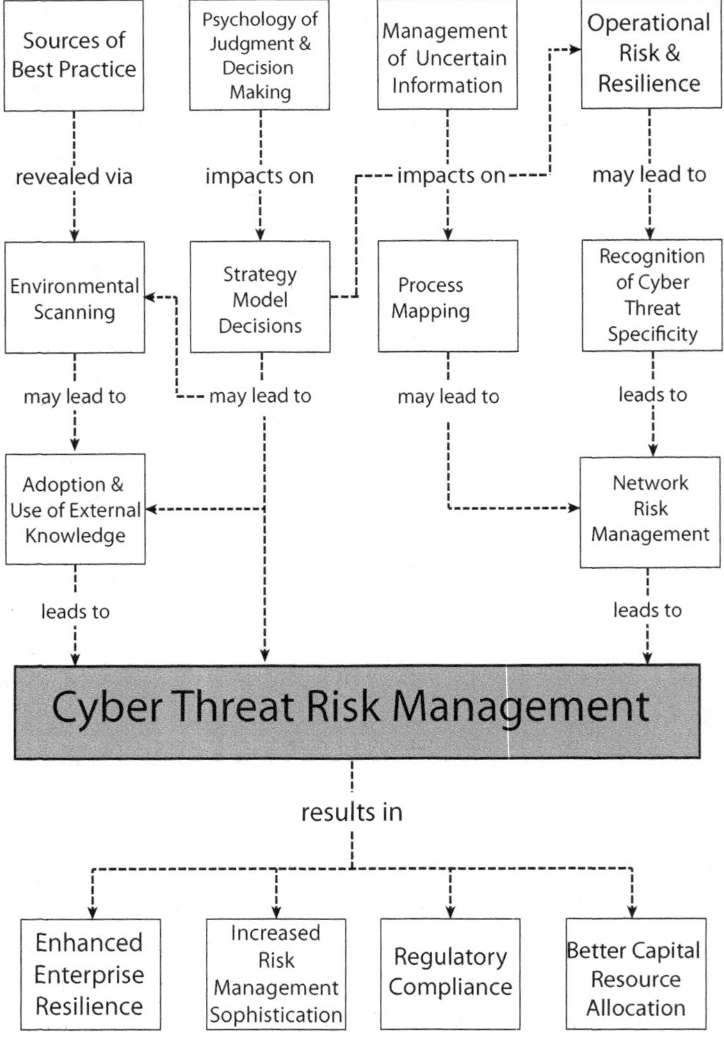

Fig. 9.19 Model for Cyber Threat Management

In taking the above into account, allied to the previous content within this book, it is possible to summarize where risk management teams can add value in the fight against cyber threats and create sustainable enterprise resilience if the following are taken into account during the creation of a cyber threat management program.

Objectives of a Cyber Risk Program

At the outset, it is imperative that there is an understanding of the differences between those risks that historically the organization is aware of and the differences between those and cyber risks. In the absence of this, there will be a reversion towards traditional risk management practices that will not be an effective form of cyber risk management.

In parallel with this is the need to determine the fit between the risk management methodologies proposed for a cyber risk program and the overall corporate strategy. An example here would be where the organization relies heavily upon IT and network uptime, but operates within a highly competitive, low margin sector. Whilst the design of the cyber risk management program may deliver a high degree of resilience, if the costs of developing and implementation are too high, the organization may place itself at risk in terms of capital reserves, free cashflows or lost opportunities going forward. It is more likely in such a case that the senior management would prefer to have a risk management strategy that transfers some of the risk to another party, rather than seek to reduce the operational risk exposures.

This of course accords with the risk appetite set for the organization by the Board generally and it is for the risk management and associated units to work within the remit whilst seeking to optimize the effectiveness of all its risk management activities. Matching the risk exposure level to the total number of risks within an organization is an extremely difficult task, and where there is misalignment the consequences of failures can be catastrophic, as can be seen in very recent times in cases of rogue trading and in market manipulation resulting from ineffective communication of the risk attitude set by senior management in banking organizations.

Whilst the above applies to risk management in general, the degree of specificity and the pervasiveness of cyber risks require ongoing and pro-active management, as opposed to a single shot approach or autopsy analysis of risk events, followed by subsequent strengthening of security.

Key Components

Clearly there is a need for identification of the risks posed to the organization in general, with cyber threats requiring data acquisition, followed by analysis of the data in order to determine through assessment, what threats are posed to the enterprise.

The impact of threats identified can only be ascertained through mapping of business processes and technology interdependencies. In many cases this information may be available via the business continuity programs organizations generally run, although it is important to ensure that the data is current and there have been no changes to, for example, technology infrastructure. There are tools available to assist in this process where the data is inappropriate or absent or requires greater detail.

Understanding the threats and the financial risk exposures will result in the development of the critical path of actions that will bring alignment with the risk appetite as well as the options available to eliminate, manage, accept or transfer risks. It is at this point that there is a pre-requisite for Board buy-in to a cyber risk management program, given the breadth and depth of reach required and access and assistance required throughout the organization.

Through the identification, assessment, and strategic approach set by the senior management for the management of cyber risks, the program must have a budget allocated to it, with normal project milestones and deliverables assigned and capital allocations at specific points agreed by the Board.

Risk Types & Valuation

The ability to reduce risk exposure is of course dependent upon all risks posed being identified as well as valued. Although most risk management teams will have clearly defined modes of operating to ensure capture of all risks, not simply key risk indicators, encapsulating operational, reputational, legal/regulatory risks and insider threats, methodologies and valuations vary largely due to sector, organization size and maturity of risk programs.

Quantification methods for example may sway towards using only either quantitative or qualitative approaches, or the weighting of importance of one to the other vary from sector to sector or dependent upon the risk appetite of each organization.

Similarly valuation methods may depend upon which items are balance-sheet permissible and therefore dependent upon geography, or how items are depreciated/amortized according to the taxation regime in place. Inputs are required from multiple sources, including process owners, legal/regulatory, audit and compliance, business continuity. The volumes and accuracy of the data used can be altered over time and the degree of granularity will generally be determined by the risk management strategy adopted e.g. whether to manage or transfer risks exposure.

Cyber Risk Options: Accept/Manage/Transfer/Mixture

Once a cost-benefit and gap analysis has been executed, it will be possible to identify those areas requiring capital and other resources allocated as a priority in managing cyber threats. Technological solutions may be at the foremost of thinking of some within the organization, but where there is a desire to transfer risk exposure outside of the enterprise, as opposed to perhaps accepting a higher risk value but cover through increasing capital reserves, then the options fall to financial products such as insurance, reinsurance and risk financing.

Such products range from cyber liability cover for small and medium sized businesses with a high online presence but little infrastructure, to large-scale manufacturers in dispersed geographical locations and with a multitude of suppliers who warrant specific risk financing structures.

Organizational Structure

With the means to manage cyber risks determined, the structure required to in order run and report requires the program management composition and roles to be established and documented. Once established, the project management group composition is similarly required.

A key component of the former is that there is a Board level sponsor of the program in order to overcome in-house political maneuvering by those who feel they should be included or who feel their control is being undermined by the program. The form of project management will vary from one organization to another and across sectors. However, at the very least there should be recourse to some well established and generally accepted project management method such as Prince2 or PMP frameworks employed by those undertaking the task.

External Information

In developing and ensuring ongoing cyber threat resilience is maintained, organizations should undertake environmental scanning and identify information external to the firm that is relevant in the context of cyber risk management. Whilst this may comprise international/national standards, professional bodies guidelines and other forms of best practice frameworks, it is worth noting that there may be other information that, whilst not necessarily targeted at cyber risks, can be adapted and leveraged for the benefit of the organization. Benchmarking can provide either a minimum standard or a level that should be attained. Data is widely available for such measurement and assessment of the effectiveness of organizations' cyber risk management programs.

Biases and Influences (including regulations)

Biases in how a cyber risk management program may be formulated, who should be within it and what areas should be addressed are all subject to psychological influences such as hindsight bias from other projects or risk management programs. Further influences can arise unwittingly from sources external to the organization.

An example here would be where senior management is briefed by strategic consultants as to where their organization lies in relation to others within the same sector and what competitors are seeking to achieve. The management then overrides whatever the original objectives were and frequently the scope too. Such mission-creep is common and this peer group pressure can arise directly or indirectly, as in the above example.

Judgment and bias can therefore derail what may be an optimal methodology along with circles of influence and external factors in favor of another that has failings within it, without this being recognized by the implementing organization. Further dangers lie in circumstances where, for example, there is a new regulatory framework imposed on an entire sector (as in the case of the banking and financial services sectors recently). In such cases, there is a very real danger of a risk management team being blindsided by the requirement to meet regulatory thresholds and standards and in maintaining these over a period of time.

This can result, as has been shown to be the case by the banking sector, in regulatory dominance determining the extent of risk management practices within a sector, with a consequent loss in risk management quality. In essence, the danger posed is that organizations purely comply with whatever their regulatory environment requires of them, as opposed to actually seeking to attain as high a degree of enterprise resilience as possible. For the case of cyber risk management, regulations relating to third party liability for causing the distribution of a computer virus, for example, can lead organizations to focus their attention on eliminating this legal liability to the exclusion of, or reduction in priority, other areas under threat from cyber attacks.

Future Trends & Impacts

So far, this book has focused upon what may be viewed as known forms of cyber threats, attacker types and motivations and against traditional firms and infrastructures. However, without requiring extreme foresight it is clear that there are current trends that will evolve into future modes of organizational and personal working that will in turn impact on what types of cyber threat will emerge and what the consequences of a successful attack may be.

There has been a vast shift towards wireless technologies in recent times and at an increasing rates as developing economies adopt wireless devices in place of traditional desktop and laptop devices for both communications and computing needs on both a personal usage and business level. This has been driven by smartphones and subsequently by tablet computers, offering increasing ability to work and control remotely.

Decentralization of applications to cloud computing has meant that a large volume of local storage and of processor speed is no longer required. There is therefore an ability to manage systems, access data in the form of files and records from any location given sufficient internet access, user authorization capability and authentication.

Risks therefore arise from a number of factors that are intrinsic to such modes of operation. As in the case of the shift from bank ATM's to internet banking, the security burden falls away from the organizations' internal security perimeter and towards the end user. With cloud computing, this is taken one step further in that if there is a security failure, there is a far greater ability to damage a vast number of users since they all use a single source.

Further, although there are an increasing number of cloud providers and most large-scale organizations will develop and deploy their own cloud infrastructure, the number of operating systems utilized within wireless devices is limited. At present, the largest rise in operating system usage has been the Android OS developed by Google Corporation, the rise in use being attributed to it being free to deploy and therefore offering cost advantages to technology providers such as Samsung and HTC in their smartphones and tablets.

Most users with smartphones and tablets do not restrict themselves to the applications that were pre-installed upon their machines. Rather, the trend is for installing apps from many different suppliers. Corporations have realized that integrating their marketing and product solutions with utilities that are valued by the customer can have a great impact for relatively little cost (when compared with traditional customer acquisition costs).

They are therefore creating interoperability between their internal systems and the external ones in the form of apps. For example, a diabetes patient can download a free app to monitor their blood/sugar levels, have the chart record linked so that a the supplier of blood test strips or lancets can generate a reminder along with a promotion that they need to top up their supply by clicking the buy function in the app. This function needs to be integrated within the organizations' order management system, customer records database, logistics and marketing departments.

In 2010, a particular form of cyber attack was undertaken against industrial process control systems developed by Siemens AG. Although such types of attack had been experienced before, this was the first instance of a computer worm being developed to also include a programmable logic controller within the malware. This was intended to offer the capability to control industrial process controls at distance. Given the rate at which apps are being rolled out and integrated within enterprise infrastructure and deployed within the cloud computing environment, allied to users installing uncertified software on the same machines, the chances of a compromise akin to the Stuxnet attacks increase.

The context is that the cloud links millions of machines that the majority run a single type of operating system that is itself open for developers to alter with development kits, these machines run software from multiple sources and intrinsically trusted. Users are storing an increasing amount of personal data in the cloud and on social networking sites. Payments, ordering systems, control of remote resources are all capable of being managed via simple and low cost electronic devices being available globally.

Banking and wireless payment functionality is increasing, allied to other transactional capabilities. There is therefore a greater motivation for hackers, either as individuals or as part of organized crime, to seek out the point of failure and extract as much as possible from as many places as possible. Personal data, plus transactional capabilities, authorization and authentication all in one place makes for targets that offer greater reward for lower risk to criminals. A final trend that will in turn increase cyber threat impact and require greater cyber risk management will be where algorithms are utilized by apps in order to reduce the number of data inputs required for a given action.

An example from the offline world is where a car accident claim form with, perhaps 30 questions, provides the risk carrier with the data required to identify fraudulent claims. This is achieved through a large number of initial questions being correlated through algorithms, so that prima facie, the accident report appears to be quite short, but the reality is a single answer is data provided to a larger body of questions.

A similar method is used in industries where there is a requirement to manage risks to a high degree and requiring voluminous reporting and auditing, such as the nuclear industry. In the case of smartphone/tablet apps, the desire is to reduce the inputs by the end user to as few as possible. However, where there are fewer commands required to achieve the same actions, the potential for data loss, and unauthorized access to accounts or systems increases over time as the number of devices and apps increases.

How these new cyber risks will be effectively managed will be the prime issue facing organizations, large and small, for the foreseeable future.

BIBLIOGRAPHY

ACH Risk Management Handbook, National Automated Clearing House Association, 1991.

ACH Risk: A Quick Reference Guide, Calwestern Automated Clearing House Association, Revised April 1990.

Adapted from Mintzberg et al., 1976

Adger, W. (2000). Social and ecological resilience: are they related? *Progress in Human Geography* 24(3): 347 – 364.

Adler P.S., and Borys, B. (1996) Two types of bureaucracy: enabling vs. coercive. *Administrative Science Quarterly* March: 61 – 89

Arthur, W. (1999). Complexity and the economy. *Science* 284 (5411): 107 – 109.

Aguilar, F.J. (1967) *Scanning the Business Environment*. New York: McMillan.

Ajzen, I., & Fishbein, M. (1977). Attitude-behaviour relations: A theoretical analysis and review of empirical research. Psychological Bulletin, 84, 888-918.

Alchian, A.A. (195) Uncertainty, evolution and economic theory. *Journal of Political Economy* **58**: 211-221.

Aldrich H. E. (1979) *Organizations and Environments*. Prentice-Hall: Engelwood Cliffs, NJ Amended from Darnton and Darnton, Business process Analysis (1997)

An Organisational Structure for Operational Risk (PriceWaterhouseCoopers 2000)

Anderson, N.H. (1965). Primacy effects in personality impression formation using a generalized order effect paradigm. *Journal of Personality and Social Psychology, 2*, 1-9.

Andrews, K. (1971) *The Concept of Corporate Strategy*. Homewood IL: Irwin.

Ansoff, H. I. (1965) Corporate Strategy. Harmondsworth:Penguin.

Argyris, C. (1997) Double loop learning in organizations. *Harvard Business Review*, September-October: 115-125.

Asch, S.E. (1946). Forming impressions of personality. *Journal of Abnormal and Social Psychology, 41*, 258-290.

Baden-Fuller, C., Stopford, J. (1992), *Re-juvenating the Mature Business: The Competitive Challenge*, Routledge, London

Bain JS. 1956. Barriers to New Competition. Harvard University Press: Cambridge MA.

Balnaves, M., and Caputi, P. (2001) *Introduction to Quantitative Research Methods; an investigative approach*, 88. Sage: London.

Bank For International Settlements. Basel Accord 1986.

Bank for International Settlements. Report December 2001.

Bansal, P, and Roth, K, supra
Bansal, P. (2000). Taking Stock of 14001 Certifications, *Academy of Management Meeting,* Toronto, Ontario, Canada.
Bansal, P. (2001) The corporate challenges of sustainable development. *Academy of Management Executive*
Bansal, P., and Bogner, W.C. (2000) Deciding on 14001: Economics, Institutions, and Context. *Long Range Planning* **35** (2002) 269-290
Barabasi, A-L, *Linked: The New Science of Networks*, Perseus Publishing 2002
Barnett, William P. & Hansen, Morten (1993).The red queen in organizational evolution. *Strategic Management Journal* 17.
Barney JB 1991. Firm Resources and sustained Competitive Advantage.*Journal of Management* 17(1): 99-120.
Barney, J.B., and Zajac, E.J. (1994) Competitive organizational behaviour: towards an organizationally-based theory of competitive advantage. *Strategic Management Journal*, Winter Special Issue 15: 5-9.
Barth, J. R., Caprio, G. Jr., and Levine, R. (2001), *The Regulation and Supervision of Banks Around the World: A New Database*, World Bank.
Bass, B.M. (1983) *Organizational Decision Making*, Irwin.
Baum J. R. (2000) A longitudinal study of the causes of technology adoption and its effect upon new venture growth. *Frontiers of Entrepreneurship Research* 1-12.
Baum, J. R., and Wally, S. (2003) Strategic Decision Speed and Firm Performance. *Strategic Management Journal* **24**: 1107-1129
Belson, W.A. (1981). *The design and understanding of survey questions.* Aldershot, England. Gower.
Bem, D.J. (1972). Self-perception theory. In L. Berkowitz (Ed.) *Advances in experimental social psychology (Vol. 6)*. New York: Academic Press.
Beranauer, T., and Koubi, V. (2006) On the Interconnectedness of Regulatory Policy and Markets: Lessons from Banking. *British Journal of Political Science,* **36**, 509-525
Berger, A. N., Herring, R. J., and Szego, G. P. (1995) *'The Role of Capital in Financial Institutions', Journal of Banking and Finance*, **19**, 393-430
Berger, P., and Luckmann, T. (1966) *The social construction of reality*. New York: Doubleday.
Bertalanffy L., von (1968) *General System Theory*, George Braziller, New York.
Bibel, W. (1993) *Deduction: Automated Logic*. Academic Press.
Bigadike, E. R. (1981) The contributions of marketing to strategic management. *Academy of Management Review*, 1981, **6**, pp. 621 -632
Bonanno, G. (2004).Loss, trauma and human resilience: have we underestimated the human capacity to thrive after extremely aversive events? *American Psychologist* 59(1): 20 -28.
Bondt, G. J. de and Prast, H. M. (2000), 'Bank Capital Ratios in the 1990's: Cross-Country Evidence', *Banca Nazionale del Lavoro Quarterly Review*, 53, 71-97
Born, G. (1994) *Process Management to Quality Improvement*, John Wiley & Sons, New York.
Bourgeois, L. J., and Eisenhardt K. (1988) Strategic decision processes in high velocity environments: four cases in the microcomputer industry. *Management Science* **34**: 816 – 835
Bourgois, L. J. III. (1980) Strategy and environment: A conceptual integration. *Academy of Management Review*, 5, 25-39.
Bowman, E. H. and Hurrey, D. (1993) Strategy through the options lens: an integrated view of resource investments and the incremental choice process. *Academy of Management Review* **18**(4): 760 – 782
Bracker, J (1980) The historical development of the strategic management concept. *Academy of Management Review* 5 (2): 219-224.
Bradburn, N.M., & Sudman, S. (1992). The current status of questionnaire design. In P.N. Beimer, R.M. Groves, L.E. Lyberg, N. Mathiowetz, & S. Sudman (Eds.), *Measurement errors in surveys* (pp29-

40). New York: John Wiley

Brandeburger AM., and Nalebuff BJ.(1996).*Cooptition*. Doubleday: New York.

Browne, F., and Gavin, C (2003), 'Regulation and its Interaction with the Macroeconomy as an Input into Asset Price Inflation', *CBFSAI Financial Stability Discussion Paper No. 3*

Burgelman, R.A. (1996) Intraorganizational ecology of strategy making and organizational adaptation: theory and field research. In Meindle, J., Stubbart, C., and Porac, J., editors, *Cognition within and between Organizations*. Thousand Oaks, CA: Sage.

Callaway, D., Newman, M., Strogatz, S., & Watts, D. (2000). Network robustness and fragility: percolation on random graphs. Physical Review Letters 85(25): 5468 – 5471.

Camp, R. C. (1989). *Benchmarking: The search for industry best practices that lead to superior performance (First)*. Milwaukee, Wisconsin, ASQC Quality Press.

Campbell J.D. & Tesser, A. (1983). Motivational interpretations of hindsight bias: An individual difference analysis.*Journal of Personality, 51*, 605-620.

Cappel, S.D. *Strategic Profiles and Performance in Service Organizations: Examining Retail Department, Variety and General Merchandise Stores.* Unpublished doctoral dissertation, Memphis State University, Memphis, Tennessee, 1990.,

Caprio, G., and Klingebiel, D. (2003), *'Episodes of Systemic and Borderline Financial Crises', World Bank Database*

Carnegie Mellon Software Engineering Institute 2005. http://www.sei.cmu.edu/publications/documents/99.reports/99tr017/99tr017chap01.html

Caves RE., and Porter, ME. (1977). From Entry Barriers to Mobility Barriers. *Quarterly Journal of Economics* 91: 241-261

Chaffee E. E. (1985) Three Models of Strategy. *Academy of Management Review*, 1985, Vol.10. No.**1**. pp.89 – 98

Chakravarthy BS.(1986). Measuring Strategic Performance. Strategic Management Journal 7(5): 437-458

Champy, J., (1995) *Re-engineering Management*, Harper Business Editions.

Chandler, A. D.(1962). *Strategy and structure. Chapters in the history of the American industrial enterprise.* Cambridge: MA: MIT Press.

Cheeseman, P. (1986) Probabilistic Versus Fuzzy Reasoning. In Kanal, L. and Lemmer, J, editors, *Uncertainty in Artificial Intelligence*, pages 85-102. Elsevier..

Chen, P.P-S. (1976) *The Entity-relationship model – toward a unified view of data*. ACM Transactions on Database Systems, 1(1) March.

Choo, Chun Wei, and Auster, Ethel (1993). "Environmental scanning: acquisition and use of information by managers", in: *Annual Review of Information Science and Technology*, edited by M. E. Williams. Medford, NJ: Learned Information, Inc. For the American Society for Information Science.

Choo, Chun Wei. (2001) Environmental scanning as information seeking and organizational learning. *Information Research*, Vol. 7 No. **1**.

Clark, D. (1990) Numerical and symbolic approaches to uncertainty management in artificial intelligence. *Artificial Intelligence Review*, 4:109-146, 1990.

Clarke, J., and Varma, S. (1999). Strategic Risk Management: the New Competitive Edge. *Long Range Planning*, Vol.32, No.4, pp 414 – 424.

Cohen, W. M. and D. Levinthal (1989). "Innovation and learning: The two faces of R&D." the Economic Journal **99**: 569-596.

Collins JC., and Porras, JI. (1994). *Built to Last: Successful Habits of Visionary Companies.* Harper Business: New York.

Collis, D.J., and Montgomery, C.A. (1995) Competing on resources: strategy in the 1990's. *HBR July –*

August 1995, pp. 40 -41

Collis, D.J., and Montgomery, C.A. (1998). Competing on resources: strategy in the 1990's. Harvard Business Review, July-August 119-128. 1998.

Computer security analysts claim that John McAfee originally inflated the figure of the Morris virus as a self-serving business publicity act.

Conner, K., and Prahalad, C.K. (1996). A resource based theory of the firm: knowledge versus opportunism. *Organizational Science* 7 (5): 477 – 501. 1996.

Coren, S., and Miller, J. (1974). Size contrast as a function of figural similarity. *Perception and Psychophysics, 16*, 355-357.

Corey, S.M. (1937). Professed attitudes and actual behavior. *Journal of Educational Psychology, 28*, 271-280.

Coutu, D. L., 2002) How Resilience Works, *Harvard Business Review May.*

Croft, B. (1993) Knowledge-based and Statistical Approaches to Text Retrieval. *IEEE Expert*, pages 8-12. April.

Cyert, R. M. and March, J.G. (1956).Organizational Factors in the Theory of Monopoly. *Quarterly Journal of Economics* 70 (1): 44-64.

Cyert, R. M. and March, J.G. (1963). *A Behavioural theory of the firm*. Englewood Cliffs, NJ: Prentiss Hall.

Daft, Richard L., & Weick, Karl E. (1984). "Toward a model of organizations as interpretation systems". *Academy of Management Review* **9** (2), 284-295.

Daft, Richard L., Sormunen, Juhani & Parks, Don (1988). "Chief Executive scanning, environmental characteristics, and company performance: an empirical study." *Strategic Management Journal* **9** (2), 123-139.

Darnton G., and Giacoletto, S. (1992) *Information in the Enterprise*, Digital Press.

Darnton, G. (1987) Automating the Generation of Functional Specifications, *proceedings of the Prise Conference, Meta Systems*, Ann Arbor, M.I.

Darnton, G., and Darnton M. (1997). *Business Process Analysis.* International Thompson Business Press. London

Darnton, G., and Giacoletto, S. (1996). Information in the Enterprise. Digital Press.

Daughtry-Weiss, D. (2002). "How to Survive Before the Fact", *Harvard Business Review* May.

Davenport T.H. (1993) *Process Innovation : Re-engineering Work Through Information Technology*, Harvard Business School Press, Boston, M.A.

Davenport T.H. and Short, J.E. (1990) The new Industrial Engineering: information technology and business process redesign, *Sloan Management Review*, Summer.

Davis, E. P., (1995), *Debt, Financial Fragility and Systemic Risk*, Clarendon Press, Oxford.

Davis, P.K. (1995). Interactive Simulation in the Evolution of Warfare Modeling. *Proceedings of IEEE*, Vol.83, No. 8, August 1995.

Deal, T. E., and Kennedy, A. A. (1982) Corporate cultures: *The rites and rituals of corporate life*. Reading, M. A: Addison Wesley.

Delurey, M., Newfrock, J., and Starr, R, (2003). *Strategy and Business* Spring.

Dembo, R.S., and Freeman, A. (1998). *Seeing Tomorrow – Rewriting the Rules of Risk*, Wiley, New York.

Dess, G. D., and Beard, D. W. (1984) Dimensions of organizational task environments. *Administrative Science Quarterly* **30**: 52 -73

De Vaus, D.A. (1985) *Surveys in Social Research,* 83. Sydney: Allen and Unwin

Dillman, D.A. (1978). *Mail and Telephone Surveys: the total design method.* New York: Willey.

Dillman, D.A. (2000). *Mail and Internet surveys: The tailored design method.* New York: John Wiley.

Dillman, T.A., & Tarnai, J. (1991) Mode effects of cognitively designed recall questions: A comparison of answers to telephone and mail surveys. In P. N. Beimer, R.M. Groves, L.E. Lyberg, N.A. Mathiowetz, & S. Sudman (Eds.), *Measurement errors in surveys* (pp367-393). New York: John Willey.

Directory of the World's Banks, Eleventh Edition, Euromoney Books, Fitzroy Dearbon: London.

Dodge, H. R., Fullerton, S., and Robbins, J. E. (1994) Stage of the organizational life cycle and competition as mediators of problem perception for small businesses. *Strategic Management Journal* **15**(2): 121 -134

Dorfman, M.S. (1994). *Introduction to Risk Management in Insurance*. Prentice-Hall, Englewood Cliffs, NJ

Dosi G,. Malerba F., and Orsenigo L. (1997). Industrial Structures and Dynamics: Evidence, Interpretations and Puzzles. Industrial Corporate Change 6(1): 3-23

Dowd, K. (1998). *Beyond Value at Risk – The New Science of Risk Management*, Wiley, New York.

Doz, Y.L. (1996). The evolution of cooperation in strategic alliances: initial conditions or learning processes? *Strategic Management Journal*, Summer Special Issue 17: 55-81.

Dubois, D., and Prade, H. (1988). An Introduction to Probabilistic and Fuzzy Logics. In Smets, Ph., Mamdami, E., Dubois, D., and Prade, H. editors, *Non-Standard Logics for Automated Reasoning*. Academic Press.

Duhaime, I. M., and Schwenk, C. R. (1985) Conjectures on cognitive simplification in acquisition and divestment decision making. *Academy of Management Review* **10**: 287 – 295.

Duncan, K. D. (1972). Strategies for analysis of the task. In J. Hartley (Ed.), *Strategies for programmed instruction: An educational technology***.** London, UK: Butterworth

Dunning, J.H. (1995). 'Reappraising the eclectic paradigm in an age of alliance capitalism'. *Journal of International Business Studies*, **26,** pp. 461 – 491.

Duysters, G., and Hagedoorn, J. (1996) The effect of core competency building on company performance. May 1996, *MERIT, Faculty of Economics and Business Administration*, University of Limburg, The Netherlands.

Dworkin, G. (1967) *Odger's Construction of Deeds and Statutes*, 5th Edn, Sweet & Maxwell

Dyer, J. H. & H. Singh. (1998). The relational view: Cooperative strategy and sources of interorganizational competitive advantage. *Academy of Management Review, 23*(4), 660–679.

Eason, K. (1988) *Information Technology and Organizational Change*, Burgess Science Press

Ehrenfelf, J. (2005). The roots of sustainability. *Sloan Management Review* 46(2): 23-25

Einhorn, H.J. and Hogarth, R.M. (1988). Behavioural decision theory: process of judgement and choice. In Bell, D.E., Raiffa, H., and Tversky, A. editors, *Decision Making: Descriptive, Normative and Prescriptive Interactions*. Cambridge: Cambridge University Press.

Evrard Corporation V Swiss Bank Corporation., 673 F.2d951 (D.C.A Ill.1982).

Farjoun, M. (2001).Towards an organic perspective on strategy. *Strategic Management Journal*, Wiley. July.

Fayol, H. (1949). *General and Industrial Management*, Pitman (Original French version 1916)

Festinger, L. (1957). *A Theory of Cognitive Dissonance*. Evanston, IL: Row, Peterson

Festinger, L., and Carlsmith, J.M. (1959). Cognitive consequences of forced compliance. *Journal of Abnormal and Social Psychology, 58*, 203-210

Fields, G., (2002). "An ominous war game", *Wall Street Journal*, December 4.

Fiksel, J. (2003) Designing resilient, sustainable systems. *Environmental Science and Technology* 37 (23): 5330-5339.

Fiksel, J. (2006) Sustainability and resilience: towards a systems approach. *Sustainability: Science, Practice & Policy*. Fall 2006, Volume 2; Issue 2.

Fitting, M. (1990). First-order Logic and Automated Theorem Proving. Springer.

Folke, C., Carpenter, S., Elmquist, T., Gunderson, L., Holling, C., & Walker, B. (2002). Resilience and sustainable development: building adaptive capacity in a world of transformations. *Ambio* 31(5): 437 – 440.

Fowler F.J. (1992). How unclear terms affect survey data. *Public Opinion Quarterly*, 56(2), 218-231.

Fowler, F.J. (1995). *Improving survey questions*. Thousand Oaks, CA: Sage

Fox, J., (1986). Three arguments for extending the framework of probability. In Kanal, L and Lemmer,

J., editors, *Uncertainty in Artificial Intelligence*, p447-458. Elsevier.

Fredrickson J. W., and Iaquinto, A. L. (1989) Inertia and creeping rationality in strategic decision processes. *Academy of Management Journal* **32**: 543 – 576

Fredrickson, J. W. (1984) The comprehensiveness of strategic decision processes: extension, observations, future directions. *Academy of Management Journal* **27**: 445 – 466

Frenkel, O.J., and Doob, A.N. (1976). Post-decision dissonance at the polling booth. *Canadian Journal of behavioural Science, 8*, 347-350

Friedman, M. (1953). The methodology of positive economics, in Friedman, M. *Essays in Positive Economics*. Chicago, IL: University of Chicago Press.

Furfine, C., (2000), 'Evidence on the Response of US Banks to Changes in Capital Requirements'. *BIS Working Paper*, No.88.

Gabbay, D., and Hunter, A. (1991). Making inconsistency respectable 1: A position paper. In Jorrand, Ph., and Keleman, J., editors, *Fundamentals of Artificial Intelligence Research*, volume 535 of Lecture Notes in Artificial Intelligence, pages 19-32. Springer.

Gabbay, D., and Hunter, A. (1993). Making inconsistency respectable2: Meta-level handling of inconsistent data. In Clarke, M., Kruse, R., and Moral, S, editors, *Symbolic and Qualitative Approaches to Reasoning and Uncertainty*, Volume 747 of Lecture Notes in Computer Science, pages 137-144. Springer.

Galbraith JR and Nathanson, DA. (1978). *Strategy Implementation: The Role of Structure and Process*. West: St Paul, MN

Galbraith, C. S. (1990) "Transferring core manufacturing technologies in high technology firms", *California Management Review,* vol.32. no. 4, 56-70

Galbraith, C., and Schendel, D. (1983) An empirical analysis of strategy types. *Strategic Management Journal*, 1983, 4, pp. 153 -173.

Galbraith, C.S. (1990). Transferring core-manufacturing technologies in high tech firms. *California Management Review*, **32**(4), 56-70.

Galbraith, J. (1973) *Designing Complex Organizations*, Addison-Wesley, Reading, MA

Galbraith, J. (1977) *Organization Design*, Addison-Wesley, Reading, MA

Gates, S., and Hexter, H. (June 2005). *From Risk Management to Risk Strategy*. The Conference Board Report Number: R-1363-05-RR

Gehani N., and McGettrick A. (1986). *Software Specification Techniques*, Addison-Wesley, Reading, M.A.

Ghemawat P., and Ricart I Costa JE. 1993. The Organizational Tension Between Static and Dynamic Efficiency. *Strategic Management Journal*, Winter Special Issue 14: 59-73

Ghemawat, P. (1991). *Commitment: The Dynamic of Strategy*. New York: The Free Press.

Gleick, J. (1987). *Chaos: Making a New Science*, Heinemann.

Glick, W. H., Miller, C.C., and Huber, G. P. (1993). The impact of upper echelon diversity on organizational performance. In *Organizational Change and Redesign: Ideas and Insights for Improving Performance*, Huber, G. P., Glick W. H. (eds). Oxford University Press: New York; 176 -214

Godiwalla, Y.M., W.A. Meinhart, and W.A. Warde. (1981). "General Management and Corporate Strategy." *Managerial Planning* **30** (1981): 17-29.

Gordon, R. G.Jr., (2000). *Ethnologue: Languages of the World*, 15th Edition, SIL Publications, Dallas.

Granovetter, M. (1985). Economic action and social structure: the problem of embeddedness. *American Journal of Sociology* 91 (3): 481-510.

Granovetter, M. (1985).Economic action and social structure: the problem of embeddedness. *American Journal of Sociology* 91(3): 481-510. 1985.

Grant, R. M. (1998). *Contemporary strategy analysis*. Oxford: Blackwell. 1998.

Gray, J., and Reuter, A. (1993)*Transaction Processing: Concepts and Techniques*, Morgan Kaufman.

Hall, A.D. (1989) *Metasystems Methodology*, Pergamon Press, Oxford.

Hall, M. J. B. (2004) "*Basel II: panacea or a missed opportunity?*" http://hdl.handle.net/2134/336

Hall, R.C. and Hitch, C.J. (1939). *Price theory and business behaviour.* Oxford Economic Papers 2: 12-45.

Hambrick, D. C. and Finkelstein, S. (1987) Managerial discretion: a bridge between polar views of organizational outcomes. In *Research in Organizational Behavior*, Cummings, L. L. Staw, B. M. (eds). JAI Press: Greenwich, CT; 369 – 406

Hambrick, D.C. (1983) Some tests of the effectiveness and functional attributes of Miles and Snow's strategic types. *Academy of Management Journal*, 26, 5-25.

Hamel, G. (1991). Competition for competence and interpartner learning within international alliances. *Strategic management journal* 12: 83-103.

Hamel, G. and Prahalad, C.K. (1989). Strategic intent. *Harvard Business Review.* May-June: 63-76.

Hamel, G., and Prahalad, C.K. (1984) *Competing for the Future.* Harvard Business School Press. Boston.

Hamilton, S., (1999). The Barings Collapse (A): *Breakdowns in Organization Culture and Management.* International Institute for Management Development, Lausanne, Switzerland, 21.06.99

Hammer, M. and Champy, J. (1993*) Re-engineering the Corporation: A Manifesto for Business Revolution*, Nicholas Brealey.

Hammer, M. and Stanton, S.A. (1995) *The Reengineering Revolution*, Harper Collins.

Hannan, M. T and Freeman, J. (1988). *Organizational Ecology*, Cambridge, MA. Harvard University Press.

Hannan, M.T.(1989) Inertia, density and the structure of organizational populations: entries in European automobile industries, 1886-1981. *Organizational Studies* 18 (2): 192-228.

Harmantzis, F. C. (2003) "*Operational Risk Management in Financial Services and the New Basel Accord*". Working Paper, Steven Institute of Technology, NJ, USA

Hamel, G., & Valikangas, L. (2003). The quest for resilience. *Harvard Business Review* 81(9): 52 – 57.

Harrington, H.J. (1991) *Business Process Improvement*, McGraw-Hill, New York.

Hart S, Banbury C. (1994). How strategy-making processes can make a difference. *Strategic Management*

Hartley, E. (1946). *Problems in prejudice*. New York: King's Crown Press.

Haspeslah, P.C., and D.B. Jemison (1991). *Managing Acquisitions: Creating Value through Corporate Renewal.* New York, Free Press.

Hausler, J. (1968). "Planning: A Way of Shaping the Future." *Management International Review* 2 12-21.

Heckerman, D., and Wellman, (1995). M. Bayesian Networks. *Communications of the ACM*, 38: 27-30.

Henderson R., and Mitchell, W. (1997). The interactions of organizational and competitive influences on strategy and performance. *Strategic Management Journal*, Summer Special Issue 18: 5-13.

Henderson, B. D. (1989). The origin of strategy. Harvard Business Review, November-December 139-143.

Henderson, R. M. and K. B. Clark (1990). "Architectural Innovation: The Reconfiguration of Existing Product Technologies and the Failure of Established Firms." *Administrative Science Quarterly* **35**: 9-30

Hendry, C., Arthur, M., & Jones, A. (1995). *Strategy through people: Adaptation and learning in the small-medium enterprise*. London: Routledge.

Henrion, M. (1995). Probabilistic and Bayesian Representation of Uncertainty in Information Systems: A Pragmatic Approach. In Smets, Ph and Motro, A., editors, *Uncertainty Management in Information Systems*. Kluwer.

Hershey, J., and Schoemaker, P. (1980). Risk taking and problem context in the domain of losses: an expected utility analysis. *Journal of Risk and Insurance, 47*, 111-132.

Hickson, D.J., Butler, R.J., Cray, D., Mallory, G.R., and Wilson, D.C. (1986) *Top Decisions: Strategic Decision Making in Organizations*, Blackwell.

Hirshleifer, Jack and John G. Riley. (1979). The Analytics of Uncertainty and Information — An Expository Survey. *Journal of Economic Literature* Vol. XVII (Dec.), pp. 1375–1421

Hoch, S.J. (1984). Availability and interference in predictive judgment. *Journal of Experimental Psychology:*

Learning, Memory, and Cognition, 11, 719-731.
Hofer, C. W. (1973) Some preliminary research on patterns of strategic behavior. *Academy of Management Proceedings*. pp. 46 -59
Hollander, S. (1987). *Classical Economics*. Oxford: Blackwell.
Hollis, M., and Nell, E J. (1975). *Rational economic man: A philosophical critique of neo-classical economics*. Cambridge: Cambridge University Press.
Holmstrom, B., and Tirole, J. (1989). "The Theory of the Firm" in Schmalensee and Willig (eds.), *Handbook of Industrial Organization*.
Horngren C.T., and Sundem, G.L. (1987) *Introduction to Management Accounting*, 7th edn, Prentice-Hall, Englewood Cliffs, NJ.
Hoskin, K. (1990). Using history to understand theory: a reconceptualisation of the historical genesis of strategy. *Paper presented to the European Institute for Advanced Studies in Management Workshop*, Venice, October.
http://www.ey.com/GLOBAL/content.nsf/International/Financial_Services_-_Risk_Management_-_Basel_II_Report_2006
http://www.kpmg.de/library/en/13329.htm
Huber, GP (1991). Organizational Learning: The Contributing Processes and the Literatures. *Organizational Science* 2:88-115
Hunter, A., (1996). *Uncertainty in Information Systems, An Introduction to Techniques and Applications*. McGraw Hill.
ISDOS *(Information System Design and Optimization System)*. Department of Industrial and Operations Engineering. University of Michigan, 1967.
ISDOS Project University of Michigan; SYCOMT Project University of Lancaster
Itami H., and Roehl TW. (1987). *Mobilizing Invisible Assets*. Harvard University Press: Cambridge MA.
Jacques, K., and Nigro, P. (1997) 'Risk-Based Capital, Portfolio Risk, and Bank Capital: A Simultaneous Equations Approach', *Journal of Economics and Business*, **49** 533-47
James, B. G. (9185). *Business Wargames*. Harmondsworth: Penguin.
Jiang, R., and Bansal, P. (2001). Seeing the need for 14001, *Academy of Management Meeting*, Washington, DC.
Johansson, H.J., McHugh, P., Pendlebury, A.J. and Wheeler, W.A. III (1993) *Business Process Re-engineering*, John Wiley & Sons, New York.
Jones, G. K., Lanctot, A., and Teegen, H. J. (2000) Determinants and performance impacts of external technology acquisition. *Journal of Business Venturing* **16**: 255 – 283
Judge, W. Q., and Miller, A. (1991) Antecedents and outcomes of decision speed in different environmental contexts. *Academy of Management Journal* **34**: 449 – 463
Jung, D. I., and Avolio, B. J. (1999) Effects of leadership style and followers' cultural orientation on performance in group and individual task conditions. *Academy of Management Journal* **42**: 208 – 218
Junker U., and Konolige, K. (1990). Computing the extensions of autoepistemic and default logics with a truth maintenance system. In *Proceedings of the Eighth National Conference on Artificial Intelligence*, pages 278-283. MIT Press.
Kahneman, D. D., Slovic, P., and Tversky, A. (1982) *Judgment Under Uncertainty: Heuristics and Biases*. Cambridge University Press: New York.
Kambil, A., and Vikram, M. (2005). *Disarming the Value Killers*. Deloitte Research, February.
Kane, E. J. (1990) 'Incentive Conflict in the International Risk-based Capital Agreement', *Economic Perspectives* (publication of the Federal Reserve Bank of Chicago), May/June (1990), 33-6
Kantola, S.J., Syme, G.J., and Campbell, N.A. (1984). Cognitive dissonance and energy conservation. *Journal of Applied Psychology, 69*, 416-421
Kapstein, E. B. (1989) 'Resolving the Regulator's Dilemma: International Coordination of Banking

Regulations'. *International Organization*, **46**, 265-87

Kaufman, G. (2006). *"Basel II has been a costly distraction on the road to minimizing the societal cost of bank failures."* Presentation, 6th Annual FDIC Research Conference, September 13, 2006.

Keeley, M. (1980) Organizational analogy: A comparison of organismic and social contract models. *Administrative Science Quarterly*, 1980, **25**, pp. 337 – 362

Keen P.G.W. (1998) *Competing in Time*, Ballinger, Cambridge, M.A.

Keynes, J. M. (1936). *The general theory of employment, interest and money.* London: MacMillan. 1936.

Klir, G.J. (1991) *Facets of Systems Science*, Plenum, New York

Knox, R.E., and Inkster, J.A. (1968). Postdecision dissonance at post time. *Journal of Personality and Social Psychology, 8,* 319-323

Kogut, B. (1985) "Design global strategies: profiting from operational flexibility." *Sloan Management Review*, pp. 27 -38

Kogut, B., and U. Zander (1992). "Knowledge of the Firm, Combinative Capabilities and the Replication of Technology." *Organization Science* 3(3): 383-397

KPMG Basel Briefing. December 2001

Krause, P., and Clark, D., (1993). Representing Uncertain Knowledge: An Artificial Intelligence Approach. Intellect, Smets, Ph., Imperfect Information: Imprecision and Uncertainty. In Smets, Ph., and Motro, A., editors, *Uncertainty Management in Information Systems*. Kluwer, 1992.

Lal, R. (1994). Sustainable land use systems and soil resilience. In D. Greenland & I. Szabolcs (Eds.) *Soil Resilience and Sustainable Land Use*. Pp. 41 – 68. Wallingford: CAB International.

Lamal, P.A. (1979). College student common beliefs about psychology. *Teaching of Psychology*, pp. 155-158.

Langley, A. (1988). "The Roles of Formal Strategic Planning." *Long Range Planning* **21**: 40-50.

Langley, A., (1995) Between "paralysis by analysis" and "extinction by instinct". *Sloan Management Review*, Spring.

LaPiere, R.T. (1930). Attitudes vs. actions. *Social Forces, 13*, 230-237.

Latham, Lanny R. and David L. Shafer, (1994). "Locking the Door on Treasury Fraud," in *Corporate Cashflow*, September.

Lauritzen, S., and Siegelhalter, D. (1988). Local Computations with Probabilities on Graphical Structures and their Application to Expert Systems. *Journal of the Royal Society B*, 50:157-224.

Leanard-Barton D., Wilson E. & Doyle J (1993) Commercializing technology: Imaginative understanding of user needs. *Harvard Business Review*

Lee A. Cheng., C.H. and Chadha, G.S. (1995) Synergism between information technology and organizational structure: a managerial perspective. *Journal of Information Technology*, March

Lessler, J., and Forsyth, B. "Coding System for Appraising Questionnaires." *Determining Processes Used To Answer Questions*. San Francisco: Jossey Bass, 1995.

Levitt B., and March JG. (1988). Organizational Learning. *Annual Review of Sociology* 14: 319-340

Likert, R. (1932) ' A technique for the measurement of attitudes', *Archives of Psychology*, 140

Lind, G. (2005), 'Basel II – The New Framework for Bank Capital', Riksbank, *Economic Review* 2/2005, 22-38

Lindblom, C.E. (1959). 'The science of muddling through', *Public Administration Review*, 19, Spring, 79-88

Lindley, D. (1987). The Probability Approach to the Treatment of Uncertainty in Artificial Intelligence and Expert Systems. Statistical *Science*. 2: 3-44.

Loewenton, I. (2003) "*Mastering and managing risks in banking and financial institutions and Basel II new Accord for Operational Risks*". Thesis. Université de Lausanne, Ecole des Haute Etudes Commerciales

Loftus, E. (1980). *Surprising new insights into how we remember and why we forget*. New York: Ardsley

House.

Long Term Credit Fund 1998 ; Enron 2001; WorldCom 2002; Tyco 2002.

Lorange, P., and Vancil, R. F. (1976) How to design a strategic planning system. *Harvard Business Review*, 54(**5**), pp. 75 -81

Lorsch, J.W. (ed) (1987) *Handbook of Organizational Behaviour*, Prentice Hall, Englewood Cliffs, NJ

Luchman, T. A.(1998). Strategy as a Portfolio of real Options, *Harvard Business Review*, September-October 1998.

Mandelbrot, B. (1982) The *Fractal Geometry of Nature*, W.H. Freeman & Co.

Manz, C. C., and Sims, H. P. (1990) *Superleadership*. Prentice-Hall: New York

March, J.G. (1976). The technology of foolishness. In Marsh, J and Olsen, J., editors, *Ambiguity and Choice in Organizations*. Bergen: Universitetsforlaget.

Markides, C. M. (2000). *All the right moves: A guide to crafting breakthrough strategy*. Harvard Business School Press.

Marsden, P. V. (1990). "Network Data and Measurement." Annual Review of Sociology **16**: 435-463.

Martin, J. with Leben, J. (1989)*Strategic Information Planning Methodologies*, Prentice Hall, Englewood Cliffs, NJ.

Mason, R. O., and Mitrof, I. I. (1981) *Challenging strategic planning assumptions*. New York

Mayer, M., and Whittington, R. (1999). Strategy, structure and "systemness": national institutions and corporate changes in France, Germany and the UK, 1950-1993. *Organizational Studies* **20** (6): 933 – 960. 1999.

McCarthy J. (1986). Applications of circumscription to formalizing common-sense knowledge. *Artificial Intelligence*, 28: 89-116.

McCarthy J., and Hayes, P. (1969). Some philosophical problems from the standpoint of artificial intelligence. In Meltzer, B., and Michie, D, editors, *Machine Intelligence* 4. Edinburgh University Press.

McKloskey D.N. (1990). *If you're so smart: The narrative of economic expertise*. Chicago IL: University of Chicago Press.

Meyer, N.D. and Boone, M.E. (1987) *The Information Age*, McGraw-Hill, New York.

Mikes, A (2005) "*Enterprise Risk Management in Action*". The London School of Economics and Political Science. Discussion Paper No. 35

Miles, R. H., and Cameron, K. S. (1982) *Coffin nails and corporate strategies*. Englewood Cliffs, N.J: Prentice Hall.

Miles, RE., and Snow CC. (1978). *Organizational Strategy, Structure and Process*. McGraw-Hill: New York.

Miller D. (1990). *The Icarus Paradox*. Harper Business. New York.

Miller N.H., and Campbell D.T. (1959). Recency and primacy in persuasion as a function of the timing of speeches and measurements.*Journal of Abnormal and Social Psychology, 59*, 1-9.

Miller, Danny, & Friesen, Peter H. (1977). Strategy-making in context: ten empirical archetypes.*Journal of Management Studies*, **14** (3) 253-280.

Mintzberg, H. (1979*) The Structuring of Organizations*, Prentice Hall, Englewood Cliffs, NJ

Mintzberg, H. (1987). Crafting strategy. *Harvard Business Review*. July-August.

Mintzberg, H. (1989). Strategy Formation: Schools of Thought, *Management Science*.

Mintzberg, H. (1989). Strategy formulation: Schools of thought. In Fredrikson, J (ed) *Perspectives on Strategic Management*. San Francisco, CA: Ballinger 1989.

Mintzberg, H. (1990). The design school: reconsidering the basic premises of strategic management. *Strategic Management Journal* 11: 171-195.

Mintzberg, H. (1994). *The rise and fall of strategic planning*. New York: Free Press.

Mintzberg, H. and Quinn, J.B. (1991) *The Strategy Process: Concepts, Contents, Cases*, Prentice- Hall, Englewood Cliffs, NJ.

Mintzberg, H., and Waters, J.A. (1985). Of strategies, deliberate and emergent. *Strategic Management Journal* 6(3): 257-272.

Mintzberg, Henry, Raisinghani, Durum & Theoret, Andre (1976). "The structure of 'unstructured' decision processes". *Administrative Science Quarterly*, **21** (2), 246-275.

Mitchell, J. (1997) '*Quantitative science and the definition of measurement in psychology*', British Journal of Psychology, 88: 355-83.

Monge, P. (1990). "Theoretical and Analytical Issues in Studying Organizational Processes." *Organization Science,* Volume 1, November, pp. 406-423.

Moore JF.(1993). Predators and Prey: A New Ecology of Competition. *Harvard Business Review* 71(3): 75-86

Moore, J.I. (1992). *Writers on strategy and strategic management*. Penguin.

Morgan (1986) *Creative Organization Theory*, Sage Publications, Beverly Hills CA

Mottro, A. (1995). Sources of uncertainty in information systems. In Smets, Ph., and Motro, A., editors, *Uncertainty Management in Information Systems.* Kluwer.

Nelson, R. (1981) "Research on Productivity Growth and Differences." *Economic Literature* (19), pp. 1029 – 1064

Nelson, R. R., & Winter, S. G. (1982). *An evolutionary theory of economic change*. Cambridge, Mass.: Belknap Press of Harvard University Press

Newgren, Kenneth E., Rasher, Arthur A. & LaRoe, Margaret E. (1984). An empirical investigation of the relationship between environmental assessment and corporate performance. Paper read at Proceedings of the 44th *Annual Meeting of the Academy of Management*, August 12-15 1984, at Washington, DC.

Niemela I., and Rintanen J. (1992). On the impact of stratification on the complexity of non-monotonic reasoning. In Nebel, B., and Swartout, W., editors, *Principles of Knowledge Representation and Reasoning*: Proceedings of the Third International Conference, pages 627-638. Morgan Kaufman.

Nord, W. R., and Tucker, S. (1987). *Implementing Routine and Radical Innovations*. D.C. Heath, Lexington

Nutter, J. (1987). Uncertainty and Probability. In *Proceedings of the International Joint Conference on Artificial Intelligence*, Pages 373-379. Morgan Kaufman.

Oakland, J.S. (1989) *Total Quality Management*, Butterworth Heinemann, Oxford.

Oatley, T., and Nabors, R (1998) 'Redistribute Cooperation: Market Failure, Wealth Transfers, and the Basel Accord', *International Organization*, **52**, 35-54

Obuchowski, J. (2006). The Strategic Benefits of Managing Risk. *MIT Sloane Management Review*, Spring Vol.47 No.3. 6-7

Ohio State Centre for Resilience 2007

Ould, M.A. (1995) *Business Processes*, John Wiley & Sons, New York.

Oxford English Dictionary; Webster's Dictionary 2002.

Pall, G.A. (1987) *Quality Process Management*, Prentice Hall, Englewood Cliffs, NJ.

Palmer, I.C. and Pot, G.A. (1989). *Computer Security Risk Management*, Van Nostrand Reinhold, New York.

Parsons, S. (1996). Imperfect information and databases. *IEEE Knowledge and Data Engineering*.

Pearce, J.A., II, E.B. Freeman, and R.B. Robinson. (1987). "The Tenuous Link Between Formal Strategic Planning and Financial Performance." *Academy of Management Review* **12**: 658-675.

Pearl, J. (1987). *Bayesian Decision Methods. Encyclopaedia of Artificial Intelligence*. Pages 48-56. John Wiley.

Pearl, J. (1987). *Fusion, propagation and structuring belief networks. Artificial Intelligence*. John Wiley.

Pennings, J. M., and F. Hariato (1992). "The Diffusion of Technological Innovation in the Commercial Banking Industry." *Strategic Management Journal* 13: 29-46.

Penrose, E.T. (1952). Biological analogies in the theory of the firm. *American Economic Review* 42 (5):

804-819.

Penrose, ET. (1959). *The Theory of Growth of the Firm*. Basil Blackwell: London.

Peteraf, M. A. (1993). "The Cornerstones of Competitive Advantage: A Resource-Based View." *Strategic Management Journal* 14 (3 (March)): 179-191.

Pettigrew A.M. (1992). The character and significance of strategy process research. *Strategic Management Journal*. Winter, Special Issue 13: 5-16.

Pettigrew, A.M. (1973). *The politics of organizational decision-making*. London: Tavistock.

Pezier, J. (2002) "A Constructive Review of Basel's Proposals on Operational Risk". *ISMA Discussion Papers in Finance* 2002-20 September, University of Reading.

Pfeffer J., and Salancik GR. (1978). *The External Control of Organizations*. Harper and Row: New York.

Plous, S. (1993) *The Psychology of Judgment and Decision Making*.McGraw-Hill. New York.

Porter ME, (1980). *Competitive Strategy: Techniques for Analysing Industries and Competitors*. Free Press: New York

Porter, M. (1996). What is strategy? *Harvard Business Review*.

Porter, M.E., (1991), Towards a dynamic theory of strategy, *Strategic Management Journal*, Winter 1991, pp95 – on

Porter, M.E., (1995), *Competitive advantage: creating and sustaining superior performance*. New York, Free Press.

Porter, Michael (1985). *Competitive advantage*. New York, NY: The Free Press.

Postrel, S, and R. P. Rumelt (1992) "Incentives, Routines, and Self-Command." *Industrial and Corporate Change* **1**(2)

Powell, Walter W., & DiMaggio, Paul J., eds. (1991). *The new institutionalism in organizational analysis*. Chicago, IL: University of Chicago Press.

Power, M. K. (2003) *The Invention of Operational Risk*. London. London School of Economics and Political Science, ESRC Centre for the Analysis of Risk and Regulation, Discussion Paper no.16.

PriceWaterhouseCoopers, UK. Growing Basel Data. 2001 Publication.

Priem, R. L., Rasheed, A. M. A., and Kotulic, A. G. (1995) Rationality in strategic decision processes, environmental dynamism and firm performance.*Journal of Management* **21**: 913 -929

Prothro, J.W., & Grigg, C.M. (1960). Fundamental principles of democracy: Bases of agreement and disagreement. *Journal of Politics, 22*, 276-294.

Quinn, J.B. (1980). *Strategies for change: Logical incrementalism*. Homewood, IL: Richard D Irwin.

Ramanujam, V., and N. Venkatraman.(1987). "Planning and Performance: A New Look at an Old Question." *Business Horizons* 30: 19-25.

Ramanujam, V., N. Venkatraman, and J.C. Camillus. (1986). "Multi-Objective Assessment of Effectiveness of Strategic Planning: A Discriminant Analysis Approach." *Academy of Management Journal* **29**: 347-372.

Raz, T. (2004) A Comparative Review of Risk Management Standards. *Working Paper No 22/2004*, Tel Aviv University, Ramat Aviv, Israel, Research No.08440100

Reinhardt, F. (1998) Environmental product differentiation: implications for corporate strategy, *California Management Review* **40**(4), 43-73.

Review of the U.S. Department of Defense Air, Space, and Supporting Information Systems Science and Technology Program (2001)

Richard P. Rumelt (1974) *Strategy, Structure, and Economic Performance*, Division of Research, Harvard Business School, Boston, (Revised edition published by the Harvard Business School Press, 1986).

Rime, B (2000) 'Capital Requirements and Bank Behavior: Empirical Evidence for Switzerland, *Swiss National Bank*, Zurich, Switzerland.

Robins, J. and M.F. Wiersema (1995), A resource-based approach to the multi-business firm: empirical analysis of the portfolio interrelationships and corporate financial performance, *Strategic*

Management Journal, 16, pp. 277-299.
Rogers, E. (1983). *The Diffusion of Innovation* (Third). New York, Free Press.
Rowan, M. 'Instant' Payback on 14001 Investment Plant.
Royston P. N. (198 9). Using intensive interviews to evaluate questions. In F. Fowler (Ed.), *Conference proceedings: Health survey research methods* (pp. 3-8). Washington, DC: National Center for Health Services Research.
Rumelt (1987) "Theory Strategy and Entrepreneurship." In D. Teece, Ed. *The Competitive Challenge,* Cambridge, Mass: Ballinger.
Rumelt, R. (1991). How much does industry matter? *Strategic Management Journal* 12 (3): 167- 185.
Rumelt, R. P. (1979) Evaluation of strategy: Theory and models. In D. E. Schendel & C. W. Hofer (Eds.), *Strategic Management.*
Russo, M. V., and Harisson, N. S. (2000) *An empirical study of the impact of 14001 registration on emissions performance*, paper presented at the 9th Greening of industry Conference, Bangkok, Thailand.
Saffiotti, A. (1987). The artificial intelligence view of the treatment of uncertain knowledge. *Knowledge Engineering Review*, 2:75-97.
Sanchez R., and Heene A. (1997). Reinventing Strategic Management: New Theory and Practice for Competence Based Competition. *European Management Journal* 15(3): 303-317
Savage, C.M. (1990) *Fifth Generation Management*, Digital Press
Schein, E.H. (1988) *Process Consultation: Its Role in Organization Development (2nd edn)*, Addison-Westley, Reading, MA.
Schendel, D. (1994). Introduction to "Competitive organizational behaviour: toward an organizationally-based theory of competitive advantage." *Strategic Management Journal*, Winter Special Issue 15: 1-4.
Schneider, B. (1999). *Secrets and Lies: digital security in a networked world.* Wiley Computer Publishing. New York.
Schuman, H., & Presser, S. (1981) *Questions and answers in attitude surveys: Experiments on question form, wording and context*. Orlando, FL: Academic Press.
Schumpeter, Joseph A. (1942). *Capitalism, Socialism, and Democracy*. New York: Harper and Brothers. (Harper Colophon edition, 1976.)
Schwenk, C.R., and C.B. Shrader.(1993) "Effects of Formal Strategic Planning on Financial Performance in Small Firms: A Meta-Analysis." *Entrepreneurship Theory and Practice* **17** (1993): 53-64.
Scott RW. (1992) The Organization of Environment: Network, Cultural and Historical Elements. In *Organizational Environments: Ritual and Rationality*, Meyer JW., Scott, WR (eds) Sage:: Thousand Oaks, CA; 155-178.
Scott, W. Richard. (1987). *Organizations: rational, natural, and open systems*. 2nd ed. Englewood Cliffs, NJ: Prentice-Hall.
Scott, W.R. (1995) *Institutions and Organizations.* Sage. Thousand Oaks, CA.
Selznick, P. (1957). Leadership in Administrative Framework. Harper & Row: New York.
Shah, Yawar. (1992). "Using the Dollar-based Global Payments System Optimally," in *Journal of Cash Management*, July/August.
Sherif, M., Taub, D., and Hovland, C.I. (1958) Assimilation and contrast effects of anchoring stimuli and judgments. *Journal of Experimental Psychology, 55*, 150-155
Sherman, S.J., and Gorkin, L. (1980). Attitude bolstering when behaviour is inconsistent with central attitudes. *Journal of Experimental Social Psychology, 16*, 388-403.
Shirley, R. C. (1982). Limiting the scope of strategy: A decision based approach. *Academy of Management Review*, **7**, pp. 262 – 268
Shoham Y. (1988). *Reasoning about change*. MIT Press.

Shrader, R. W., and McConnell, M. (2002). Security and Strategy in the Age of Discontinuity: A Management Framework for the post-9/11 World. *Strategy and Business*, First Quarter 2002

Shrader, R. W., and McConnell, M. *Security and Strategy in the Age of Discontinuity: A Management Framework for the post-9/11 World*. Strategy and Business, First Quarter 2002

Sieber J. (1992). *Planning ethically responsible research: Developing an effective protocol*. Newbury Park, CA. Sage

Simmons, B. A. (2001), 'The International Politics of Harmonization: The Case of Capital Market Regulation'. *International Organization* 55 (**3**); 589-620

Simon H.A. (1965). The science of muddling through. *Public Administration Review*, 19, Spring, 79-88.

Simon, H.A. (1965). *The New Science of Management Decision in Management Decision Making* in Welsch, L.A.., and Cyert, R.M. (eds), Penguin Books.

Simons, H. W., N. Berkowitz and R. J. Moyer (1970). "Similarity, credibility, and attitude change: A review and A THEORY." *Psychological Bulletin* **73**: 1-16.

Sissell, K. (1998) Certification: an essential element? *Chemical Week* **160** (36), 46

Slevin, D. P., and Colvin, J. G. (1995) Entrepreneurship as firm behavior. In *Advances in Entrepreneurship, Firm Emergence, and Growth*, Vol. 2, Katz, J. A. Brockhaus Sr. R. H. (eds). JAI Press: Greenwich, CT; 175 – 224

Sloan, A P. (1963). My years with General Motors. London: Sedgewick & Jackson.

Slovic, P., & Fischhoff, B. (1977). On the psychology of experimental surprises. *Journal of Experimental Psychology: Human Perception and Performance, 3,* 544-551.

Slovic, P., Fischhoff, B., & Lichtenstein, S. (1982b). Response mode, framing, and information-processing effects in risk assessment. In R.M. Hogarth (Ed), *New directions for methodology of social and behavioral science: Question framing and response consistency* (no. 11). San Francisco: Jossey-Bass.

Smets, Ph. (1992). Imperfect Information: Imprecision and Uncertainty. In Smets, Ph., and Motro, A., editors, *Uncertainty Management in Information Systems*. Kluwer, 1992.

Smith, A. (1776). An Inquiry into the Nature and Causes of the Wealth of Nations. Meuthen and Co. London.

Source: KPMG Basel Briefing. 2001.

Source: PriceWaterhouseCoopers. Notes on Basel. 2000.

Source: Risk Books (Online Journal)

Source: Scott, W. R. (1995). *Institutions and Organizations*. Thousand Oaks, CA, Sage

Stacey, R. (1992) *Managing Chaos*, Kogan Page.

Stacey, R. (1993). 'Strategy as order emerging from chaos', *Long-range Planning*, 26(1).

Starr, R., Newfrock, J., & Delurey, M. (2003). Enterprise resilience: managing risk in a networked economy. *Strategy + Business* 30(1): 1- 150.

Stebbins, M.W.., Sena, J.A. and Shani, A.B.R. (1995) Information technology and organization design. *Journal of Information Technology*, June

Stern LW., and El-Ansary AI. (1988). *Marketing Channels*. Prentice Hall: Englewood Cliffs, NJ.

Stewart, T.A. (1991) Brainpower. *Fortune* 123 (11).

Stewart, T.A. (1995) Trying to grasp the intangible. *Fortune*, 2 Oct.

Strassman, P.A. (1990) *The Business Value of Computers*, Information Economics Press.

Subramanian, Ram, Fernandes, Nirmala & Harper, Earl (1993). "Environmental scanning in US companies: their nature and their relationship to performance." *Management International Review* **33** (3), 271-286.

Subramanian, Ram, Kumar, Kamalesh & Yauger, Charles (1994). "The scanning of task environments in hospitals: an empirical study". *Journal of Applied Business Research* **10** (4), 104-115.

Sutton, Howard. (1988). *Competitive intelligence*. New York, NY: The Conference Board.

Swedberg, R., Himmelstrand, W., and Brulin, G. (1987). The paradigm of economic sociology. *Theory and Society* 16 (2): 169-213.

Szulanski, G. (1996). "Exploring internal stickiness: Impediments to the transfer of best practice within the firm." *Strategic Management Journal* **17**: 27-43.

Teece D, Pisano G, Shuen A. (1997). Dynamic capabilities and strategic management. *Strategic Management Journal* **18**(7): 509–534.

Teece, D. (1977) "Technology Transfer by Multinational Corporations: The Resource Cost of Transferring Technological Know-How." *Economic Journal* (87), pp 242 – 261

Teece, David (1981). The multinational enterprise: market failure and market power considerations. *Sloan Management Review*, **22** (3): 3-17

Teichroew etc al. (1980). *Application of the Entity-Relationship Approach to Information Processing Systems Modeling*.

Teichroew, D., and Hershey, E.A. (1977) PSL/PSA: A Computer-aided Technique for Structured Documentation and Analysis of Information Processing Systems. *IEEE Transactions on Software Engineering*.

Teichroew, D., Macasovic, P., Hershey, E.A., and Yamamoto, Y. (1980) Application of the entity-relationship approach to information processing systems modeling, in *Entity-Relationship Approach to System Analysis and Design*, North Holland, Amsterdam.

Thompson, James D. (1967). *Organizations in Action*. New York: McGraw-Hill.

Thorelli HB. (1986). Networks: Between Markets and Hierarchies. *Strategic Management Journal* 7 (1): 37- 51.

Thorndike, E.L. (1920). A constant error in psychological ratings. *Journal of Applied Psychology, 4,* 25-29.

Thurston, C. W. (1998) Latin America finds Profit in 14000, *Chemical Market Report* **253**(7), 18

Tichy, N. M., and Sherman S. (1993) Jack Welch's Lessons for Success. *Fortune*. pp. 68 -72

Toffler A. (1990) *Powershift: Knowledge, Wealth and Violence at the Edge of the 21st Century*. Bantam Books

Tsoukas, T. (1996). The firm as a distributed knowledge system: a constructionist approach. *Strategic Management* Journal 17, Winter Special Issue: 11 –26.

Tversky, A., and Kahneman, D. (1974). Judgement Under Uncertainty: heuristics and Biases. *Science*, 185: 1124-1131.

Van de Ven, A.H., Poole, M.S. (1995). Explaining development and change in organizations. *Academy of management review*, 20(3), 510-540.

Van Opstal, D. (2006). Cutter IT journal May 2006, Cutter International LLC

Vander Heijen, K. (1996). *Scenarios: The Art of Strategic Conversation*, Wiley, New York

Veliyath, R., and S.M. Shortell. (1993). "Strategic Orientation, Strategic Planning System Characteristics and Performance." *Journal of Management Studies* **30**: 359-381.

Venkatraman, N. (1994) IT-enabled business transformation: from automation to business scope redefinition. *Sloan Management Review*, Winter

Vincent D.R. (1990) *The Information Based Corporation*, Dow Jones Irwin.

Vogel, S. K. (1996) *Freer Markets, More Rules: Regulatory Reform in Advanced Industrial Countries*. Ithaca, N.Y.: Cornell University Press.

Von Neuman J., and Morgernstern, O. (1994). *The theory of games and economic change*. Cambridge, MA: Harvard University Press.

Wallace, A. (1991). nne. Corporate Treasury Guide to UCC Article 4A. Bethesda: Treasury Management Association.

Webb, D. and A. Pettigrew, (1999). "The temporal development of strategy: Patterns in the U.K. Insurance Industry." *Organization Science*. 10 : 601-621.

Weick, K. E. and Daft, R. L. (1983) The effectiveness of interpretation systems. In K. S. Cameron & D. A. White (Eds.), *Organizational effectiveness: A comparison of multiple models*. New York: Academic Press, 1983, pp. 71 -93.

Weick, K.E. (1990). Cartographic myths in organizations. In Huff, A., editor, *Mapping Strategic Thought*. London. Wiley.

Weiner, N. (1954) *The Human Use of Human Beings* – Cybernetics and Society, Houghton Mifflin & Co.

West, Joseph John. (1988). *Strategy, environmental scanning, and their effect upon firm performance: an exploratory study of the food service industry*. Blacksburg, VA: Virginia Polytechnic Institute and State University. (Ph.d. thesis)

Whittington, R., and Whipp, R. (1992). Professional ideology and marketing implementation. *European Journal of Marketing* 26 (1): 52-63.

Wicker, A.W. (1969). Attitudes versus actions: The relationship of verbal and overt behavioral responses to attitude objects. *Journal of Social Issues, 25*, 41-78.

Wicker, A.W. (1971). An examination of the "other variables" explanation of attitude-behavior inconsistency. *Journal of Personality and Social Psychology, 19*, 18-30.

Wilensky, Harold. (1967). *Organisational intelligence: knowledge and policy in government and industry*. New York, NY: Basic Books.

Williamson, O.E. (1967). *The economics of discretionary behaviour.* Chicago, IL: Markham.

Williamson, O.E. (1991). Strategizing, economizing and economic organization. Strategic Management Journal 12:75-94.

Willis, G.B., DeMaio, T., & Harris-Kojetin B. (1999). Is the bandwagon headed to the methodological promised land? Evaluating the validity of cognitive interviewing techniques. In M.G. Sirken et al (Eds.), *Cognition in survey research* (pp133-154). New York: John Wiley.

Yourdon, E. (1989*) Modern Structured Analysis*, Prentice-Hall, Englewood Cliffs, NJ.

Zack, M. (1999). Developing a knowledge strategy. *California Management Review* 41 (3): 125 – 146.

Zadeh, L. (1986). Is Probability Theory Sufficient for Dealing with Uncertainty in Artificial Intelligence? In Kanal, L. and Lemmer, J, editors, *Uncertainty in Artificial Intelligence*. Elsevier.

Zadeh, L. (1994). Fuzzy Logic, neural networks and soft computing. *Communications of the ACM,* 37 (3): 77-84.

Zaltman, G., R. Duncan and J. Holbek (1973). *Innovations and Organizations*. New York, John Wiley and Sons.

Zevitt, A.M. (1997). *Disaster Planning and Recovery*, Wiley, New York.

Zuboff, S. (1988) *In The Age of The Smart Machine*, Heinmann Professional Publishing.

INDEX

Actual Cyber Threat Data, 218
Adaptive Strategy, 116
Algorithmic Modeling of Cyber Threats, 212
Alternative Risk Transfer, 235
Analyzing Organizations, 185
AS/NZS 3931:1998, 44
AS/NZS 3931:1998 – Risk Analysis of Technological Systems, 249
AS/NZS 4360:1999, 39
Attack Lifecycle, 33
Attack Types, 15

Basic Process Map, 178
Bayesian Networks, 104
Best Practice Adoption, 36
Best Practice Transfer, 53
Biases and Influences (including regulations), 267
Bottom-up, 170
Branch Approach, 87
Brand Equity Risk, 261
Brand Risk, 259
Branding League, 262
BS 25777:2008 - Information and Communications Technology Continuity Management, 249
BS ISO/IEC 17799:2005: Information Technology. Security techniques, 249
BS25999: Business Continuity Management 2006 / ISO 22301: 2012, 250
Business Continuity Planning, 246
Business Process Mapping, 173
Business Process Themes, 180

Categories of Attacker, 23
Categories of Intangible Assets and Accounting Treatment, 259
Causal and Predictive Models, 167
Causal models, 167
Characteristics of Non-Proportional (Excess of Loss) Reinsurance, 234
Characteristics of Pro Rata and Excess of Loss Reinsurance, 232
Classes of Attack, 31
Classical Formalisms, 102
Classical Theory, 121
COBIT, 45
COBIT: Control Objectives for Information & Related Technology, 246
Cognitive Dissonance, 72
Comparison with Certified Standards, 48
Concepts of Security, 29
Conceptual Security Measures, 29
Conditional Expected Shortfall, 223
Conditioned Viewing, 66
Confidence Level, 223
Context Dependence, 76
Contrast Effect, 76
Controls and Insurance Mitigation, 164
Corporate Environment, 30
Countermeasures, 209
Cyber Risk Management Model, 7
Cyber Risk Options: Accept/Manage/Transfer/Mixture, 266
Cyber Risk Program Development, 92
Cyber Risk Valuation Systems, 217

Decision Making, 70
Decision Making Under Chaos, 91
Default Information, 99
Default Reasoning, 108
Denial of Service, 32
Digital/Virtual Security, 26
Direct Estimation Method, 162
Discovery, 67
Diversification Benefits, 166

Economic Rents from Existing Knowledge, 56
Enacting, 66
Enterprise Resilience, 154
Enterprise Resilience Positioning, 2
enterprise resilience program, 157
Enterprise Topology and Earnings Driver Classification, 158
Environmental Scanning, 61
Environmental Scanning as Organizational Learning, 61
Evolutionist Theory, 122
Example Brand Valuation Models, 261
Example of Qualitative Assessment, 205
Examples of Survey Development, 251
Excess of Loss Reinsurance, 233
Exploiting Vulnerabilities, 32
External Information, 243
Extrapolation of Data for Future Threats Prediction, 224

Formal Approaches to Uncertainty, 101
Forms and Operation of Alternative Risk Transfer, 237
Four Approaches to Strategy, 119
Four Stages of Knowledge Transfer, 57
Framework for Shorter Term Decision Making, 89
Future Trends & Impacts, 268
Fuzzy Information, 105

Gap Analysis, 199
Group and Segment Risk Distributions, 164

Hackers, 17
Halo Effects, 79
Host-based Intrusion Detection Systems, 211

I.T. Risk Management, 154
Inconsistent Information, 99
Incrementalism, 86
Individual Risk Distributions, 160
Individual Risks, 163
Industrial Espionage, 20
Information as an Asset, 189
Information Classification, 97
Information External to the Organization, 69
Information Technology and Business Processes, 188
Infowarriors, 23
Insurance Derivatives, 239
Intellectual Property Risk Management, 258
Internal Enterprise Assessment, 251
International Standards, 35
Interpretive Strategy, 117
Intra-firm Transfers of Best Practice, 55
Intrusion Detection Systems, 210
Intrusion Detection Technologies, 210
IP Packet Manipulation, 33
ISO 14001, 49
ISO 31000:2009 Published November 2009, 246
ISO/IEC 17799, 249
ISO/IEC 27002: Information Security Management, 246

Judgement and Decision Making, 70

Levels of Uncertainty, 100
Life Cycle of a System, 27
Linear Strategy, 116
Logical Incrementalism, 88
Loss Modeling Method, 161

Malicious Insiders, 19
Malicious Software, 32
Managing Cyber Threats, 192
Managing Uncertain Information, 93
Measurement Methods, 160
Memory and Hindsight Biases, 75
Meta-level Information, 100
Mitigation Strategies and Options, 228
Model for Cyber Threat Management, 264
Models of Strategy, 115
Monte Carlo Simulations, 165

National Intelligence Organizations, 22
Network & Cyber Risk Assessment, 199
Network Intrusion Detection Systems, 210
Normative Model, 83

Objectives of a Cyber Risk Program, 264
OCTAVE, 47
OCTAVE: Operationally Critical Threat and Vulnerability Evaluation, 245
Operational Risk, 149
Operational Risk Correlations, 166
Operational Risk Framework, 153
Order Effects, 80
Organic Perspective of Strategy, 130
Organization and Practical Analysis, 187
Organizational Learning, 61
Organizational Structure, 267
Organizational Structure for Cyber Risk Programs, 194
Organized Crime, 21

Patterns and Motives & Adversaries, 17
Per Process Risk Exposure, 227
Plasticity, 79
Police Forces, 21
Possibilistic Logic, 106
Possibility Theory, 105
Predicate Logic, 102
Predictive Models, 167
Prepositional Logic, 102
Primacy Effect, 77
Probabilistic Information, 99
Probability Theory, 103
Process Map of Service Delivery, 183
Processualist Theory, 124
Professional Body Frameworks and Guidelines, 45
Proportional and Non-Proportional Agreements, 232
Pseudo-Opinions, 80
Publicity Attacks, 16

Qualification Problem, 107
Qualitative Analysis Pros and Cons, 206
Quantitative Analysis Pros and Cons, 206

Ramification Problem, 107
Recency Effect, 77
Regulations, Standards and Professional Bodies, 243
Reinsurance, 228
Reputational Risk, 262
Resilience Profiling and Baselining, 158
Resilience Strategy, 185
Return on Investment and Risk Equation Examples, 208
Risk Assessment, 199
Risk Consolidation, 169
Risk Identification, 168
Risk Management, 162
Risk Management Objectives, 4
Risk Management Operational Risk and Enterprise Resilience, 139
Risk Profiling, 169
Risk Quantification, 169
Risk Standards, 36
Risk Types & Valuation, 266
Root Approach, 87
Root Semi Variance, 222
Sarbanes Oxley, 243
Scanning and Performance, 62
Secondary Exposure Factor, 208
Security Model, 30
Security Threats Posed, 8
Security Threats Summary, 10
Self-Perception Theory, 73
Strategic Benefits of Managing Risk, 143
Strategic Decision Making, 84
Strategic Decision Speed and Firm Performance, 134
Strategic Planning, 113
Strategy and Managing Risk, 111
Strategy; Definitions, Models, Theories and Perspectives, 111
Structural Risk, 262
Systemic Theory, 128
Technical Solutions, 209
Technology-Process Interdependency Mapping, 225
Terrorists, 21
The Press, 20
Theories of Strategy, 138
Top-down Risk Profiling, 168
Traditional Versus Internet/Network, 11
Treaty and Facultative Reinsurance, 231
Trends Environment, 193
Trust Model, 27
Types of Uncertain Information, 98

Uncertainty in Information, 98
Underlying Exposed Assets, 208

Underwriting Reinsurance, 234
Undirected Viewing, 65

Vulnerabilities, 26
Vulnerability Landscape, 26
Vulnerability Path, 28

Weaknesses Common to Both Modelling Methods, 170
Weaknesses Specifically Related to Cyber Threats, 170